Study skills

Critical Reading
and Writing *for*
Postgraduates

Mike Wallace and Alison Wray

SAGE Publications
London • Thousand Oaks • New Delhi

First published 2006

SAGE Publications Ltd
1 Oliver's Yard
55 City Road
London EC1Y 1SP

SAGE Publications Inc.
2455 Teller Road
Thousand Oaks, California 91320

SAGE Publications India Pvt Ltd
B-42, Panchsheel Enclave
Post Box 4109
New Delhi 110 017

British Library Cataloguing in Publication data

A catalogue record for this book is available
from the British Library

ISBN-10 1-4129-0221-5   ISBN-13 978-1-4129-0221-2
ISBN-10 1-4129-0222-3   ISBN-13 978-1-4129-0222-9 (pbk)

Library of Congress Control Number 2005936728

Typeset by C&M Digitals (P) Ltd., Chennai, India
Printed on paper from sustainable resources
Printed in Great Britain by TJ International, Padstow, Cornwall

Contents

How to use this book   vii

Author biographies   xi

Acknowledgements   xiii

Part One: Becoming a critical reader and self-critical writer   1

  1 What it Means to be Critical   3

  2 Making a Critical Choice   15

  3 Getting Started on Critical Reading   26

  4 Getting Started on Self-Critical Writing   39

  5 Creating a Comparative Critical Summary   48

Part Two: Developing an in-depth analysis   59

  6 A Mental Map for Exploring the Literature   61

  7 Components of your Mental Map   71

  8 Developing a Critical Analysis of a Text   91

  9 A Worked Example of a Critical Analysis   100

 10 Developing your Argument in Writing a
Critical Review of a Text   115

Part Three: Constructing a critical review of the literature   127

 11 Focusing and Building up your Critical Literature Review   129

 12 Integrating Critical Literature Reviews into your Dissertation   147

13 Tools for Structuring a Dissertation   166

14 Building your Academic Career on Critical
        Reading and Self-Critical Writing   177

Appendices   **183**

1 Abridged article: 'One word or two?'
       (Wray and Staczek)   185
2 Abridged article: 'Sharing leadership
       through teamwork' (Wallace)   195
3 Blank form for the Critical Analysis of a text   209
4 Checklist: developing a logical overall
       argument in a dissertation   219

Index   **222**

How to Use this Book

This book is primarily aimed at postgraduate students and early-career academics in the social sciences who recognize the need to enhance the quality of their research writing by becoming critical readers of the literature and by honing their skills as self-critical writers. We address ourselves directly to postgraduates embarked on written work that requires an engagement with the published (and unpublished) literature. This written work includes the coursework essay, Masters dissertation and Doctoral dissertation (also called a 'thesis' in some countries). However, anyone undergoing the process of academic apprenticeship, or guiding others to do so, will be able to relate to the structured approach that we offer: research methods lecturers, supervisors, mentors, experienced practitioners making a mid-career transition into an academic post, or indeed any academic who missed out on study skills and research methods training.

Critical reading and self-critical writing are highly transferable skills. A critical literature review may be prepared for a course assignment or for publication. Critical reviews may be incorporated into a larger project as part of a Masters or Doctoral dissertation, an academic book, or a research grant proposal. So the same basic ideas and techniques are equally applicable to postgraduate and academic work.

The book is suitable for self-directed learning, for use as a class textbook in a research methods module and as a handbook from which supervisor and student can work side-by-side. In addition, peer mentors within the academic profession may find a role for it in supporting their less experienced colleagues. Amongst today's postgraduate students are tomorrow's academic researchers, teachers, trainers, supervisors, examiners and mentors. The book thus offers a firm foundation for the generic professional training of future and current academic staff.

Our structured approach to learning critical reading and self-critical writing skills is underpinned by two core ideas. The first is the recognition of academic discourse as a two-way constructively critical process of enquiry where:

- as a critical reader, one evaluates the attempts of others to communicate with and convince their target audience by means of developing an argument; and

- as a writer, one develops one's own argument, making it as strong and as clear as possible, so as to communicate with and convince one's target audience.

The parallel is clear. The tangible product of critical reading is, typically, a written account of what has been read. Assessors take such accounts as the basis for judging an individual's ability to engage critically with the literature in the field of enquiry. Successful writers, therefore, are those who can apply their critical reading faculties equally to the research literature and to their own commentaries upon it. The techniques introduced in this book will make it easier to respond effectively and positively to constructive feedback on assessed work, and to emulate the good practice (and avoid the worst practice) observed in published materials.

The second core idea is that arguments are viewed as comprising two components: a set of claims or assertions (the conclusion), and the backing for them (the warrant) that is needed to render the conclusion convincing to a sceptical audience. In other words, for a conclusion to be convincing, it must be warranted by evidence that adequately justifies why this conclusion should be accepted. Sources of such evidence include research findings, professional experience and the definition of a theoretical idea.

The material in the book is organized into three parts:

1   Getting started on critical reading and self-critical writing.

2   Developing a mental map for navigating the literature, analysing texts in depth and writing critical reviews of them.

3   Structuring critical reviews of the literature and incorporating them into a dissertation, and taking forward the skills of critical reading and self-critical writing in an academic career.

The material in the book is designed to build up skills and confidence gradually as the reader works sequentially through each chapter and the associated exercises. Several of these exercises could either be used as classroom activities or could form the basis of assessed critical review assignments. In the two most central exercises, readers are invited to analyze and review two abridged academic journal articles, supported by worked examples, as a preparation for writing their own reviews of texts that they have chosen.

We chose these two articles from amongst our own research publications because they raise contrasting generic issues for critical readers, and because the content of each is likely to be of general interest. The main focus of the article in Part One, by Wray and Staczek (2005), is a conceptual model of how different people might process the same linguistic material in different ways. The exemplification comes from a court case that assessed the intended and received meaning of the American dialect term 'coonass', which the plaintiff found racially offensive. Wray and Staczek's interest lies in applying their theoretical model to this real-life case, as a means of accounting for what happened, without engaging directly with the substantive issues of the case. Thus, through this paper Wray and Staczek exemplify for readers how to engage critically with the argument pursued in a published work, while maintaining a distance from their personal views about the substantive issue. This is an important academic skill.

The article in Part Two, by Wallace (2001), also focuses on the link between theory and empirical evidence. However, whereas Wray and Staczek apply a general model of language processing to illuminate an empirical case, Wallace derives a model from empirical cases of teamwork within senior management teams in UK schools. Also, whereas Wray and Staczek adopt a relatively impartial standpoint towards the substantive issue, Wallace adopts an explicitly value-laden approach. Wallace exemplifies for readers how an author's own views can be appropriately expressed within an academic paper, to make a normative argument and offer proposals about what should be done.

The chapters and appendices offer a range of practical tools for tackling particular critical reading and reviewing tasks, including forms to complete when analyzing texts, checklists to prompt thinking and structures for planning reviews. Two blank forms included as appendices are designed to be photocopied for readers' use. Alternatively, electronic versions may be downloaded from the Sage website (www.sagepub.co.uk/wallace).

The guidance material in each part develops a progressively more sophisticated engagement with texts and the target written product. Attention is paid to both single-text analysis and the integration, in a review, of comments on several texts. From first steps into critical reading and self-critical writing, to the preparation of competitive research bids and academic peer reviews, the text explains and exemplifies in logical stages these necessary skills of sound academic practice.

Parts and Chapters	Insights and techniques	Target written product
Part One (Chapters 1–5) Becoming a critical reader and self-critical writer.	• Critical reading for self-critical writing. • Critical choice of texts to read. • Developing an argument. • Critical Synopsis Questions. • Critical Synopsis of a text.	• Critical Summary (one text). • Comparative Critical Summary (several texts).
Part Two (Chapters 6–10) Developing an in-depth analysis.	• Mental map. • Critical Analysis Questions. • Critical Analysis of a text.	• Critical Review (one text). • Comparative Critical Review (several texts).

(Continued)

(Continued)

Parts and Chapters	Insights and techniques	Target written product
Part Three (Chapters 11–14) Constructing a critical review of the literature.	• Structuring a Critical Literature Review via Critical Analyses and Critical Synopses. • Integrating Critical Literature Reviews into the structure of a dissertation. • Transferring critical reading and self-critical writing skills to the professional academic sphere.	• Self-contained Critical Literature Reviews. • Structure for a dissertation incorporating several Critical Literature Reviews. • Academic journal articles incorporating a Critical Literature Review. • Research grant proposals incorporating a Critical Literature Review. • Peer reviews and assessment reports.

Author biographies

Mike Wallace is a Professor of Education at the University of Bath. He is series editor of the Sage *Learning to Read Critically* edited books, and is currently AIM (Advanced Institute of Management Research) Lead Fellow responsible for research capacity-building. He researches the management of change in education and other public services, and has authored several books reporting his research. He is co-author, with Eric Hoyle, of the 2005 book *Educational Leadership: Ambiguity, Professionals, and Managerialism* (Sage).

Alison Wray is a Professor of Language and Communication at Cardiff University. She is lead author of the popular undergraduate research methods textbook *Projects in Linguistics* (Arnold). Her research centres on the modelling of lexical storage and processing, particularly in relation to formulaic phrases, and it has been applied to language learning, evolution of language and language disability. Her 2002 book *Formulaic Language and the Lexicon* (Cambridge University Press) won the Annual Book Prize of the British Association for Applied Linguistics.

Acknowledgements

Our thanks to postgraduate students at the University of Bath and Cardiff University for feedback on materials used in this book. Ray Bolam's ideas were a key influence on our thinking about mental map components and structuring a dissertation. Louise Poulson kindly gave us permission to draw on material (co-authored with Mike Wallace) that previously appeared in Chapters 1 and 2 and Appendix 2 of:

Wallace, M. and Poulson, L. (eds) (2003) *Learning to Read Critically in Educational Leadership and Management*, London: Sage.
Poulson, L. and Wallace, M. (eds) (2004) *Learning to Read Critically in Teaching and Learning*, London: Sage.
Goodwin, A. and Stables, A. (eds) (2004) *Learning to Read Critically in Language and Literacy Education*, London: Sage.

Thanks also to John Staczek and Equinox Publishing Ltd for permission to reproduce in abridged form the material in Appendix 1, and to Sage Publications Ltd and the British Educational Leadership, Management and Administration Society (BELMAS) for permission to reproduce the material in Appendix 2. The full references are:

Wray, A. and Staczek, J. (2005) 'One word or two? Psycholinguistic and sociolinguistic interpretations of meaning in a civil court case.' *International Journal of Speech, Language and the Law* 12(1): 1–18, published by The University of Birmingham Press © 2005. Reproduced with the permission of Equinox Publishing Ltd.

Wallace, M. (2001) 'Sharing leadership of schools through teamwork: a justifiable risk?' *Educational Management, Administration and Leadership* 29(2): 153–167. Published by the British Educational Leadership, Management and Administration Society (BELMAS) © 2001. Reproduced with the permission of Sage Publications Ltd.

Part I　Becoming a Critical Reader and Self-Critical Writer

1 What it Means to be Critical

You may already be a more critical reader than you realize. Take a look at this fictional advertisement and think about how you would respond to it.

WHY DO IT THE HARD WAY
when you can be rich NOW!!!

It took me five years to make my first million. I made my second million in six weeks. Now I just can't stop making money. I own four luxury villas on three continents, five top-of-the-range sports cars and my own helicopter. Most important of all, the financial security of my family is ensured.

Now I want to share my good fortune with you. By following my simple instructions you too can be a millionaire within just a few months. There is no risk and it just can't fail. I have already helped hundreds of people attain their dream of a new life. They are so grateful to me – no longer do they worry about domestic bills, healthcare or their children's education. Their future is certain. And yours can be too.

Just call me on the number below, and I will send you my introductory pack *free of charge*. It will explain to you how my failsafe method can bring you guaranteed wealth and happiness. Call now, and let your life change forever for the better.

The advertisement promises to make you a millionaire. Would you call the phone number? If not – or if you are not sure whether you would – why is that? The introductory pack is free. Your financial worries could soon be over. What would stop you picking up the phone?

The fact is that we do not necessarily take everything we read at face value, nor should we. Our life's experiences make us suspicious of advertisements like this. We might ask: 'Are you as rich as you claim? Why do you want to help people you have never met? Is your method legal and ethical? Is there really no risk? Would I just end up making you richer, at my own expense? If your method is so wonderful, why have I never heard of it before? What will you do with my personal details once I give them to you? How much will the phone call cost?'

These are all critical questions. They indicate that you can see more in a text than is presented on the surface. You are looking for a hidden agenda, the author's real purpose. You are relating what you read to what you already know about the world. It is a sad reflection upon that world, perhaps, but we rarely expect to get something for nothing and we sometimes expect that people will try to trick us.

Learning to be critical in academic enquiry

Academic writing is generally much more benign. We do not normally expect authors to be lying or trying to swindle us. But that does not mean there are not hidden layers to a piece of academic text. A critical approach to the reading of a journal article or book is therefore essential if we are to assess the value of the work it reports. Certain expectations underpin the way in which academic writing operates. The most fundamental expectation is that when a claim is made, it will be backed up by reasons based on some form of evidence. In other words, the reader asks at every point: 'Have you given me sufficient grounds for accepting your claim?' Such a question need not imply that authors are untruthful. In most fields of enquiry it is not a matter of truth, but of viewpoints, interpretation and significance. As readers we are attempting to find common ground between our own understandings and beliefs, and those of the authors. That can only be done by thinking about the extent to which the claims and supporting evidence in a text – which presumably satisfy the authors – also satisfy us.

Since each person has different knowledge and experience, it is sensible for the reader to adopt a critical frame of mind that maintains a distance from, and friendly scepticism towards, what authors say. Thus, in reading an academic article, we might keep in our mind the following sceptical provisos:

- The authors mean to be honest, but may have been misled by the evidence into saying something that I consider untrue.

- The authors mean to be logical, but may have developed a line of reasoning that contains a flaw.

- The authors mean to be impartial, but may have incorporated into the account some assumptions that I do not share.

- The authors mean to tell me something new, but may not have taken into account some information that I already possess from elsewhere.

Reasonable scepticism means being open-minded and willing to be convinced, but only if authors can adequately back up their claims. It entails striking a balance between what one expects and what one accepts. No single study can achieve everything and no author can tell you everything that could possibly be told. The critical reader is not put off by the limitations of a study, but will expect authors to interpret their study in a way that takes account of those limitations. Accomplished authors will clearly signal to the reader the basis on which their conclusions have been drawn and the confidence they have in any generalizations they make.

It takes most novice critical readers a while to learn how to interpret authors' signals, and to work out how to respond to them. As a result, part of the learning process is often that one goes a little too far towards one or both extremes – uncritical acceptance or overcritical rejection of authors' claims – before finding a happy medium. Learning the knack of reasonable scepticism is, of course, particularly challenging because published material really does vary quite considerably in its rigour and reliability.

In order to assess your current ability to evaluate what you read, consider the short (fictional) extract below, from a paper published in 2005 by someone we have called Browning. What questions might you, as a critical reader, want to ask of the author in relation to the claims made? The account refers to a study in which some children were taught to read using the *phonics* method (sounding out words on the basis of the component letters) and others were taught using the *whole word* method (learning to recognize and pronounce complete words).

> In the reading test, the five children who were taught to read using phonics performed better overall than the five children taught using the whole word method. This shows that the phonics method is a better choice for schools.

Your questions might include:

- Is a study of just ten children sufficient to draw such a strong conclusion?

- What does 'performed better overall' signify? Did some children taught using the whole word method perform *better* than some children taught using phonics and, if so, what does this mean for the results?

- Were the differences between the two groups sufficiently great for us to be satisfied that they would occur again in a re-run of the experiment with different subjects?

- How were the two teaching programmes administered, and might there have been 'leakage' of whole word teaching into the phonics teaching and vice versa?

- What was the reading test actually testing, and might it have been unintentionally biased to favour the children taught using phonics?

- What care was taken to check how parental involvement at home might have influenced what and how the children learned?

- Were the two sets of five children matched for intelligence, age, gender, or other factors?

- Is it reasonable to infer that what works well in a small experimental study will work well in all school environments?

- How does Browning envisage phonics being used in schools? Would there still be a place for the whole word method?

Some such questions asked of a short, decontextualized extract like this will almost certainly be answered elsewhere in the text. That is where to look first. But other questions may remain unanswered, leaving you to seek your own answers or to consider the risk involved if you accept the report without answering them. Suppose the text is central to your study for an essay, so that you want to comment on it in detail. Then you will need to include some account of the weaknesses that your critical questions raise, as a balance to your description of what the authors are claiming. Here is an indication of how, in an essay, you might comment on a published text that is useful, but not perfect.

> Browning (2005) found that children taught to read using phonics did better in a reading test than children taught using the whole word method. However, the study was small, the test rather limited, and the subjects were not tightly matched either for age or gender. An examination of Browning's test scores reveals that, although the mean score of the phonics group was higher, two of the highest scorers in the test were whole word learners. Since this indicates that the whole word method is effective for some learners at least, Browning is perhaps too quick to propose that 'the phonics method is a better choice for schools' (p. 89).

Your critical reading of others' work will usually be in preparation for producing your own written text. There are several benefits to this marriage of reading and writing. First, you will develop a sense of what is and is not a robust piece of research – essential when you come to plan your own empirical investigation (for a dissertation, say). Second, you will soon begin to identify where the existing research has left a gap that your investigation can fill. Third, the attention you pay to the writing of others will naturally affect the quality of your own writing. You will soon:

- demand of yourself evidence to back up your claims;

- be alert to the possibility of making an illogical jump in your reasoning;

- become sensitive to your own assumptions and how they might affect your claims;

- realize the importance of checking the literature thoroughly to ensure that your understanding is sufficiently deep.

In short, you will develop a mature academic style of writing that is both fair and astute in its accounts of the work of others, and that maximizes the opportunity for others to take seriously what you have to say.

The skill of critical reading lies in assessing the extent to which authors have provided adequate justification for the claims they make. This assessment depends partly on what the authors have communicated and partly on other relevant knowledge, experience and inference that you are able to bring into the frame.

The skill of self-critical writing lies in convincing your readers to accept your claims. You achieve this through the effective communication of adequate reasons and evidence for these claims.

Academic traditions and styles

All academic traditions require a critical engagement with the works of other scholars. However, some traditions emphasize it more than others. Depending on where you have been educated till now, you may have been encouraged to take predominantly one or another approach to what you read and write. Let us point to the opposite ends of a particular dimension in these traditions: student-centred learning versus knowledge-centred learning. Both have a role for the balanced learner, but neither should be taken to an extreme. Table 1.1 illustrates what can happen at the extremes, and how mature academics must strike a reasonable balance between their own ideas and those of others. Try using these descriptions to help you judge where your educational experience to date has located you on the continuum.

The purpose of student-centred learning is to help individuals gain confidence in developing their own ideas. This is achieved by using existing knowledge as a stepping-stone on the way to originality. In knowledge-centred learning, individuals are encouraged to become aware of existing scholarship and to value it above their own ideas as a novice. Ultimately, both traditions are really just two aspects of the same thing: individuals make a personal effort to contribute something new to an existing bank of respected knowledge. However, the assumptions underlying each tradition do make a difference to how scholars operate. Typically, the rhetoric of the western-style tradition

Table 1.1 Targeting an effective balance between different academic traditions

Too student-centred (Values imaginative thought even if not fully grounded in established theory and knowledge.)	Target balance (Appropriately reflects fair and constructively critical reading.)	Too knowledge-centred (Values traditional wisdom over the views and experience of the academic apprentice.)
Too easily dismisses the expertise of others.	Assumes authors are knowledgeable, while remaining alert for possible flaws in the reasoning.	Takes too much at face value.
Fails to see the big picture.	Juxtaposes the overall picture with the specifics of particular situations.	Fails to see implications of generalized ideas for a specific context.
Underestimates the task of becoming truly knowledge-able about a model or idea.	Is prepared to criticize a model or idea, while retaining a sense of what authors might say in reply.	Believes it is sufficient to be knowledgeable about a model or idea.

tends to emphasize the importance of the individual. Western-educated students can easily over-interpret this emphasis and forget to give sufficient importance to the work of others. In contrast, non-western-educated students may be intimidated by the sudden emphasis on what they think.

The term 'critical reading' is inevitably associated with the idea of the individual trying to show why his or her own interpretation of some idea or observation is better than someone else's. It may seem, then, that someone from a student-centred learning tradition is at an advantage in mastering the skills of critical reading. However, this is not necessarily the case. Students from both traditions bring something useful to the task and have pitfalls to avoid. The techniques introduced in this book bring together skills from each tradition.

Being critical as a requirement of academic study

Just what is expected, then, in postgraduate study? Here is an example description, with key features in bold type.

An Official Statement of Expectations Placed on Postgraduate Students

Critical thinking and creativity: managing creative processes in self and others; **organizing thoughts, analysis, synthesis, critical appraisal**. This includes the capability to **identify assumptions, evaluate statements in terms of evidence, detect false logic or reasoning, identify implicit values, define terms** adequately and **generalize** appropriately.

(Extract from 'Skills for all Masters Programmes', subject benchmark statement for the Master's level award in Business and Management, Quality Assurance Agency for Higher Education (UK), http://www.qaa.ac.uk/academicinfrastructure/benchmark/masters/MBAintro.asp)

The lengthy list of critical skills here can be boiled down to just two: the capacity to evaluate what you read and the capacity to relate what you read to other information. Applying these skills to any academic text involves looking out for its potential strengths and weaknesses.

Evaluation is important. If knowledge was simply a set of facts, we could take all that we read at face value. However, knowledge is only partly about the facts themselves. Knowledge also entails their interpretation and the use of past facts to help us make predictions about future facts. It often also entails the evaluation of facts against certain assumed values. For instance, it was taken for granted in the earlier illustrative discussion about phonics and whole word reading that it is desirable for children to learn to read efficiently and effectively. If you take away that assumption, then the facts will be open to different interpretations. It can be a shock to the university student when first discovering that facts can be interpreted in diverse ways, leading to very different predictions about what will happen in the future, or judgements about what should happen.

The critical reading of a text is rarely about questioning the facts as such. Mostly it is about assessing the quality of the case that has been made for interpreting and evaluating the facts in some way. Thus, the critical reader is interested in whether there is sufficient evidence to support a claim, whether there is another possible interpretation that has not been considered, and perhaps whether the authors have argued convincingly that their interpretation applies to other cases.

The critical reader can achieve this by focusing on several potential objects of scrutiny, addressing one or more of them at any time. They include:

- the evidence provided in the account;

- whether the reasoning of the author's argument follows logically to the conclusion that has been drawn;

- explicit or implicit indications of the author's values and assumptions;

- the match between the author's claims and those of other authors;

- the match between the author's claims or predictions and the reader's own research evidence or knowledge.

To engage fully and appropriately with a written text, the reader ideally needs to have a clear understanding of what the authors are doing, sufficient knowledge of the field of enquiry and (where possible) reliable evidence of his or her own, or at least some reliable intuitions about the way things work in the real world. But no readers have the necessary time or expertise always to put themselves in this advantageous position. The art, then, is to know how far to go with any particular text. This, in turn, will depend on how central the text is to the study activity that one is involved in, and what one's specific goals are in reading it. Reading is done for a reason, and maintaining a clear sense of what that reason is makes evaluation much easier.

Task-driven critical reading

It should always be possible, before you start reading a book or journal article, to state why you are doing so. Here are some possible reasons:

- you have been told to read it in preparation for a class;

- you are doing background reading on a particular subject, just to get your bearings;

- it reports a particular approach or technique that you want to see in action;

- it addresses a particular question that you want to know the answer to;

- you are looking for evidence to counter-balance something else that you have read;

- you have a particular story to tell, and you need some supporting evidence for it.

Irrespective of your reason for reading a text, it is generally helpful to approach it with one or more questions that you want to answer in order to progress your own work. A broad question addressed to the author such as 'What did you do, and what did you find out?' will be best answered with a straight description of the content of the paper. However, more finely-tuned questions will help you focus on specific issues, while automatically providing a direct route into critical reading. For example: 'Is this author's method of investigation the best one for me to emulate in my own work? How does this author's position compare with that of another author whose work I've read? Would this author be likely to challenge the claims that I am making in my own work?'

Other than at the initial background reading stage, you will rarely have the luxury of reading for reading's sake. There is simply too much literature out there. You will have to make choices about what you read and how thoroughly you read it. These choices will be based on your best guess about what you might use the information for: usually some written task of your own. So the questions you bring to the text, as illustrated above, can help you decide what to read and in how much depth.

It may seem like a bad idea to decide, *before* you read something, what you are going to get out of it. How can you know until you have finished reading? If you start with a particular question in mind, will that not prevent you from seeing what else the material has to offer? The danger is not as great as it may seem. If you are alert, you will tend to notice other things that are relevant to your task, even if you did not expect to find them there. The single-minded approach will help you to separate out the different kinds of information you are seeking and deal with them at the right time.

Imagine you are reading a paper that reports a questionnaire study because you want to get some hints on how to design a questionnaire of your own. In the course of the reading you realize that one of the results of the study has a bearing on what you are researching. The fact that you already have a focused question regarding the study design will encourage you to make a note to return to the paper later, when you are specifically working on a data-related question. Doing so will help you avoid distracting yourself from the matter in hand so that you end up achieving neither task properly.

This disciplined strategy means that you may often read the same work more than once, for different purposes. It also means that any notes you make on that work will tend to be in different places, under topic headings, rather in the form of a single, bland and unfocussed summary of what the paper says.

Linking critical reading with self-critical writing

One person's writing is another person's reading. Whatever you write as a student will be read critically by your assessors. If you progress to writing for publication, anonymous reviewers and then the general academic community will also be critical readers of your work. A secret of successful writing is to anticipate the expectations and potential objections of the audience of critical readers for whom you are writing. That means that you must have a sense of who your readers are and what they expect. What you learn from this book about the techniques of critical reading in the academic context can be directly applied to making your own academic writing robust for other critical readers like you – who are intelligent, well-informed and fair-minded, who are ready to be convinced, but who expect high standards of scholarship and clarity in what they read.

As you work through this book, identifying effective ways of interrogating what you read, you will find that some of the techniques are familiar because you already apply them to your reading and writing. Others you will now be able to apply for the

Table 1.2   Linking a critical approach to your reading with a self-critical approach to your writing

How critical a reader and self-critical a writer are you already?

A   Tick each element of critical reading in the list below that you already employ when you read academic literature.

B   Tick each element of self-critical writing that you already employ when you write. (You may find it helpful to look at assessors' comments on your past work, to see what they have praised and criticized).

C   Then add up the number of ticks for each column, and consider your response to our statement at the end of the exercise.

Element of critical reading		Element of self-critical writing	
When I read an academic text I:	*Tick*	**When I write an academic text I:**	*Tick*
1 try to work out what the authors are aiming to achieve;		1 state clearly what I am trying to achieve;	
2 try to work out the structure of the argument;		2 create a logical structure for my account, to help me develop my argument and to help the reader to follow it;	
3 try to identify the main claims made;		3 clearly state my main claims;	
4 adopt a sceptical stance towards the authors' claims, checking that they are supported by appropriate evidence;		4 support my claims with appropriate evidence, so that a critical reader will be convinced;	
5 assess the backing for any generalizations made;		5 avoid making sweeping generalizations;	
6 check how the authors define their key terms and whether they are consistent in using them;		6 define the key terms employed in my account, and use the terms consistently;	
7 consider what underlying values may be guiding the authors and influencing their claims;		7 make explicit the values guiding what I write;	
8 keep an open mind, willing to be convinced;		8 assume that my readers can be convinced, provided I can adequately support my claims;	
9 look out for instances of irrelevant or distracting material, and for the absence of necessary material;		9 sustain focus throughout my account, avoid irrelevancies and digressions, and include everything that is relevant;	

(Continued)

Table 1.2 (Continued)

Element of critical reading		Element of self-critical writing	
When I read an academic text I:	*Tick*	**When I write an academic text I:**	*Tick*
10 identify any literature sources to which the authors refer, that I may need to follow up.		10 ensure that my referencing in the text and the reference list is complete and accurate, so that my readers are in a position to check my sources.	
Total number of ticks		**Total number of ticks**	

The more ticks you have for both columns, the further you have already progressed in becoming a critical reader and self-critical writer. Look back at any boxes that you have not ticked. Consider how you might incorporate these elements of critical and self-critical writing into your habitual approach to study.

first time. If you need certain things in what you read, it makes sense that you should supply them to your target audience in what you write. If you want clarity, then you yourself should be clear. If you need authors to be explicit about their assumptions, then you should be explicit about yours. If you want authors to provide evidence to support their claims, then you should provide evidence for your own.

No two readers want quite the same things, and you will probably never fully anticipate all of the requirements and preferences of your assessors. But you can certainly get a long way towards that goal. How far have you progressed so far in becoming a critical reader and self-critical writer? Try the exercise in Table 1.2.

In Table 1.2 we have highlighted the link between elements of critical reading and their counterparts in self-critical writing. Whatever you look for as a critical reader of literature, your assessors may also look for in your writing when judging how far it meets their assessment criteria. The elements of self-critical writing relate to meeting the needs of your readers, so that they can grasp what you are trying to communicate. But just as importantly, they enhance your capacity to make your argument convincing to your readers. This is why it is to your advantage to develop a strong sense of your audience. Meeting your target readers' needs and convincing them will help to ensure that your account meets the assessment criteria. During your studies, you will find it useful to refer back to this exercise occasionally, to monitor your progress in developing critical reading and self-critical writing skills.

Where now?

Having discussed how to make the most of what you read, the next step is to consider how to select effectively from the vast array of literature available. That is the topic of the next chapter. Then, in Chapter 3, we introduce the basics of critical reading, in the form of five Critical Synopsis Questions that you can ask of a text. Chapters 4 and 5 use these insights to introduce some simple techniques for self-critical writing: presenting your own ideas in a well-supported way. Part One thus prepares you for the more detailed engagement of Parts Two and Three, where we revisit the same approach at a more advanced level.

2 Making a Critical Choice

What you choose to read in preparing for your assessed written work is as important as how critically you read it. Becoming a critical reader must entail becoming a critical selector of those texts that promise most centrally to suit your study purposes. There is far too much literature out there, especially with the advent of the Internet, for you to read everything that may be relevant. So making critical choices about what to read is the first step in critical reading.

Our chapter begins with techniques for deciding what to read. We then distinguish between different types of literature that you may come across in the course of your studies. Finally, we consider how the Internet offers you a very potent but sometimes unreliable literature source.

Deciding what to read

Suppose it is time to start reading for an essay or a longer piece of work. Where do you begin? You may have been supplied with an indicative reading list and perhaps some set texts. If so, someone else has made some decisions on your behalf to get you started. But whether or not you have that initial helping hand, there still comes a point when you have to make decisions about what to read. The more principled you can make your choices, the better.

Strategy is paramount. Apart from planning ahead – getting to the library before the crowd for instance – it is useful to operate a two-stage process when identifying what to read. First, draw up a long-list of texts that look important. Then select carefully from within that list those texts that you will aim to obtain and read. An advantage of this approach is that you can easily compensate if an item you had targeted is not available. You can work out from your long-list what other text might fulfil the same function. Drawing up the long-list is relatively straightforward. You might consider any of the following tactics:

- Use any recommended reading list that has been issued for your module or subject area, including those from past years.

- Search on the Internet for reading lists posted up for similar modules at other universities, and identify texts that are repeatedly recommended.

- Look up one or two important texts in the library catalogue. Then do a search using their subject code to see what else has been classified as covering the same topic.

- Go to the library shelves and see what is physically stored under the same class mark as the key recommended texts.

- Note how many copies the library has of a particular text. If there are plenty, this has evidently been a recommended text at some point.

- As you begin to read, note texts that are often cited by others, and whether positively or negatively (both may be useful).

- Make a list of the three or four journals most often carrying papers that have been recommended or frequently cited, then check the back and current issues of those journals for other papers of the same kind.

- Use abstracts databases to search for papers via keywords and author names that you associate with the topic.

- Look through the catalogues (on paper or on-line) of the leading academic publishers to see what has come out recently.

- Check what books have been reviewed in recent academic journals.

In this way, you can soon build up your list of *possible* reading, from which you can choose what you actually read and in how much detail.

Yet you might reasonably ask why you should consider reading anything that has not been specifically recommended to you. There are many reasons why a relevant text may not be included on your reading list. There may not have been room for all the possible items. Or your topic may be one of several covered in the module, so it has not been given many entries of its own. By keeping the reading list small, the lecturer may even be encouraging you to take some responsibility for seeking out appropriate literature. In short, it is up to you to find out what else might be worth reading and add it to your long-list.

From long-list to short-list

How should you decide which items on your long-list to prioritize? Your reading has to achieve several aims that your selection of texts must take into account. A convincing essay (or dissertation) is likely to cover some or all of the following in relation to the literature:

- An overview of what the key issues in the field are and why they are important.

- An overview of what has been done and found out, and a summary of where the field of enquiry currently stands.

- Some specific examples of the sorts of methodology, results and analysis reported by individual researchers.

- Answers to one or more specific questions that you have been required, or have chosen, to address.

No single text can support all of these agendas. You may need one set of texts to help you develop your overview, another set to help you interpret the work to date within its wider context, yet another to give you specific information about methodology and analysis, and so on. To target your reading you need to ensure that you short-list a variety of texts that between them will help you achieve each of your goals. But how can you tell what a particular text is most likely to be useful for? One way is by categorizing texts according to their main purpose.

Support literature

Textbooks

Most students turn to textbooks early on in their academic studies. There are two basic types of textbook. Skills textbooks aim to help you learn such things as how to design a robust investigation, analyze data statistically, and so on. Skills textbooks are not usually problematic to use, since it is clear that they are a tool rather than a resource. The other kind of textbook, to which we shall direct our focus in what follows, is the subject textbook. Subject textbooks generally introduce readers to a field of academic enquiry, and are explicitly designed to support students' learning. The features of textbooks may include:

- relatively cheap compared with research books;

- words like 'introduction', 'guide' or 'study' in the title or the series title;

- available in softback, with an eye-catching cover;

- a title that evidently encompasses a field or sub-field rather than a particular research agenda (e.g., *A Short History of the English Language*) or else that covers a particular skill (e.g., *Statistics in the Social Sciences*);

- cover-blurb that indicates a student target readership;

- multiple copies in academic bookshops and libraries. Also, popular textbooks often run to more than one edition.

Although they are of crucial importance to any student, textbooks are something of an exception in the academic literature, falling largely outside the central realm of research activity. As a result, they should be used with care. At postgraduate level you will be expected to have more on your reference list than textbooks. They can be an excellent place to start, but inherent limitations mean that they are usually *only* a starting place.

One difficulty with using a subject textbook is that it can be so like a literature review that it is difficult for you to find something new to say. It is important, therefore, to view the textbook author as just one interpreter of the facts. Expect that there will be other ways of interpreting the facts too, and look for those ways, both in other textbooks and by thinking things through for yourself. If you view a textbook as just the account of one commentator, rather than a summary of some unassailable truth, it becomes possible to pitch one account against another and discuss the reasons for the differences.

A second difficulty with a textbook is that it normally tells you *about* research without you getting to see the original research report. It is essential, at postgraduate level, to make every attempt to read for yourself anything that you judge to be of central importance. You cannot guarantee that textbook authors have interpreted research in the same way that you would have, or have focused on the aspects that are of significance for you. The only way you can be sure is to read the original works. Most textbooks provide full references to their sources, and you should aim to follow them up so that you have had sight of everything you discuss. Occasionally you may have to compromise and simply identify a particular work as 'cited in' some other work – that is, admitting that you have read *about* it but not actually *read* it. But aim to keep such references to an absolute minimum.

A third limitation of some textbooks is that, in the interests of offering the reader a clear story, authors may make strong claims that are not backed up with sufficient evidence and they may over-simplify complicated issues. This is not necessarily inappropriate, given the introductory nature of a textbook. But it can be a hazard for students, who may fail to appreciate the complexity underlying an apparently simple observation, or fail to realize that opinion is divided on a matter that is presented as fact. Again, the solution is to see the textbook as a signpost to information, rather than a fully reliable source, and to read the original works that it cites wherever possible.

Readers, handbooks and encyclopaedias

Other forms of support literature include readers, handbooks and encyclopaedias. Readers are collections of classic papers on a particular subject. While a few of the papers may have been written especially for the collection, most will be articles or extracts from books that have previously been published elsewhere. The editors will have selected what they consider to be the most important work for students to read. But their selection is a personal one and other academics may not consider it to be fully representative of key works in the field. If a paper in a reader has been reproduced in full, it is acceptable to reference its appearance there and not to have seen the original. However, it is a good idea to give the original date as well as the date of the reader, so that it is clear when the paper was written.

Handbooks and specialist encyclopaedias are like readers, except that the articles will normally have been especially commissioned. Leading academics will have written a comprehensive overview of the current state of research, theory or methodology in their area. Such articles are, in consequence, immensely useful for gaining a solid understanding of the state-of-the-art in a field. Remember, however, that even top researchers can give only their own perspective and there are likely to be other perspectives that you should also consider.

'Front-line' literature

This book deals predominantly with the critical reading of *front-line* publications: theoretical descriptions and explanations, reports of original research, accounts of current practice and policy statements. Such works are the direct link between you and a researcher, practitioner or policy-maker. They report what has been done, how, why, what it means and what should be done next. You can use them to help you answer questions arising from all aspects of your own work, from its conceptualization, through its design, implementation and interpretation, to its presentation in written form.

A rough-and-ready distinction may be made between four types of front-line literature: theoretical, research, practice and policy. Most texts are easily identifiable as belonging to one type or another. For example, a journal article reporting an empirical investigation is obviously research literature. But you should bear in mind that any individual text may feature aspects of more than one literature type. Thus a journal article which is mainly reporting an empirical investigation may also discuss implications for the development of theory. Here is a brief description of each type, which shows how all four can be used to impart one or more kinds of knowledge. (In Part Two, we explore types of literature and kinds of knowledge in more detail.)

Theoretical literature models the way things are (or appear to be), by using evidence to identify patterns. The evidence may include experiments, observations, experience or ideas, and may not be work that the theorizers have conducted themselves. The patterns, once formalized into a theoretical model, may enable researchers to make predictions about what will happen in future scenarios. Such predictions are called *hypotheses* (Figure 2.1).

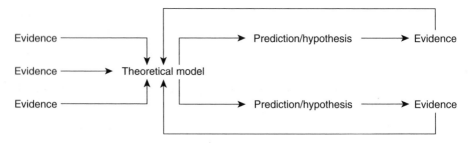

Figure 2.1   How theory and evidence interact

When neutrally presented, a theoretical model can help readers to deepen their understanding of the social world and to anticipate what range of things might be observed in the future, and under what circumstances. Theoretical literature can also be used to present the case for a particular point of view or to recommend changes. Recommended changes might be at an international, national, institutional or personal level and, accordingly, readers may be more or less able to respond directly to them. Consider the case of a journal article putting forward a predictive model about the consumption of the earth's natural resources. The model predicts that, at current rates of consumption, some resources will be used up within fifty years. In itself, such an account is merely a statement of what the facts appear to be. However, it could be used to criticize national or international policy, to make recommendations for change, to influence the way people are educated, or to encourage individuals to take greater responsibility for their personal use of resources.

Research, or data-driven, literature reports observations about the real world, often relating them to a prediction or hypothesis derived from a theory or model. Data falls broadly into two types, observational and experimental, though there is some overlap. The major difference relates to whether or not the researcher manipulates the situation. In a classic experimental design, a comparison might be made between two groups or situations that are identical except in one specific regard determined by the experimenter. It is assumed that any difference in the outcomes will be due to that one contrast. In a classic observational design, the researcher might gather data that will indicate how a particular individual or group operates, but without intervening. Between the two lies a range of options, including:

- Observing two contrasting groups or situations that occur naturally (a natural experiment).

- Observation in which the researcher participates in the observed activity or situation (participant observation).

- Detailed observation of one or more individuals or groups with the same, or contrasting, profiles (case studies).

As with theoretical literature, data-driven research may be presented neutrally, in order to augment a general understanding about how particular phenomena operate. However, it can also be used to help explain where things are going wrong, to demonstrate a method that seems to work well (or better than some other method), to convince trainers or policy-makers to effect changes in present methods, or to enable individual readers to gain fresh insights into their own behaviour or practice.

Practice literature relates to accounts of how things are done, and will often be written by experienced practitioners who feel that others might benefit from an understanding of how they operate. This type of literature features most strongly in applied fields of enquiry that focus on a domain of practical activity in the social world, such as nursing. A neutral account might, for instance, offer a personal illustration of how a particular nurse working for a relief agency has learned to cope with the extreme demands of over-crowded refugee camps in times of famine. But the account might also be put to use in identifying shortcomings in existing systems, recommending practices that have been found to be effective, training others who will soon encounter similar situations or, at the personal level, influencing readers to reflect on similarities between their own situation and the one reported.

In *policy literature* (also featuring most strongly in applied fields) the emphasis is on effecting major changes in existing patterns of practice. A neutral report might recount how something is currently done, along with indications of any predictable outcomes from that approach. A less neutral report might propose alternative approaches that would lead to more desirable outcomes, outline how a particular policy is to be implemented through training provision, or offer individuals specific insights relating to their own approach in relation to existing or new policy. For instance, a policy document might prescribe changes in practice in the recruitment and training of interpreters for the law courts. Proposed improvements might include measures for obtaining better qualified interpreters, rolling out a successful pilot scheme to more areas, and training court officials and police officers in the new procedures. Individual readers of the document might, according to their role in the process, decide to pay more attention to how potential interpreters are identified, how they are approached and dealt with, or how individuals requiring interpreters fare under the current policy.

Using the Internet: opportunities and dangers

Much support and front-line literature is available in electronic format as well as in hard copy. If you have Internet access, you will also have access to powerful search engines that direct you to myriad websites and downloadable files. However, care must be taken in using the Internet. On the one hand, it is a huge resource offering enormous opportunities to gather information but, on the other, it carries certain dangers.

Many of these dangers are obvious. Leaving aside such things as computer viruses, there are two major potential pitfalls that you need to know how to avoid. One is using

Internet resources as a convenient replacement for work you should be doing yourself, in particular the construction of text. Copying and pasting material from the Internet into your own work is regarded as cheating, or *plagiarism*, and usually carries very heavy penalties. You need to resist the temptation to take this short cut. Your assessor's critical eye is very likely to spot what you have done and, more fundamentally, you will not learn as much as you would by doing the work yourself. What is the point of postgraduate study if you do not attempt to maximize your learning? Plagiarism is a huge issue in higher education, and we recommend that you inform yourself fully about it and scrupulously avoid it in your work.

The question of *unreliability* is another aspect of Internet usage and is directly relevant to our key concern with critical reading. However critically you aim to read, it makes sense to favour texts that you have reasonable confidence in. The support literature and front-line publications discussed earlier have been written by people with a commitment to truth and accuracy. In addition, all such texts have undergone some level of scrutiny by others to ensure that they live up to that commitment. The Internet, on the other hand, is a huge, amoral, uncoordinated dissemination forum. On the one hand, it includes some of the support literature and front-line publications whose reliability is assured by the means we have just described. On the other hand, there are no safeguards to assure the quality of everything else that can be posted on websites. As a result, the content of the Internet overall, and its reliability, is very variable.

Given the potential benefits, we strongly advocate using the Internet if it is available. But you need to be critical in sorting the good material from the bad. Since this is not always easy, you need techniques for ensuring that your use of the Internet only enhances, and never diminishes, the quality of your academic work. These techniques include applying all the standards of critical reading that we describe in this book and not assuming that the confidence with which something is said is a reliable guide to how true it is.

When you are learning about a new topic, it is often difficult to evaluate the quality of an argument or of evidence. So you may not feel confident about whether a claim you find on the Internet is reliable. A technique for avoiding this difficulty is to think of the Internet not as a repository of knowledge but as a catalogue. When you find something on the Internet, try to avoid making that the endpoint of your search. Take the information and use it to locate another kind of material in which you can have more confidence.

For instance, you might find on a webpage the following claim: 'Metaphors are central to how we navigate the world (Lakoff and Johnson)'. Rather than accepting this claim without any further investigation, it would be much safer to check out who Lakoff and Johnson are, and to see if they have written an academic paper or book making the claim. (Indeed they have: Lakoff, G. and Johnson, M. (1980) *Metaphors We Live By*, Chicago: University of Chicago Press.) If so, obtain the text from the library and use that as your resource. The Internet has been a springboard, much as your supervisor might be when recommending that you look at a particular text.

INTERNET MATERIAL – THE GOOD, THE BAD AND THE UGLY

Likely to be very reliable:
1   Journal articles that have gone through peer review and are also published in an academic journal. In fact, these should be referenced according to their paper details, rather than as an Internet resource.
2   Journal articles published in genuine electronic journals and subject to the same peer review processes as paper journals. These need to be referenced using their volume number and date, plus the full web address. It is possible that they will not have page numbers.
3   Journal articles and book chapters that have already been published and have been posted, usually in PDF, on an academic's home page. Check, however, that it is the published version you have. If it says 'submitted to' a journal, or 'draft', then it has not yet been peer-reviewed. It will be worth trying to find out if it has since been published.
4   Official materials published on a recognized institutional website, e.g., the British Museum site, or the Institute of Linguists' site. You can find out what site you are on by going to the home page.

Likely to be fairly reliable:
1   Pre-peer-reviewed material, as described in (3) above – but track down the published version if possible.
2   Lecture or research notes on the site of an academic working at a recognized institution.

Likely to be unreliable:
1   Material on the home pages of individuals.
2   Material on organization websites that is written by enthusiasts rather than experts.
3   Free-for-all post-your-views sites (unless restricted to a recognized set of academic contributors).
4   Web-logs, chatroom pontifications, etc.

REFERENCING INTERNET SOURCES: GOLDEN RULES

1   Attribute the material to a person if possible, not just a web address. Giving the web address alone is like referencing a book by describing where you found it in the library.
2   If (and only if) no author is named (and you may need to explore the site to be sure), give the institutional details instead. If you can't find an author or an institution, do you really want to trust this material?

(Continued)

(Continued)

3   Give the date when it was posted or last updated, if available, otherwise the year in which you saw it.
4   Indicate the date on which you last accessed it.
5   Always check that the URL you have given will indeed take someone to the exact material you are citing.

An example of how to reference an Internet source:
In the text:

… there is no single agreed definition of formulaic language (Wray 2004) …

In the reference list:

Wray, A. (2004) 'What is formulaic language?' *http://www.cf.ac.uk/encap/clcr/flarn/formulaiclanguage.html*. (Last accessed 28th August 2005.)

Academic authors who aim to convince a critical reader that their work is robust will *only* reference Internet sources where:

- The material is robust and reliable.

- There is no equivalent published paper version.

- The Internet resource has been the legitimate end-of-the-line, not the means to finding a published paper resource.

Being choosy about the literature you read

To sum up, in postgraduate studies there is no avoiding the necessity, sooner or later, of selecting what to read and deciding what *not* to read. The support literature is frequently a good place to begin. But you cannot expect support literature to provide the full detail, depth of argument and backing for claims contained in the front-line literature that this support literature is designed to introduce. At postgraduate level, the assessors of your written work will expect you to have engaged critically with the front-line literature. So we suggest that you use the support literature to gain an initial overview of any topic, and as one way of identifying the key front-line literature sources that you should read. The Internet is another good place to begin. But you cannot expect all material that you turn up to be as reliable as peer-reviewed journal articles and official publications. So we recommend that you simultaneously maximize your use of the Internet to find out what there is that you should read, but minimize your reliance on the Internet as your final destination.

Enough said about what to read. Once you have a text in your hands, how are you to read it critically, rather than just absorbing its content? That is the focus of the next chapter.

3 Getting Started on Critical Reading

Critical reading as part of academic study is a very active process. Although it is tempting to conceive of reading simply as a matter of passively transferring information from the page into your head, what actually occurs is much more complicated. You cannot avoid being affected by your own expectations, prejudices and previous knowledge, and these will shape your understanding of the literature you read.

It is vital to realize that authors also have prejudices, assumptions and beliefs. These too will tend to influence your understanding of a text. Therefore a key critical reading skill is that of identifying authors' underlying aims and agendas, so that you can take them into account in your evaluation of the text in hand. Occasionally you will have to think carefully and 'read between the lines' to establish authors' values and aims. More often the authors will not be hiding anything, whether deliberately or accidentally, and you will easily be able to establish their purpose, provided you realize the importance of doing so.

We have already noted that critical reading for postgraduate study is task-driven: usually the task culminates in a written product for assessment. In the previous chapter we discussed the first step in taking charge of your response to a task: making your own critical choice about what you read. Once you have done that, your second step is to make the texts work for you. Far from having to absorb slavishly everything the authors have written, you can *focus* your reading by asking questions of a text and looking for answers that will help you to achieve your goals.

In this chapter we first briefly consider how asking carefully formulated questions can help you to focus on what you are looking for in a text, even before you start reading it. Next we explore how you might evaluate what you have read – by identifying authors' arguments and judging the adequacy of the backing they offer for them. Finally we bring together the skills of focusing and evaluating, by offering a simple way to structure the questions you ask of any text. (This approach paves the way for a more detailed analysis of texts in Part Two.)

Focusing through a central question and review questions

In Chapter 1 we saw that asking questions as you study a text enables you to focus your reading effort. For literature-related tasks that draw on a number of texts, you can gain additional focus by formulating a broad *central question*. It will underlie the entire piece of work or a substantial thematic section. A central question is expressed in general terms and asks a question about something in the social world that will almost certainly need to be answered by asking more specific questions. An essay title is often framed as a central question (e.g., 'Does perceived social status affect how pharmacists address their customers?'). An essay title that is not framed as a question (e.g., 'Discuss the impact of perceived social status on the ways in which pharmacists address their customers') can usually be turned easily into a question. Doing so is a very effective tactic for finding and keeping focus in your work.

A *review question* is a more specific question that you ask of the literature. Review questions that are derived from a broader central question will ask something that directly contributes to answering the central question (e.g., 'What does research suggest are key factors determining how pharmacists would be likely to address their customers?'). However, review questions can also help with theoretical questions (e.g., 'Whose model can I use to investigate style shift in speakers?'). Similarly, review questions may arise in justifying the methodology of your own developing research for, say, a dissertation (e.g., 'What can I learn from published studies about how to observe interaction in shops?'). The review question, or questions, you ask of the literature will therefore vary according to your purposes and the type of literature you deem a particular text to be.

Evaluating the usefulness of what you read

Working on the assumption that not all texts are going to be equally useful, how can you establish the merits of what you read? Obviously, you want to take most notice of the works that contribute something directly relevant to your task, and that you feel are reliable and plausible. Not all opinions are worth taking seriously and extreme views might need to be treated with caution.

To find out how reliable the material in a text is, you need to identify and evaluate its *arguments*. An argument consists of a *conclusion* (one or more claims that something is, or should be, the case) and a *warrant* (the justification for why the claim or claims should be accepted). A warrant is likely to consist of evidence from the author's research or professional experience, or else it will draw on others' evidence, as reported in the literature. A robust conclusion, then, is one that is sufficiently warranted by some form of evidence. Only with such evidence should you be convinced of a conclusion's validity.

OPINION = UNWARRANTED CONCLUSION

ARGUMENT = CONCLUSION + WARRANT

The *conclusion* is only half of an argument. You can legitimately ask of any set of claims: 'Why should I believe this?' The other half of the argument is the *warrant*. The warrant is the reason for accepting the conclusion. Demand a convincing warrant for every conclusion that you read about. Also, demand of yourself that every conclusion you draw is adequately warranted.

It is the authors' job to provide you with the best available warrant for their conclusion. Your job is to judge whether the warrant is enough to make the conclusion convincing, and so whether that conclusion should be accepted or rejected. By way of illustration, we will unpack the argument and the evaluation of it that formed our example in Chapter 1. Here is the (fictional) extract from Browning again:

> In the reading test, the five children who were taught to read using phonics performed better overall than the five children taught using the whole word method. This shows that the phonics method is a better choice for schools.

The conclusion is a single claim: 'the phonics method is a better choice for schools'. Browning offers research evidence as the warrant for his conclusion: 'the five children who were taught to read using phonics performed better overall than the five children taught using the whole word method'. But we saw that Browning's claim was vulnerable, at least as depicted in the extract, because it was not clear how he could justify his claim that the phonics method was best for any school on the basis of this small amount of evidence. What Browning's claim illustrates is the drawing of a conclusion without *sufficient* warrant. Here is the example commentary from Chapter 1:

> Browning (2005) found that children taught to read using phonics did better in a reading test than children taught using the whole word method. However, the study was small, the test rather limited, and the subjects were not tightly matched either for age or gender. An examination of Browning's test scores reveals that, although the mean score of the phonics group was higher, two of the highest scorers in the test were whole word learners. Since this indicates that the whole word method is effective for some learners at least, Browning is perhaps too quick to propose that 'the phonics method is a better choice for schools' (p. 89).

The commentator evaluates the claim by critically assessing whether Browning's warrant is strong enough to make his conclusion convincing. First, the limitations of the empirical investigation are noted: 'the study was small, the test rather limited, and the subjects were not tightly matched either for age or gender'. Second, a notable degree of overlap is highlighted between the range of findings for the two groups of subjects, something that was evidently reported by Browning but was ignored by him in warranting his conclusion: 'An examination of Browning's test scores reveals that, although the mean score of the phonics group was higher, two of the highest scorers in the test were whole word learners'.

Note that these two evaluatory comments comprise the *commentator's own evaluatory warrant*. The commentator's evaluatory warrant is used to *back the commentator's own conclusion* that: 'Since this indicates that the whole word method is effective for some learners at least, Browning is perhaps too quick to propose that "the phonics method is a better choice for schools"'. The commentator is implying that Browning's warrant is insufficiently robust to make his sweeping conclusion convincing.

Importantly, in your role as commentator, you should be cautious about how you make counter-claims – you, yourself, must have sufficient warrant to support them. It would be unfortunate to write: 'Browning is unable adequately to justify his conclusion that "phonics is the best choice for schools", therefore, we can conclude that phonics is *not* the best choice for schools'. It is rather easy to criticize the shortcomings of others' conclusions, and then to draw similarly flawed conclusions oneself!

This potential for a commentator to draw insufficiently warranted conclusions makes its own impact on your reading. Thus far, you will have identified yourself with the commentator in this example. However, suppose that you, as a critical reader, are reading this commentary on Browning's work as one of your texts. You need not accept at face value the conclusions that the commentator draws. Has the commentator supplied sufficient warrant to justify the conclusion that Browning's claim should be rejected? In order to decide, you might choose to go and read Browning's work for yourself and see whether you feel that the commentator has been fair or not.

Tracking down and reading the original work is of great importance for evaluating the arguments in a text that reports it second-hand. Every retelling of a story tends to simplify it and second- or third-hand accounts can end up appearing much more definitive than the original. Thus, even though Browning offers too little warrant for his conclusion about phonics being the best choice for any school, this does not necessarily mean that phonics is the worst choice, or that the whole word method is the best choice. A range of possibilities opens up regarding alternative claims. One is that Browning is right, but just has not been able to provide satisfactory evidence from his own study. Another is that Browning has failed to see certain patterns, or to relate his findings to others that might have supported his conclusions. Our commentator has not chosen to provide the kind of information that you would need in order to see what options there are. So only by reading the original study for yourself, rather than relying on an intermediary, could you ensure that you were fully informed in making your own evaluation.

Identifying the warrants and conclusions of arguments

Academic discourse offers us several ways of relating ideas to each other. As a result, there is more than one formulation that can connect a conclusion and its warrant. Key indicators are the words or phrases that link the conclusion to the warrant, such as: *therefore, because, since, so, it follows that, it can be concluded that*, and so on. For instance, the following formulations all say essentially the same thing:

- *Since* research shows that girls mature faster than boys, studies should take age and gender into account when exploring child development.

- Child development studies should take age and gender into account *because* research shows that girls mature faster than boys.

- Research shows that girls mature faster than boys. *Therefore*, studies of child development should take age and gender into account.

Other variations may weight the warrant, implying that it is reliable in its own terms but not necessarily universally true:

- *Insofar as* girls are believed to mature faster than boys, studies of child development should take age and gender into account.

- *In conditions where* girls mature faster than boys, studies of child development should take age and gender into account.

- *Where it is relevant to the investigation that* girls mature faster than boys, studies should take age and gender into account.

Incomplete or flawed arguments

In your reading (and your own writing) look out for incomplete arguments. Here are some common flaws and the ways in which you can ask questions to identify where the problem lies (Table 3.1).

As these illustrations suggest, when you adopt the role of critical reader you are, in a sense, interrogating the author, to answer the questions that your reading has raised in your mind.

Table 3.1 Identifying flaws in arguments

Flaw	Questions that indicate the flaw
Conclusion without a warrant.	Why? How do you know?
Warrant without a conclusion.	So what? Why are you telling me this? What does it imply?
Conclusion with an inadequate warrant.	Does this evidence really mean as much as you claim? Is this evidence robust enough?
Warrant leading to an illogical conclusion.	Does this reasoning add up? Aren't there other more plausible conclusions?
Conclusion that is not explicitly linked to its warrant.	What are you trying to claim? What is the causal relationship between the factors?

THINKING YOUR WAY INTO THE MIND OF THE AUTHOR

How can you focus on *your* questions when the author's agenda may be different? Imagine that you have the opportunity to talk to the author face to face. What questions would you ask to pursue your own agenda? Use the author's text to try and work out how the author would answer your questions.

Five Critical Synopsis Questions

The five questions introduced here map onto the more detailed approach to critical reading that we explore in Part Two. As will become clearer then, the extent to which you apply the in-depth level of engagement will vary, depending on how central a given text is to what you are trying to achieve. In many cases, the five basic Critical Synopsis Questions are all you will need and, even where you undertake a more detailed analysis, they may well have been your starting point:

A   Why am I reading this?

B   What are the authors trying to do in writing this?

C   What are the authors saying that is relevant to what I want to find out?

D   How convincing is what the authors are saying?

E   In conclusion, what use can I make of this?

Critical Synopsis Question A: Why am I reading this?

In Chapter 2 we reviewed some of the most likely answers to this question. In the early stages of your study of a new area you may be reading something because you were advised to or because you want to gather some background. However, the more you work in an area, the more you will be choosing what to read with attention to your own agenda in relation to a specific study task. This is where a review question, as discussed above, could valuably come in. It would offer you a focusing device that ensures you take charge of your critical reading and are not distracted into following the authors' agenda at the expense of your own.

Critical Synopsis Question B: What are the authors trying to do in writing this?

If you are to assess the value of authors' findings or ideas for your own interests and priorities, you need to have a clear understanding of what the authors were trying to do. It should be fairly clear what their purpose is, often from the abstract or introduction and, failing that, the conclusion. These are the places where authors tend to make most effort to convey to the reader why their piece of work should be taken seriously. Authors may be trying to do any of the following:

- Report their own research.

- Review others' work.

- Develop theory.

- Express particular values or opinions.

- Criticize what is currently done.

- Advise on what should be done in the future.

It is also useful to consider who their target readers might be. As regards the level of knowledge that is assumed, while textbooks are written primarily for students, journal articles and research monographs are not. While they are read by students, the primary readership is other academics and sometimes the student will feel rather like an onlooker as a debate rages. Edited books vary in their target readership, according to what they cover. Some offer an up-to-date overview of a field. Others are based on presentations made at a particular conference and can be so eclectic as to be quite misleading to the student entering the field for the first time. Besides the level of knowledge, the target readership is also defined by the *scope* of knowledge. Students from a non-psychology background will find a book written for psychologists less easy to understand than one targeting readers with expertise in the subject.

Critical Synopsis Question C: What are the authors saying that is relevant to what I want to find out?

This simple question covers several aspects of any text that may be important to you:

- What the text is actually *about* – what it reports, how any empirical work was carried out, what was discovered and what the authors conclude about it.

- Where any overlap lies between the authors' concerns and your own interests – the authors are unlikely to have been asking exactly the same questions as you are.

Critical Synopsis Question D: How convincing is what the authors are saying?

We have already touched on this crucial question for the critical reader. It invites you to evaluate the quality of the authors' data and arguments, particularly with regard to the strength and relevance of the warrant for any claims that are made. Other things that you might keep an eye on are any underlying assumptions made by the authors that you do not share, and whether the claims are consistent with other things that you have read or that you know about from your own research or professional experience.

Critical Synopsis Question E: In conclusion, what use can I make of this?

For the purposes of fulfilling your study task, does this text count amongst the many that you will refer to quite briefly, or the few that you will want to discuss in depth? Are you minded to write about this work positively or negatively, and would you want to imply that, overall, you agree or disagree with the claims the authors make? If your reading is guided by a review question, how (if at all) does the text contribute to answering it?

A Critical Synopsis of a text

The sequence of five Critical Synopsis Questions provides a structure for ordering your critical thoughts in response to any text you read. Writing down your answer to each Critical Synopsis Question will help you firm up your responses, especially when you are at an early stage of learning to become a more critical reader. Critical Synopsis Question A can be written before you start reading, Critical Synopsis Questions B, C and D as you go along and E once you have finished reading. Taken together, your answers comprise your Critical Synopsis of the text, available for you to refer to when moving from preparatory reading to writing your account for assessment.

The blank form for a Critical Synopsis of a text can be photocopied. Alternatively, you may wish to download the Critical Synopsis template from the Sage website (www.sagepub.co.uk/wallace). Or you could type out the form to create your own electronic template. The template enables you to write as much as you like in answering each Critical Synopsis Question. We recommend that you fill in a copy for each text that you read. If you attach a copy of the completed Critical Synopsis form to the original text, you can quickly remind yourself of the key points. The accumulated set of completed forms will provide you with a summary of what you have read and how it relates to your developing interests. The evaluative code at the end of the form is useful for sorting the forms later – a rapid means of generating a short-list of texts that you want to return to for a more in-depth consideration.

Trying out a Critical Synopsis of a text

We invite you now to familiarize yourself with this structured approach to developing a Critical Synopsis by completing one for yourself. The text for you to read is in Appendix 1. It is an abridged version of a paper by Wray and Staczek (2005), exploring possible reasons why a mismatch in two people's knowledge of an expression led to an expensive court case. In order for you to focus your reading, and to complete Critical Synopsis Question A, let us imagine that you have been given the task of writing an essay entitled: 'Discuss the ways in which language can be the focus of a court dispute'. Following our earlier advice, you have turned the essay title into a review question to help you focus your reading: 'In what ways can language be the focus of a court dispute?' You have made the critical choice to read the paper by Wray and Staczek because it looks like a piece of research literature about a court dispute where language is the focus. Turn now to Appendix 1 and, as you read, complete the blank Critical Synopsis form.

FORM FOR A CRITICAL SYNOPSIS OF A TEXT

Author, date, title, publication details, library code (or location of copy in my filing system):

A   Why am I reading this?

B   What are the authors trying to do in writing this?

C   What are the authors saying that is relevant to what I want to find out?

D   How convincing is what the authors are saying?

E   In conclusion, what use can I make of this?

Code:

(1) = Return to this for detailed analysis; (2) = An important general text; (3) = Of minor importance; (4) = Not relevant.

When you have finished, reflect for a moment on how well you have got to know the paper as a result of having to answer the Critical Synopsis Questions. The more Critical Synopses of texts that you complete, the more naturally you will ask these questions. As critical reading in this way becomes automatic, you will eventually find that you no longer need the prop of the Critical Synopsis form. But since this is your first Critical Synopsis, you may not yet feel sure how to answer each Critical Synopsis Question. So, for comparison, you may wish to look at our answers when we completed the Critical Synopsis form for this paper.

FORM FOR A CRITICAL SYNOPSIS OF A TEXT

Author, date, title, publication details, library code (or location of copy in my filing system):

Wray, A. and Staczek, J. (2005). 'One word or two? Psycholinguistic and sociolinguistic interpretations of meaning in a civil court case.' International Journal of Speech, Language and the Law 12 (1): 1–18 [abridged as Appendix 1 in Wallace, M. and Wray, A. (2006) Critical Reading and Writing for Postgraduates. London: Sage.]

A   Why am I reading this?

Part of reading to answer the review question 'In what ways can language be the focus of a court dispute?'

B   What are the authors trying to do in writing this?

They provide an explanation, from psycholinguistic theory (Wray's), for why two people had different understandings of the same word or phrase. They show that sociolinguistics and psycholinguistics play a role in how we understand language. But they don't propose that court cases should always take these things into account.

C   What are the authors saying that is relevant to what I want to find out?

An African-American woman sued her employer after she was sent a certificate calling her a 'Temporary Coon Ass'. 'Coonass' (usually one word) is a dialect word that does not relate historically to 'coon' or 'ass', and refers to white people from Louisiana. The case revolved around whether the sender should have realized that she

(Continued)

(Continued)

would find 'coonass' offensive because it contains 'coon'. The authors' 'Needs Only Analysis' model shows how the sender could fail to notice 'coon' inside 'coonass', because he had never had to break the term down into its components. Meanwhile the recipient, not knowing the dialect word, would automatically break it down to reveal two offensive words.

D   How convincing is what the authors are saying?

Their argument is convincing in itself, but draws only on one theory. They don't mention any other court cases, so it is not clear how common this sort of dispute is. There is no mention of other kinds of disputes in the courtroom either. There is good quality evidence about what happened and what the individuals believed 'coonass' to mean: original court transcripts, other court documentation. Other supporting evidence from dictionaries and a survey is offered.

E   In conclusion, what use can I make of this?

(a)   It will be useful for demonstrating that one way in which language can be the focus of dispute is when two people fundamentally disagree on what a word or phrase means – but is this case representative? I need to find other cases that are similar and also cases that illustrate different kinds of dispute.

(b)   It could inform a discussion of what causes disputes, bringing in psycholinguistics and sociolinguistics – but I may need to look at alternative theories too.

Code: (2) or (1)

(1) = Return to this for detailed analysis; (2) = An important general text; (3) = Of minor importance; (4) = Not relevant.

Our reading was driven by the review question posed above. Bear in mind that our answers may differ from yours, since they reflect our perceptions and evaluatory judgements. But what we have written can help you to gauge which aspects of the Critical Synopsis process you are most confident about, and which aspects you may need to concentrate on when undertaking Critical Synopses on your own.

From Critical Synopsis to Critical Summary

In Chapter 4 we will take this Critical Synopsis of Wray and Staczek's paper as a starting point for developing a Critical Summary of a text, thus moving seamlessly from critical reading into the art of self-critical writing. You may, understandably, be more concerned with writing than with reading, since it is what you write that will be assessed. But your capacity to develop a convincing argument in your account is heavily dependent on the quality of your preparatory critical reading. It is important that you feel confident about the ideas presented in this chapter before moving on, since they are the foundation of your self-critical writing.

4 Getting Started on Self-Critical Writing

Writing a good account of the literature requires care, otherwise you can waste a lot of words covering irrelevant issues (for hints on spotting irrelevant material, see the Linkage Tracker Test, Chapter 13). As with your critical reading, remember that you are in charge. You must decide, and map out, the story that *you* need to tell. This skill may not come easily. Initially, you may be tempted to write descriptively, just summarizing the work in the order in which it was presented in the original. A straight summary like this, however, will draw you into the concerns of the author and away from your own. In order to keep your focus, look for where the text intersects with your review questions. Then you can extract solely the information that relates to these questions, and weave it together into answers. Your evaluatory views on the validity and relevance of the claims you read about will be highly relevant, because they will determine what you tell your target readers about the text. Your readers should be able to tell why you have mentioned the work and what you think of it.

This chapter shows you how to make a text work for you by using a Critical Synopsis (Chapter 3) as the basis for a written account. We begin with an exploration of the role you adopt as commentator. We next examine some characteristics of the target readers for whom you are writing. Many students are so concerned with what they have to say that they forget that they are not writing for themselves. When your critical readers are also your assessors, it is vital to understand how to communicate a convincing argument. We conclude the chapter by showing how the answers to Critical Synopsis Questions can be incorporated into the writing of a Critical Summary of a text, whether as a short review or as part of a more extensive piece of work.

Developing your own argument

When you are instructed, for an essay or longer assignment, to give your own view on an issue, this does not mean simply giving your instinct or opinion. Rather, it implies assessing evidence in published material or elsewhere, to build up a coherent and convincing position. That is, you construct an *argument* using the available evidence as the *warrant* for your *conclusion*. In Chapter 3 we suggested that, as a critical reader, you should be convinced only when authors' conclusions are adequately backed by their warrant. Now, in becoming a more self-critical writer, you should apply the same standards to your writing so that you can convince your target readers.

Compare the following extracts from two essays entitled 'Should phonics be adopted for teaching reading in schools?'

1 'There are many different opinions about this question, but I think that phonics should be taught.'

2 'Taking into account the various arguments in the literature that I have discussed, it seems reasonable to conclude that phonics is a sufficiently reliable method to be adopted in schools.'

In (1) the claim is not backed up by evidence. Even the mention of the 'many different opinions' is not being used as a warrant (to act as a warrant it would have to be more directly linked to the conclusion, e.g., 'On the basis of the many different opinions ... I think'). As a result, the reader gains the impression that the author is probably just presenting the same opinion, maybe biased and uninformed, that she or he had before beginning to read. Of course, the author might in fact have developed this view on the basis of reading the literature but unless that is made explicit in the account, a reader will not know.

In (2) the author makes clearer how the literature has been used: the various arguments have been discussed in the course of the essay. Additionally, the author has made the relationship between the warrant and the conclusion rather tentative ('it seems reasonable'), suggesting that he or she feels that it is inappropriate to take a strong view. This impression is taken further by the proposal that 'phonics is a *sufficiently* reliable method', which is much less extreme than, say, 'phonics is entirely reliable' or 'phonics is methodologically very sound'. Indeed, it sets a tone implying that no one could hope to find a perfect method and a reasonable compromise is to select a method that stands a good chance of working satisfactorily.

Where the sweeping statement in (1) could disguise a greater insight than the reader can detect, the reverse is not true of (2). The statements in (2) would be difficult to construct convincingly unless one really had discussed the arguments and come to a balanced conclusion. It follows that a reader or assessor will tend to have confidence that a wording like (2) is an accurate reflection of what the author really knows and thinks.

Writing for your audience

As the discussion above indicates, successful academic writing entails anticipating what your target readers will need to know and ensuring it is delivered in the most effective way. To write convincingly for your audience entails knowing something about who

SELF-CRITICAL WRITING IN THE WIDER CONTEXT

Awareness of audience is a generic skill. It demands different emphases according to the purpose and destination of the material. However, in all cases, unless you can adequately back up your claims, your readers will find them unconvincing. If they do, it will undermine the achievement of your purpose in writing the text.

your readers are: what they know, what they believe, what they expect, what they are likely to find convincing. It also entails understanding what their purpose is in reading your work. In other words, if they were to complete the five Critical Synopsis Questions (Chapter 3) about your essay (or dissertation), how would they answer Critical Synopsis Question A: 'Why am I reading this?' During your postgraduate study, their answer is likely to be 'in order to assess it' or 'because it is my job to provide feedback on a draft'.

HOW STRONG IS YOUR SENSE OF THE AUDIENCE FOR YOUR ACADEMIC WRITING?

Look carefully at each of the statements in our profile of the academics who may assess a postgraduate's written work. Then consider the two questions at the end of the exercise.

Profile of the postgraduate student's target readers (assessors):

Age	**Old enough** to have read plenty of other postgraduate work, so they will have a measure by which to judge yours.
Lifestyle	**Busy**, so they will appreciate a logical structure, clear focus and fluent writing style that communicates efficiently.
Attitudes	**Fair and respectful**, concerned solely with the quality of your argument.
	Sceptical, so they won't accept your argument unless you can adequately back your claims.
	Open-minded, so they will be ready to be convinced by a well-backed argument, even if their own views are different.
	Empathetic, having once been a postgraduate student themselves, they will have a sense of how you're feeling and how difficult it can be to navigate a new topic.

(Continued)

(Continued)

Best subject	**The field of enquiry**: knowledgeable about the area in general but possibly not about detailed issues or your professional experience. Therefore, they will welcome a brief description of specific context and content, but only insofar as it is relevant to your argument.
Likes	**Logic**, as expressed in an account that is carefully constructed, well-argued, balanced, meticulous on detail and reflective. **Books and journals**, so they know the literature well and will expect you to have read what you write about and to report it accurately (and they may wish to follow up some of your references to extend their own knowledge). **Evidence that you have met the assessment criteria**, since no work, however imaginative, can pass unless it fulfils the requirements that are laid down. **Signposting**, indicating what you're doing, what you've done and what you're doing next, and making clear how parts of the written account fit together in supporting your argument.
Pet hates	**Waffle**: ill-structured writing that is unfocused and leads nowhere. **Avoidable errors** that careful proofreading could have picked up, whether in spelling, punctuation, word choice or grammar. **Over-generalization**: sweeping conclusions that are unconvincing because they go far beyond the backing provided. **Free-floating recommendations for practice**: insufficiently justified proposals about what should happen. **Poor referencing**: failure to acknowledge authors or inaccurate and incomplete reference lists. **Plagiarism**: using chunks of someone else's text as your own work, passing off others' ideas as your own or failing to acknowledge your sources adequately.
Believe that	**Conclusions must be warranted** by evidence from research, literature or experience, if they are to convince. **Everything in a written account should be relevant** to the focus and the conclusions.

A   To what extent are you already aware of the characteristics of your assessors and their concerns as they read your work?

B   Which of their concerns could you take more fully into account as you prepare written work for them to assess?

Let us focus on the immediate target readership of someone completing assessed work at postgraduate level. We can profile the postgraduate assessor quite specifically, though surprisingly little needs to change for it to fit other kinds of academic reader that you might target. Academics may play a range of roles in regard to the reading of other people's writing, whether as consumers of published literature for their own research, reviewers for academic journals, or panel members for research funding bodies. They may be more indulgent of students, who are still in the academic apprentice stage. However, they will nevertheless be looking for evidence of the same critical approach to reading and self-critical approach to writing that they expect generally from members of the academic profession.

Structuring a Critical Summary of a single text

Here we focus on a short account of the kind that you will need in an essay-length work, or might use in a dissertation where the text you are reviewing is not the focus of detailed examination. (How to do a more in-depth review will be discussed in Part Two.)

We have previously suggested that you should rarely, if ever, write a purely descriptive summary of a text. Even when you are writing about a single publication, it is possible to keep a focus on your own agenda rather than that of the authors whose work you are critically summarizing. Wherever you choose to focus on a single text sufficiently to offer a Critical Summary of it, aim to introduce your readers to the text and then, in the role of commentator on this text, develop your own warrant as backing for your conclusion.

One approach is to structure your account according to the order of the five Critical Synopsis Questions. The projected length of our illustrative Critical Summary structure is up to 500 words. We have indicated the approximate number of words for each component, though this is flexible. (If you were writing a review of a different length you could adjust the length of components proportionately.) Your answers to each Critical Synopsis Question relate to each component, so you can refer to them when writing your Critical Summary of the text and also refer back to the original text as necessary.

STRUCTURE FOR A CRITICAL SUMMARY OF AN ARTICLE OR CHAPTER REPORTING RESEARCH (500 WORDS)

- *Title*
- *Introducing the text* (50–100 words), informed by your answers to Critical Synopsis Question:

  A   Why am I reading this?

- *Reporting the content* (100–200 words), informed by your answer to Critical Synopsis Questions:

  B   What are the authors trying to do in writing this? and C — What are the authors saying that's relevant to what I want to find out?

- *Evaluating the content* (100–200 words), informed by your answer to Critical Synopsis Question:

  D   How convincing is what the authors are saying?

- *Drawing your conclusion* (100–150 words), informed by your answer to Critical Synopsis Question:

  E   In conclusion, what use can I make of this?

To learn how this structure works, we invite you to write a 500-word Critical Summary, based on your completed Critical Synopsis of the Wray and Staczek article from Chapter 3. You will need to provide your own title. Try to keep fairly close to the word length allocations in the outline above. Your answer to each Critical Synopsis Question will form the starting point for completing each component, and you can also revisit the original Wray and Staczek article in Appendix 1.

When you have written your Critical Summary, you can compare what you wrote with our effort below. (Do try writing your own Critical Summary first, to maximize your learning opportunity.)

Building up a Critical Summary: an illustration

Our Critical Summary reflects our purposes and the answers contained in our completed Critical Synopsis (Chapter 3), so it will differ from yours in places. We are imagining that our task is not just to write a Critical Summary of the Wray and Staczek article, but to incorporate it as one section in an essay on the ways in which language can be a focus of dispute in a court case. Here is how we proceed to introduce the text, develop our warrant and draw our conclusion.

Introducing the text

The first thing to do is indicate to the target readers why this text is worth mentioning (informed by the answer to Critical Synopsis Question A). The reason why we are writing a Critical Summary of the Wray and Staczek article is because it contributes towards answering our review question 'In what ways can language be the focus of a court dispute?' by offering evidence about one of these ways. Since our Critical Summary of this text is to be part of something larger, we also need to provide a link from what was under discussion previously. We assume here that our essay has begun with some broad observations about how and why language can be a matter of dispute generally. These observations are brought to a summary, as a way of leading into the main discussion of language disputes in the courtroom. (Alternatives to this particular introduction might include talking about the importance of language in the oral proceedings of a courtroom, or beginning with a concrete example of what can happen when language falls into dispute in the courtroom, as a means of setting the scene for a structured account of the phenomenon.)

> ...As this brief discussion has demonstrated, language can be the basis of dispute when there is an unintentional mismatch between the beliefs of speaker/writer and hearer/reader. This may occur when the hearer/reader mishears/misreads or misunderstands a word, or when the literal or implied content of a sentence is misconstrued. We have seen that such 'disputes' are usually resolvable through repetition/rereading or explanation. It follows that only particularly difficult cases will get as far as the law court. Wray and Staczek (2005) report such a case, in which there was a fundamental difference between what two people believed the same piece of language to mean.

The link-in illustrated here enables readers to see why, given what has gone before, it makes sense to consider the Wray and Staczek paper now. It also makes a basic statement about the content of the paper, drawing out the essence of the story it tells. Here we have managed, already, to tell readers that what we think is most interesting about this text is the kind of dispute that it illustrates.

Reporting the content

More needs to be said about the text itself, but without getting distracted into merely retelling the account in the source text. The basis of what is to be written lies in our answers to Critical Synopsis Questions B and C. We require only that part of the answer to Critical Synopsis Question B that is relevant to our developing account. The other part of our original answer to that question, about how courts should respond, would be a distraction here (but it might be mentioned later in the essay, if and when the issue of policy arises). Next, the answer to Critical Synopsis Question C is needed, so that readers have a rough idea of what the paper is about. This is the passage that may be most like a straight description. It needs to be kept short, with a firm eye on why this text is being critically summarized at all. Here is our account, bringing out the features that relate to our interest in how language can lead to legal disputes.

> Wray and Staczek aim to provide a theoretically informed commentary on a past court case, in order to explore the possible psycholinguistic and sociolinguistic causes of the dispute. The case was one of alleged racial harassment, after an African-American woman was sent a certificate calling her a 'Temporary Coon Ass'. The dispute hinged on the fact that the sender knew 'coonass' (usually spelled as one word) to be a dialect term referring to white people from Louisiana. In contrast, the recipient found the term offensive because it contains 'coon'. On the basis of their theoretical psycholinguistic model, 'Needs Only Analysis', Wray and Staczek claim that the sender could have failed to notice 'coon' inside 'coonass' because he had never needed to break the term down into its components. Meanwhile, the recipient, not knowing the dialect word, would automatically have broken it down to reveal two offensive words.

Note some of the details that have not been mentioned because they are irrelevant to the purpose of the essay (e.g., how the sender came to send the certificate and why the woman received it, the detailed etymological history of 'coonass', how the different regional backgrounds of the expert witnesses for the prosecution and defence affected the positions they took).

Evaluating the content

The next component of the Critical Summary is informed by the answer to Critical Synopsis Question D. Readers need to know whether we accept the authors' claims that we have just summarized: are they adequately warranted? This is the place to give a balanced view, identifying any reservations that are relevant to our story. Here is our evaluation.

> The 'coonass' dispute is a particularly interesting one, since both parties appear to have had a plausible position. Wray and Staczek convincingly argue that unless the two interpretations have actually been pointed out, one or the other is likely to be overlooked. This explanation well-accounts for the details of the case, though the authors do not offer an alternative with which it could be contrasted. Being a single case study, there is little indication of whether disputes of this kind are common or rare. Although the authors are obliged to speculate about the internal linguistic knowledge of the individuals involved, the court transcripts do provide a reliable source of direct evidence for what both parties said about their understanding of the disputed term.

(If our reservations had not been relevant to our interests, we would have just mentioned them in passing. For example, 'Although one shortcoming is…, nevertheless this work seems to demonstrate that…'.)

Drawing a conclusion

Critical Synopsis Question E concerns what use can be made of the text in pursuing the summarizer's purposes. In our case, it has helped with answering our review question. This is where we can demonstrate to our readers what we have gleaned from this text and how we view its worth and relevance. The set of claims in the conclusion is warranted by our earlier account of the content and our evaluation of it. It is often also possible to use the conclusion component to provide the impetus into the next section of the work. Here is how we did so, leading into the next part of our essay.

> The focus of interest here is the kinds of disputes that can arise in the courtroom on account of language. Wray and Staczek's paper well-illustrates one type. It demonstrates that disagreements about what a word or phrase means may not be easy to resolve, even in the court. What remains unclear is the extent to which their model of how such disputes happen would apply to other cases, and other kinds of disputes.

> Central to Wray and Staczek's case was the attempt to apportion blame. In other cases, however, it is not the question of blame that is at issue. Rather, it is a question of how serious the offence is judged to be. For instance …

Having worked through the development of our Critical Summary, you may wish now to re-read the components one after another to see how the Critical Summary looks as a whole.

Structuring an account to develop a convincing argument

The basic structure for a Critical Summary is flexible, but there are limits. Your target readers need to know what the text is about before reading your critical assessment. They also need to know how the Critical Summary contributes to what you are trying to achieve in your account, and they must be able to see that your conclusion is well-backed by an adequate warrant. It is the combination of these components that is necessary for rendering a Critical Summary convincing to critical readers. In the next chapter we will show you how this approach can be extended to enable you to compare several texts on the same topic.

5 Creating a Comparative Critical Summary

We have aimed to show that, in writing for assessment, it pays to focus your reading via a review question. You can then construct a convincing answer to that question by using your critical evaluation of relevant texts as the warrant for a robust conclusion. In the previous chapter we concentrated on dealing with a single text. However, it is not always appropriate for your review question that you write sequentially about one text after another. You may be required to review texts whose authors develop contrasting arguments related to your topic, and to evaluate which is most persuasive and why. The amount you write will almost certainly be governed by an imposed word limit. However, the good news is that comparative writing is much more economic on words than a sequential account.

Comparing and contrasting evidence from several texts in relation to your own agenda is more complex than focusing on one text at a time. You have to make all the texts work for you, yet the authors of each text are attempting to convince their target readers about their own argument and are pursuing different (and possibly incompatible) agendas. It is easy to be swayed one way by one argument, then a different way by the next. So how can you pick your way between these different accounts and develop your own argument, as commentator, about whichever aspects of the various works are relevant to your purpose?

You will need to interrogate the texts quite determinedly to work out how each one relates to the issues that interest you. You will also need to probe beneath the surface: should you believe this claim? If you do, what does it imply about this other author's quite different claim? Are they compatible? What would each author be likely to say about the other's work? By comparing the arguments of each, can you see a pattern, contrast or similarity that neither of them could see alone?

This chapter examines how a Comparative Critical Summary may be built up. First, we indicate how a comparative account can be structured. Then we talk you through a worked example of a Comparative Critical Summary.

Structuring a Comparative Critical Summary

This structure parallels the one we presented in Chapter 4 for a single text. Your comparative account should be based on a Critical Synopsis of each text that you are evaluating. These Critical Synopses will have been completed during your preparatory reading. Your argument will be developed by comparing the different answers that each text has provided for a given Critical Synopsis Question. Effective comparisons are possible only if you have prepared all your Critical Synopses with the same review question or questions in mind. This is why it is important to identify your review questions as early on as possible.

Placing your completed Critical Synopses side by side will enable you to scan across them to see how your answers to the same Critical Synopsis Question compare with each other. Doing this as you go along will help you to firm up your thinking while you work on developing your argument. If you have attached the Critical Synopses to the original texts, you will easily be able to refer back to them if necessary.

As with the Critical Summary of a single text, the most straightforward structuring option is to follow the order of the five Critical Synopsis Questions. This time you will be comparing two or more texts within each section of the account in developing your own argument as commentator.

STRUCTURE FOR A COMPARATIVE CRITICAL SUMMARY OF SEVERAL TEXTS

- *Title*
- *Introducing the texts*, informed by your answers to Critical Synopsis Question A for all the texts.
- *Reporting the content*, informed by your answers to Critical Synopsis Questions B and C for all the texts.
- *Evaluating the content*, informed by your answers to Critical Synopsis Question D for all the texts.
- *Drawing a conclusion*, informed by your answers to Critical Synopsis Question E for all the texts.

This structure is only a guide. The extent to which a comparative account is fully integrated can and should vary. Use your own sense of what works best for answering *your* questions. It might suit your purposes, on one occasion, to integrate and compare the findings of research (informed by your answers to Critical Synopsis Question C for all the texts together). However, you might then talk separately about the limitations of each piece of research (informed by your answer to Critical Synopsis Question D) for one text at a time. On another occasion, it might make most sense to start by contrasting the aims of each researcher (informed by your answers to Critical Synopsis Question B) for all the texts together. Next, discuss the findings of each study separately (informed by your answer to Critical Synopsis Question C for one text at a time). Then jointly evaluate what they tell you about your own concerns (informed by your answers to Critical Synopsis Question D for all the texts together). In short, our guidelines are not a formula, but pointers that can help you make informed decisions about what will serve your purpose best. You are in charge, not us.

Building up a Comparative Critical Summary: an illustration

Here we demonstrate how to integrate a discussion of three texts. Accordingly, our example combines information on three publications. One is the Wray and Staczek (2005) paper (for which we wrote a Critical Summary in Chapter 4). Our completed Critical Synopsis for that paper is in Chapter 3. The other two texts are papers by Butters (2004) and Langford (2000), for which we have provided our completed Critical Synopsis forms below. At the top of the respective forms is the full reference to the papers, so you can obtain them for yourself if you wish. However, we shall assume that you have access only to our Critical Synopses.

FORM FOR A CRITICAL SYNOPSIS OF A TEXT

Author, date, title, publication details, library code (or location of copy in my filing system):

Butters, R. R. (2004) 'How not to strike it rich: semantics, pragmatics, and semiotics of a Massachusetts Lottery Game Card'. Applied Linguistics 25(4): 466–490.

A   Why am I reading this?

Part of reading to answer the review question 'In what ways can language be the focus of a court dispute?'

B   What are the authors trying to do in writing this?

Butters analyzes the basis of two different interpretations of the instructions on a lottery scratch card. He raises theoretical questions about how linguistic and non-linguistic (semiotic) features relate to each other: specifically, how does the position of words on a card affect how the words are understood?

(Continued)

(Continued)

C   What are the authors saying that is relevant to what I want to find out?

Butters describes a court dispute hinging on language in its broader context. A State Lottery Commission was taken to court by two apparent winners of $1m. The instructions on the scratch card said that if they revealed the $1m prize in any location on the card, they had won. But the intention was any location within the relevant game (there were two games on the card). The author looks at both sides of the argument. The words were not in dispute, only whether the buyer should infer from the design features of the card that there were two games, not one. He shows (p. 483) how there is no ambiguity in the 'small print' rules and that the addition of the word 'in' in two places on the card would have been enough to prevent the ambiguity. He concludes: 'A linguist who attempts to analyze the interpretations of the game card will be severely and unnecessarily restricted if he or she limits the linguistic testimony to evidence that does not clearly make use of semiotics' (p. 487). He explains why the line is drawn differently for a lottery card than for warning instructions.

D   How convincing is what the authors are saying?

Butters shows convincingly that language is not in a vacuum in real use: language is interpreted in the context of its presentation, including design features, customary practice and general knowledge (e.g., that there are different rules for roulette and dice). Butters had a vested interest in the case, as expert witness, but balances both sides. He includes evidence from the court case. He does not attempt to draw a strong conclusion about what is right or wrong.

E   In conclusion, what use can I make of this?

It helps identify the boundaries between language and other things in legal disputes. Butters raises several general issues and provides a helpful literature review of other studies on language disputes in the courtroom. It will be useful as a contrast to other language-related court cases because there was no question of what the disputed language was, or what it meant, just how it should interact with non-linguistic information.

Code: (2)

(1) = Return to this for detailed analysis; (2) = An important general text; (3) = Of minor importance; (4) = not relevant.

FORM FOR A CRITICAL SYNOPSIS OF A TEXT

Author, date, title, publication details, library code (or location of copy in my filing system):

Langford, I. (2000) 'Forensic semantics: the meaning of 'murder', 'manslaughter' and 'homicide'. Forensic Linguistics 7 (1): 72–94.

A   Why am I reading this?

Part of reading to answer the review question 'In what ways can language be the focus of a court dispute?'

B   What are the authors trying to do in writing this?

Langford demonstrates a way of making clearer the meaning of three important legal terms: 'murder', 'manslaughter' and 'homicide', using a particular method of simple meaning expression.

C   What are the authors saying that is relevant to what I want to find out?

Langford talks about words that are used in the court, but maybe are not properly explained. It is one way in which (unintentional) disputes might arise (e.g., in the jury discussions about whether the defendant technically did commit murder or not). He provides a solution: complex terms could be defined through a series of simple descriptions using only 59 key words. This makes it possible to pin down exactly where the differences lie between words with similar meaning, and also where there are differences between the normal (e.g., juryperson's) understanding of a word and the official legal one. He claims that this approach lets you translate the definitions accurately between languages.

D   How convincing is what the authors are saying?

He shows convincingly that there is a potential problem with current legal definitions but no evidence is cited that there ever has been a misunderstanding of these terms in practice. His proposed solution seems effective, though it may not be practical (people might feel patronized if they got explanations of the kind he proposes). No evidence is given that it has been tried.

E   In conclusion, what use can I make of this?

Language is the medium of the court case, not the focus of the dispute (as with Wray and Staczek (2005) and Butters (2004)). But it is still important because different interpretations of the language could affect the outcome of the case. It might be interesting to see how his solution would work on the language-dispute cases. This is a useful pivot resource that I could use as one focus in a discussion on dispute resolution.

Code: (2), maybe (1)

(1) = Return to this for detailed analysis; (2) = An important general text; (3) = Of minor importance; (4) = not relevant.

Introducing the texts

To help the reader understand the purpose of the Comparative Critical Summary, it is necessary to indicate why the publications under discussion are being introduced now. In our example we need to identify how, together, the three papers present useful material relating to our review question: 'In what ways can language be the focus of a court dispute?' (informed by our answers to Critical Synopsis Question A). In the example in Chapter 4, we also demonstrated how one can link the introduction with a previous section. This time, instead, we show how an essay or substantive section of a longer work might *begin* with the introduction of the texts, illustrating one technique for creating a platform to do so.

> Since human beings so often misunderstand each other, it seems inevitable that, from time to time, language will become the focus of legal dispute. In this essay, evidence will be reviewed to establish the ways in which that can happen. First, two cases of legal disputes about meaning (Wray and Staczek (2005) and Butters (2004)) are reviewed. Then, themes from these cases contextualize the discussion of a third paper, Langford (2000), which highlights a different kind of linguistic problem in the court and proposes a radical solution to it.

The scene has been set with the general observation that human beings often misunderstand one another. This observation is used as a warrant for the claim that there is likely to be something interesting to say about linguistically based legal disputes. Note that no attempt is made to provide a warrant for the observation about people often misunderstanding each other. As part of the opening statement, readers are being expected simply to accept it. There is something of a risk here. If readers were to immediately think 'who *says* that humans often misunderstand each other?', then there would be a credibility problem with everything that depends upon this opening assumption. Therefore, it is advisable to make unwarranted claims only when you are very sure that readers are not going to feel uncomfortable about them. If in doubt, you can hedge the unsubstantiated claim by limiting its scope. In our example, we could have begun: 'Insofar as human beings…'.

Next, we have told the reader about the scope of the essay: how the broad issue of misunderstandings is being narrowed down into something manageable. Finally, we introduce the reader to the three papers, indicating how each is relevant to our theme and how they relate to each other. We reveal that two of the papers will be compared head-to-head and a third one will be brought in afterwards. This is a response to the way that these particular papers help us answer the review question effectively, and it is just one of the options for presenting material within the basic structure for a Comparative Critical Summary.

Reporting the content

If readers are to follow the comparison, some basic content information must be offered. However, it is often unnecessary to describe first and compare later. Answers to Critical Synopsis Question B, 'What are the authors trying to do in writing this?', are arguably of more importance in a comparative account than in a single – text analysis, because it could be that differences in content (e.g., data, method, conclusions) are explained by differences in what the respective authors were trying to achieve. In our present case, the aims of Wray and Staczek and of Butters are rather similar in this regard but the aims lead them to different outcomes.

> The accounts by Wray and Staczek (2005) and Butters (2004) are a useful starting point because both aim to locate specific linguistic disputes within a broader theoretical perspective. However, there are also differences between them. Although Wray and Staczek explicitly deny any intent to comment on how a court should judge a linguistic dispute, their model does offer a means of explaining why misunderstandings might arise unwittingly. In contrast, Butters concludes that there is no theoretical framework that can help the court easily to characterize and resolve the kind of dispute that he is dealing with.

By now, readers have been told that these two papers can be compared and contrasted in a number of ways but have yet to be told what they actually report, so this must come next (informed by our respective answers to Critical Synopsis Question C). The essential story of each text can be kept separate. However, it is then useful to point readers specifically towards the issues that the authors jointly address, corresponding with the review question.

> Wray and Staczek (2005) report a case of alleged racial harassment, after an African-American woman was sent a certificate calling her a 'Temporary Coon Ass'. The dispute hinged on the fact that the sender knew 'coonass' (normally spelled as one word) to be a dialect term referring to white people from Louisiana. In contrast, the recipient found the term offensive because it contains 'coon'. Wray and Staczek's theoretical psycholinguistic model, 'Needs Only Analysis' demonstrates how the sender could fail to notice 'coon' inside 'coonass' because he had never had to break the term down into its components, while the recipient, not knowing the dialect word, would automatically break it down to reveal two offensive words.
>
> The case reported by Butters (2004) was brought against a State Lottery Commission by two apparent winners of one million dollars. The instructions on the scratch card they bought said that if they revealed the $1m prize logo 'in *any* location', they had won. But the intention of the Commission was that the winning logo must be in any location *within the relevant game* and there were two games on the card. Butters discusses whether the design features of a card can reasonably be said to contribute to the interpretation of an ambiguous wording and concludes that the relationship between semiotics and language is too little understood for a model to be offered.
>
> There are notable similarities between these cases. Both were brought by aggrieved parties who believed that their interpretation of a text was valid and reasonable. However, the focus of the two disputes is not the same. The defendants in the Lottery card case at no point denied the meaning of the word 'any'. Thus, unlike the Wray and Staczek case, no difference of opinion occurred in relation to the language. Rather, the Lottery card dispute related to how a non-linguistic factor, the design of the card, might contribute to understanding which physical space 'any' refers to.

The paragraph comparing the two cases has homed straight in on the central issue of the review question: what sorts of disputes can occur? The narrative has shown a fundamental difference between the two texts. Now we bring in the third text, which is different again, so much so that it brings out the similarities between the first two. First we create a link and then give Langford's article the same short summary description, before bringing all three papers together into a discussion that draws on features of each.

Despite these differences, both cases do feature a linguistically based dispute that comes to court. However, this is not the only way in which language can be disputed in the courtroom. Langford (2000) draws attention to the way in which language, as a courtroom tool, is open to different interpretations. Technical terms that are understood by the professional legal teams may not be understood – or worse, may be differently understood – by those less experienced in the courtroom, including the jury. He argues that different beliefs about what words mean might create problems in reaching a verdict. His proposed solution is the adoption of a method for defining terms such as 'murder', 'homicide' and 'manslaughter' that uses only 59 key words. He argues that this method makes it possible to pin down exactly where the differences lie between words with similar meaning, and also where there are differences between the jury member's understanding of a word and the official legal meaning.

Taken together, the three accounts demonstrate the potential for misunderstandings about word meaning to have far-reaching effects on people's lives. Language can impact on the litigants and defendants in direct disputes, and on any defendant who is the subject of a jury's unwittingly variant readings of significant technical terms. The argument that Langford makes for simplified definitions of technical terms resonates also in the real world, where greater explicitness in what we write and say might prevent others misinterpreting our intention.

Evaluating the content

The final paragraph above draws out some potential points of contact between the studies. But what we have not yet done is offer any opinion on which of the studies, if any, is really robust enough to withstand the critical eye. We draw for this on the answers to Critical Synopsis Question D.

However, it would be hasty to propose that Langford's system is the panacea for all misunderstandings. Although he provides a robust demonstration of how the simplified definitions reveal the source of the problem, the reader is left unsure about whether they would really work in practice. He offers no evidence that they would and one might anticipate that these simplified definitions could appear patronizing to a jury. Furthermore, he supplies no warrant, even anecdotal, to support his initial claim that there really is a problem in the courtroom with how technical terms are understood. In similar vein, Wray and Staczek's psycholinguistic insights are offered without any clear evidence that they would, in reality, clarify a complex picture in any reliable way, or that they could be generalized to other similar disputes. Indeed, although Langford's and Wray and Staczek's studies draw the stronger conclusions, it is Butters' solution to the dispute he describes that is most succinct. He reveals that the ambiguity did not extend to the 'small print' instructions and that the simple insertion of the word 'in' in two places would have prevented ambiguity on the scratch card (p. 483). In doing so, he only heightens interest in the question of why, then, it should have occurred. He wisely concludes that 'A linguist who attempts to analyse the interpretations of the game card will be severely and unnecessarily restricted if he or she limits the linguistic testimony to evidence that does not clearly make use of semiotics' (p. 487).

Here, the limitations of the accounts are presented in a way that continues to inform the question of what a dispute is. It is revealed that in Langford's case there might not, in reality, even be a dispute at all. Next it is pointed out that Wray and Staczek's model works for their case, but might not be applicable to others – an issue of how representative the 'coonass' dispute is. Butters fares better and this is in part because his claims are more moderate, so there is less to challenge. Our sympathy with Butters' stance, as commentators, is indicated by our use of the qualitative judgement term 'wisely'.

Drawing a conclusion

If you succeed in writing a critical review that focuses, at every stage, on your review question, you may wonder what there is new to say at this final stage. But we have reached a crucial point in our Comparative Critical Summary. Readers need to be given an answer to the 'so what?' question. In effect, all that has gone before is one big warrant and now it is necessary to present the conclusion that derives from it. Your answers to Critical Synopsis Question E should give you hints as to how you considered each text, as you read it, to play a role in answering your review question.

The first thing is to remind readers of what the review question was. Next, threads may be drawn out from what has gone before, to provide a succinct answer to that question. It need not be a final answer, of course, because there may be other texts to consider. It is important to avoid writing a straight repetition, even in summary, of what has already been said. Readers have only just finished reading it and hardly need reminding. What they do need is a different viewpoint.

In exploring the question of how language can be the focus of a legal dispute, we have examined three cases in which the basis of the dispute is meaning. These cases reveal that meaning-based disputes are complex. Firstly, it seems that disputes about meaning are often in the eye of the beholder. In neither the coonass nor the Lottery case did the defendants believe that there was a dispute at all and in the coonass case it was, perhaps, less of a genuine dispute about the meaning of 'coonass' than of whether responsible managers should realize that the term might be interpreted in more than one way (Wray and Staczek, 2005: 18). Meanwhile, Langford has supposed that there is a potential for unrecognized disagreement about the meanings of words, without actually providing evidence that there is any. Secondly, Langford's and Wray and Staczek's papers both show that a dispute does not need to be about one person being correct and the other incorrect. Rather, both interpretations can be genuine, yet different. Finally, Butters shows that language is not an island and that its interpretation is different according to how it is presented. This opens up the possibility that linguistic disputes will overlap with other kinds of dispute: how and where something was said, why something was written in one place or in one typeface rather than another, and whether it is part of our communicative competence to interpret a linguistic signal as part of a larger signal that has non-linguistic parts as well.

We turn now to a different kind of linguistic dispute found in legal cases: differing claims about what was said...

Our Comparative Critical Summary has concluded with three observations that address the question of how language can figure in legal disputes, focusing specifically on disputes about meaning. The conclusion is fully based on what has been previously said, yet makes new points, by coming at things from a different angle.

Having completed the exploration of disputed meaning, the account moves on to deal with disagreements about linguistic form. Here, if we were continuing, we would begin a new Comparative Critical Summary, based on reviews of other texts. After one or more such additional sections, we might aim to pull together the range of evidence that we had accumulated, to draw some general conclusions about the nature of linguistic disputes and why their intrinsic nature makes them difficult to resolve.

Making progress as a critical reader and self-critical writer

In Part One, we have introduced you to insights and techniques that can help you become a more critical reader and self-critical writer. These ideas can give you confidence that you are using your time productively. You can enhance your own learning by increasingly noticing good and bad practice in what you read and understanding how to model your own writing on what you find most effective in the writing of others. You can organize your approach to study by knowing how to choose what texts to read, identifying your purpose in reading them and making succinct, orderly notes that can be drawn upon for writing your critical account of the literature. You can easily compare across texts, knowing that your approach to reading has highlighted the key points that you need for an effective comparison. Your expectation of finding an adequate warrant for every conclusion in what you read will transfer into your own writing, so that you expect of yourself, as a self-critical writer, a justification for any claim you make. As a result, you will be equipped to present your assessors with what they are looking for: robust arguments that reflect how your own interpretation of a range of evidence leads you to a particular, warranted, conclusion.

There is a lot more to be learned, however. We move on in Part Two to explore how to engage critically with one or more texts in greater depth.

Part II   Developing an In-Depth Analysis

6 A Mental Map for Exploring the Literature

In Part Two we develop further the ideas from Part One by demonstrating how critically to analyze texts in greater depth. As you embark on reading a range of literature using the Critical Synopsis Questions in Part One, you will probably identify a small number of texts as being particularly central for your topic. These are the texts with the greatest potential to inform your thinking and your subsequent writing. So it will be a good investment of time to scrutinize these texts in greater depth. Doing so successfully and efficiently requires a refined grasp of how academic enquiry works and a more extensive array of questions to guide your critical engagement.

To help you sharpen your in-depth critical analysis skills we show you how to develop a *mental map* that can guide your thinking as you explore the social world. The map will enable you to find patterns in the ways that authors discuss their topics and in how they try to convince their target audience. For many of our illustrations we draw on the abridged version of the journal article by Wallace (2001) in Appendix 2.

We begin the present chapter by introducing the mental map, consisting of a key and four components. We then explore the key in more detail. Chapter 7 sets out the four mental map components and demonstrates how, in principle, they can be used to inform an analysis. Then, in Chapter 8, the mental map is put to work on a real example. We use it to demonstrate a structured approach to the Critical Analysis of Wallace's article, inviting you to try it out for yourself. In Chapter 9 we provide our own completed Critical Analysis of this article as an illustration. It includes an accompanying commentary explaining our reasons for each step we have taken. Finally, in Chapter 10 we begin by exploring how a Critical Analysis of this kind can be used as the platform for writing a Critical Review of a particular text. By way of illustration, we offer our own Critical Review of Wallace's article, drawing on the earlier Critical Analysis. Thus, we mirror, with an in-depth analysis, the procedures we illustrated in Part One using the five Critical Synopsis Questions to create a less-detailed Critical Summary. As in Part One, the approach that we first describe and illustrate for one text can be expanded to cover multiple texts. We end the chapter with structured advice on how to conduct a Comparative Critical Review, making the transition from one text to several at the in-depth level. We suggest you turn now to Appendix 2 and read the abridged article by Wallace once through, before you tackle Part Two.

Developing your mental map

A mental map means simply a way of thinking about the social world, so that different aspects can be considered and evaluated independently. You can use the mental map we describe to explore and account for patterns in what you read, and also to understand the nature of your own work. The map has a key and four related components (which elaborate on ideas introduced in Part One). Between them, the key and components help you see not only what authors have done in their research and why but also how they are attempting to convince their readers about it.

Of course, no mental map is definitive and a philosopher could offer something much more detailed and discriminatory than we use here. We offer an approach that is sufficiently defined to navigate by, while being streamlined enough to be usable. Here we focus on the key (leaving the four components till the next chapter).

The key to the mental map: one set of tools for thinking

Tools for thinking are necessary for understanding the social world because our experience of it, and our ability to communicate that experience, do not rest on our senses alone. The social world is only 'real' insofar as we create a conceptual reality that gives meaning to interaction between people and the social structures that they create to facilitate or control that interaction. Furthermore, we can share these concepts only through language.

The notion of 'education', for example, is a social construct. 'Education' is an idea employed conventionally to refer to various experiences and activities, and even to the state of being of an educated person. There is no one-to-one correspondence between whatever social world might exist 'out there' and people's interpretation of it in their minds. It is common to find that other people understand a social phenomenon differently from the way that we do. One person's 'valuable educational activities' (say, opportunities for children to learn through play) might be another person's 'deplorable waste of time' (if such activities are interpreted as merely playing around without learning).

The tools for thinking that we describe are embedded in the language of the literature you read, as they will also be in the literature that you produce when writing for assessment or publication. Therefore, what we are introducing here is not new but a way of focusing your attention onto something that you have already encountered and used. By becoming more conscious of concepts that you have an implicit familiarity with, you will be able to ask questions that reveal hidden features of a text, including unspoken assumptions, logical flaws and unwarranted conclusions.

TOOLS ARE CONSTRUCTS TOO!

Be warned – these tools are themselves constructs that rely on the interpretation of language. As you will see, authors differ in what they mean when they talk about them: how they intend a term to be defined, how they employ it, how they conceive of the relationship between the tools. No idea, even a tool for thinking, has a fixed and universally agreed definition. All the same, since academic communication fundamentally depends on common understandings of the discourse, there is an area of general agreement and shared meaning for most terms, which we have aimed to capture in our descriptions. Compare your existing understanding of each term against the way that we define it. Any differences may shed light on things that have puzzled you up to now (for instance, where your understanding of a term has been rather narrower, or rather broader, than is customary in academic usage).

The tools for thinking that comprise our key are: concepts, perspectives, metaphors, theories, models, assumptions and ideologies.

What are concepts?

Ideas like 'education' are *concepts*. The word (or term) *education* is used as the bridge between the abstract concept 'education' in the minds of the author and the reader. Using the term to refer to the concept, we can write about how we classify, interpret, describe, explain and evaluate aspects of the social world. One concept will be defined in relation to other concepts, so 'education' might be defined in relation to concepts like 'instruction', 'creativity', 'training' or 'skill formation'.

It follows that the extent to which concepts can be successfully shared by an author and a reader depends on the extent to which they both interpret the term in the same way. Suppose an author states an opinion about a concept (e.g., adult education is of little benefit to the economy) and the reader disagrees with it. This could be for one of at least three reasons:

1 The author and reader differently understand what the term refers to (e.g., 'adult education' means evening classes in flower arranging, versus 'adult education' means mature student access to full-time university study).

2 They have different conceptualizations of the underlying phenomenon (e.g., adult education is largely about giving retired people access to pastimes, versus adult education is an opportunity for people to make up for previously missed opportunities).

3 The reader does not share the author's view about the concept (e.g., adult education is expensive and makes no difference to employability, versus all education is beneficial, because it stimulates the individual to make life-changing decisions).

If no one has a monopoly on the definition of concepts, there is great potential for confusion. This will result in a failure to communicate, one major reason why authors may not convince a reader about some issue that seems obvious to them. In order to see things through the author's eyes, the reader needs to find a way of working out what the author means by the terms used. What authors can do to help the reader is to offer an explicit 'stipulative definition' of the main concepts they are dealing with. In this way, readers can see where their own understanding is different and also make a deliberate, if temporary, change to their own conceptualization, so as to see things through the eyes of the author.

EXPLICIT AND IMPLICIT DEFINITION OF CONCEPTS

Wallace's (Appendix 2) definition of *power* (page 201) is **explicit**:

> Following Giddens (1984), a definition of power as 'transformative capacity' – use of resources to achieve interests – is employed.

Definitions can also be **implicit**, yet are easily detected if the first mention of the concept is followed by detail that contributes an account of what is meant by it. Wallace (Appendix 2) indicates what 'senior management teams' are by describing their role, typical membership and involvement in decision-making (pages 195–6):

> ... senior management teams (SMTs) in British primary schools, whose role is to support the headteacher in leading and managing the institution. Typically, they consist of the headteacher, deputy head and other teachers with the most substantial management responsibility. Team members are variably involved in making policy and routine management decisions on behalf of other staff, whose views are represented in some measure.

Just as you, as a reader, need authors to define their key concepts, as a writer you risk confusing your readers unless you give a stipulative definition of the key concepts that you employ.

Since the social world is infinitely complex, concepts are used by an author to focus the attention of the reader on particular features, while others are backgrounded. Furthermore, where several concepts are to be considered together, it is often useful to bundle them under a single label. A researcher interested in the impact on literacy of poverty, family instability and parental drug-abuse might variously discuss them individually and also bundle them under the group-heading 'social problems'. There they do not need to be differentiated, because the earlier discussion has indicated what the term 'social problems' is intended to cover.

Grouping concepts has the advantage of enabling us to attend to patterns in the phenomenon. But it will also obscure other patterns, which a different grouping would have drawn to our attention. This compromise is inevitable, since no one is capable of attending to everything at once. The key thing is to be aware when a group concept is being used and to expect the author to provide sufficient information for you to know what is encompassed within it.

What are perspectives?

Sets of concepts are often combined to form *perspectives*. A perspective is a device for filtering an examination of social events and processes, so that certain things are excluded, while others appear particularly prominent. A cultural perspective, for example, brings to the fore facts, values, assumptions and codes governing what is, and can be done within, a culture. But the adoption of a cultural perspective will tend to push out of the way other factors, such as the individual's psychological motivations, even though they, too, will determine how a person behaves. A writer can pick out different features of the social world using different filters but nobody can look at something from all possible perspectives simultaneously.

The university degree ceremony provides an illustration. A behavioural perspective would draw to our attention the actions and words of the participants. A social relations perspective would examine the reasons why students elect to attend, perhaps in order to share one last special day with their friends and so that their parents can come and watch. A motivational perspective might reveal why individuals feel that it is 'worth' attending and how it affects their sense of identity and achievement to participate in the event. A cultural perspective could examine how, through ritual, the academics symbolically acknowledge their students' achievements and the vice chancellor formally accepts them into the ranks of graduates of the institution.

Although multiple perspectives are difficult to manage, it is possible to combine perspectives to a limited extent. A common approach is to examine a phenomenon first from one perspective, then from another. However, difficulties can arise when the two perspectives embody concepts that are incompatible with each other. If a cultural perspective on what happens in meetings emphasizes how people share beliefs and values to reach consensus, but a political perspective on the same meetings emphasizes how individuals use power to achieve their personal goals at others' expense, which explanation are you to accept? A solution is to combine the different perspectives rather than deal with them independently by adopting compatible stipulative definitions of the key concepts. That is, the analyst makes a choice from within the range of possible definitions for a concept, in order to home in on one that is shared across the perspectives being used.

COMBINING PERSPECTIVES

Wallace (Appendix 2) employs a combined cultural and political perspective on teamwork within the senior management teams that he researched. He justifies the combined approach as follows (page 200).

> The cultural and political perspective guiding the research integrates concepts about teacher professional cultures and micropolitics. It focuses on the reciprocal relationship between culture and power: cultural determinants of differential uses of power and uses of power to shape culture...

In order to make the combined perspective work, Wallace has selected stipulative definitions of the core concepts 'culture' and 'power' that are compatible with each other. His stipulative definition of 'culture' is: 'the way we do things around here', and allows for the possibility that different people may hold overlapping or contradictory beliefs and values about the culture. Equally, his stipulative definition of power as 'transformative capacity' is neutral and so allows for power to be used collaboratively or conflictually.

What are metaphors?

A *metaphor* is a way of describing one unfamiliar or complex phenomenon in terms of another, more familiar or simpler one. The characteristics of something familiar and easy to understand are used to explore, by analogy, the nature of the more difficult phenomenon. In the previous section, we likened the 'perspective' to a filter. A light filter selects certain wavelengths and excludes others. An industrial filter holds back large particles while allowing small ones to pass through. Using these images, it becomes easier to think about the 'perspective' as something that allows certain aspects of a phenomenon to be seen while others are left aside.

**A GRAPHIC METAPHOR: THE 'GARBAGE CAN'
IMAGE OF DECISION-MAKING**

March and Olsen (1976) used the metaphor of a 'garbage can' to characterize how ambiguity and unpredictability feature in organizational decision-making. The 'garbage can' metaphor captures the idea of various types of input (such as individuals' presence and interest, issues that need deciding, or local conditions)

(Continued)

(Continued)

being 'thrown' into the decision-making process in a rather haphazard, unpredictable way. What comes out of the decision-making process is a product of that mix.

(March, J. and Olsen, P. (1976) *Ambiguity and Choice in Organizations*. Bergen: Universitetsforlaget.)

A metaphor maps onto the concept that it describes, but not exactly. There are aspects of the concept that lie outside the bounds of the metaphor and also aspects of the metaphor that lie outside the bounds of the concept. In our 'Garbage Can' example, the metaphor draws attention away from the possibility that decision-making will sometimes be orderly and predictable. Conversely, a garbage can is periodically emptied out, whereas decision-making tends to be built on accumulated past decisions.

The boundaries marking where the metaphor and concept no longer overlap are important. Pushing at them can be useful for exploring the phenomenon in new ways. But over-extending them will lead to 'shoehorning' things into unhelpful images. Consider what would happen if one explored an aspect of garbage can usage that March and Olsen could scarcely have included back in 1976: recycling. Would it help us understand more about decision-making in organizations if we thought metaphorically about how some items in a garbage can could be rescued and recycled? Or would that be an unhelpful step too far?

As a critical reader, you will often find yourself engaging with an account in which a metaphor has been adopted. It is important for you to reflect on which aspects of the social phenomenon being discussed are highlighted and which underplayed or ignored, and how the metaphor could be further exploited or is already being pushed beyond its usefulness.

What are theories and models?

The terms 'theory' and 'model' refer to explanatory and often evaluative accounts of one or more aspects of the social world, incorporating a bundle of related concepts defined in a particular way. Theories and models may or may not be informed by research or practical experience.

Theories are widely viewed as a coherent system of connected concepts, lying within one or more perspectives. They may be used to interpret and explain what has happened and to predict what will happen. In some fields, theories can be employed normatively, to prescribe what should be done to improve an aspect of the social world. Thus, a 'progressive theory of education' will make proposals about how education ought to be. It might be couched within a psychological perspective on individual development and employ the metaphor of 'nurturing growth'.

Models generally entail a small bundle of concepts and their relationship to each other. They tend to refer to a specific aspect of a phenomenon, which may form part of a broader theory. It is common, therefore, to see a specific phenomenon being modelled on the basis of the predictions or prescriptions of a more general theory.

MODELLING INTERACTION: CLARITY VERSUS COMPREHENSIVENESS

Wallace (Appendix 2) develops a model of interaction between headteachers and other members of their senior management teams (pages 204–6). The core concepts are represented diagrammatically as a simple 'two by two' matrix of cells and arrows:

- The norm of belief in a management hierarchy contrasted with the contradictory norm of belief in making an equal contribution to teamwork.
- Subscription to each norm by the headteacher contrasted with subscription to each norm by other team members (under the assumption that the same headteacher or other team members might subscribe to either norm at different times).

The four cells contain descriptions of the different outcomes of each combination, and they fall along a continuum from no synergy between the headteacher and other team members (when the headteacher subscribes to a belief in a management hierarchy and the other SMT members do not), to high synergy (when everyone adopts the norm of equality in the contribution to teamwork). Moderate and low synergy outcomes are also represented in the other two cells.

Note how Wallace has deliberately simplified even this quite specific aspect of teamwork by contrasting the headteacher's position with that of all the other members of the senior management team lumped together. The advantage of clarity that is gained through this simplification comes at a price. It ignores the possibility that amongst the other SMT members, individuals may differ over which norm they subscribe to at any given time. A more realistic model would have to consider multiple subgroups of team members, more linkages and more positions – but doing so would sacrifice clarity.

What are assumptions and ideologies?

Any interpretation of the social world rests on certain *assumptions*: taken-for-granted beliefs of which the writer may be fully aware or quite unaware. The validity of any assumption is always open to question, often by considering whether there is evidence to support or challenge it, or by checking whether the assumption is logically consistent with the claims being made.

IDENTIFYING AND CHALLENGING ASSUMPTIONS

Wallace (Appendix 2) identifies assumptions which, he claims, underlie normative theories of educational leadership (page 197).

1 Principals possess freedom to determine their vision, their strategy for inspiring colleagues to share it, and the means for implementing it through their practice.
2 It is possible to engineer change in a teacher culture with predictable results.
3 Elements of the teacher culture are mutually compatible and individual interests are reconcilable, facilitating transformation that results in unity of purpose.
4 Empowerment of teachers leads to their actions to realize the vision proffered by principals.

He challenges these assumptions, developing the argument that they are unrealistic for the context of schools in the UK. As his warrant he draws on evidence from policy and research literature. Then he reports his own research findings and uses these as a warrant for his further conclusions (pages 206–7).

Authors tend not to justify their own assumptions because those assumptions are the starting point for whatever argument they wish to develop. But critical readers may identify and challenge assumptions in the literature, in order to develop their own counter-argument, as Wallace does. (Whatever assumptions Wallace makes are, of course, just as open to challenge as those of the authors whose claims he criticizes.)

The term *ideology* implies a system of beliefs, attitudes and opinions about some aspect of the social world, based on particular assumptions. An ideology guides action towards the realization of particular interests or goals. Ideology-driven action may prevent others from realizing their own interests. Many teachers and lecturers espouse an 'educational philosophy'. This is an ideology built upon their beliefs, attitudes and opinions about education. One such ideology might be that 'education is about developing a life-long love of learning'. This ideology is intrinsically value-laden because it cannot be based on fact alone. Rather, it additionally draws upon views about the purposes, content and methods of education, and about the ideal balance of control between the different participants in deciding what should and should not be done.

IDEOLOGY AS A NEUTRAL OR A CRITICAL TERM

The notion of an ideology is often employed neutrally, referring to any system of beliefs whether true or false. However, it is sometimes used critically to imply a false or distorted set of beliefs, representing a partisan interest that is not being made fully explicit. For instance, Marxists point out that the superficially neutral educational philosophy that 'the purpose of formal education is to provide the skilled workforce necessary for our nation's economic competitiveness in a global economy' is not, in fact, neutral. The Marxist identifies this ideology as one that protects the employers' position of advantage, by deflecting employees' from a recognition that they could better their economic position.

In your critical reading, it is important first to identify when authors' claims about the social world reflect their ideology, and then to question the assumptions and values that underlie the ideology itself.

A key to help you make sense of what you read

We have introduced the prospect of developing your own mental map for making sense of the literature that you come across. Our metaphor of a map draws attention to the possibility that you can find your way around what can otherwise be a bewildering variety of material. So far we have concentrated on the key, the *set of tools for thinking*. As you engage with these tools, you will quickly see how authors use them to build up different arguments and how the tools' limitations can affect the robustness of an argument. You will gradually sharpen your ability to question critically whether the tools have been put to convincing use or not (e.g., whether core concepts have been adequately defined). In the next chapter we progress to the other aspect of the mental map: the four components to which the tools for thinking are applied in making and justifying claims to knowledge.

7 Components of your Mental Map

Having presented the key to the mental map (a set of tools for thinking), we now introduce the four mental map components. How do the components relate to the tools? The authors whose work you study will have employed the different tools for thinking in order to develop a convincing argument. The components of the mental map will help you evaluate a range of factors that contribute to the content and robustness of that argument:

- The authors' tentativeness or certainty about their claims and their willingness to generalize.

- The kinds of knowledge they draw upon and create.

- The type of literature they produce and some common weaknesses that might render it less than convincing.

- Their reasons for studying, reflected in the questions they address and the answers they claim to have found.

In short, your mental map will enable you to home in on what authors were trying to do, why, and with what success. In this chapter we explain what each component is and how it relates to the key and other components of the mental map. (In the next chapter we will discuss the application of the mental map in critical reading.)

Each mental map component provides a means of interrogating a text. The components are:

- Two *dimensions of variation amongst knowledge claims* about the social world, affecting their vulnerability to criticism.

- Three *kinds of knowledge* that are generated by reflecting on, investigating and taking action in the social world.

- Four *types of literature* that inform understanding and practice.

- Five *sorts of intellectual project* that generate literature about the social world.

Two dimensions of variation among knowledge claims

In Part One we saw that an argument is constructed from one or more *claims to knowledge* – assertions that something is, or normatively should be, true. These claims are supported by some form of backing that warrants the drawing of that conclusion.

Knowledge claims are made with varying degrees of *certainty* and it is possible to question whether the degree of certainty that the author asserts is justified. The academic literature is not short of highly speculative claims to knowledge of the social world, made with enormous confidence that they are certain truths. Yet, as we have already seen, no knowledge of the social world can ever be beyond all doubt. It is always appropriate for the critical reader to ask whether there is sufficient evidence to support the degree of certainty with which a claim has been made.

Certainty about a claim

Authors sometimes make explicit their own lack of certainty by stating that their claims are tentative or cautious. A formal means of signalling tentativeness is through *hypotheses*. A hypothesis is a claim consisting of a proposition or statement that something is the case but which is as yet unproven. It will often be predictive (as we saw earlier in Figure 2.1), implying that a particular outcome will flow from a particular action. An enquiry into an aspect of the social world might begin with a hypothesis, the validity of which is then tested by checking whether evidence supports it or not. Alternatively, an enquiry may produce hypotheses as outcomes, amounting to predictions that could be tested in future. However, many hypotheses in the study of the social world are so general that they are not amenable to straightforward testing. For instance, how could we convincingly test the hypothesis that 'learning how to learn is a more effective preparation for adult life than learning lots of facts'? What would count as sufficient evidence to warrant the conclusion that the hypothesis was supported or should be rejected?

Generalizing a claim

Claims are also made with varying degrees of *generalization*. The issue here is the extent to which findings from within the context that has been studied also apply to other contexts. Some level of generalization is normally expected in research: one examines a phenomenon in a limited way in order to find out something that is likely to be true in other similar circumstances. Generalization, in part, is about how one judges what counts as a similar circumstance. A claim about, say, the effectiveness of whole-class teaching might be made on the basis of studying five British primary schools. A judgement must then be made about whether it holds true for all British primary schools, and whether it might be extended to all schools and other educational arrangements anywhere.

Frequently, when sweeping generalizations are made, the author is not explicit about the range of contexts to which the claim applies. Rather, the extent of the claim is implied rather than stated, as in the assertion mentioned earlier, that 'learning how to learn is a more effective preparation for adult life than learning lots of facts'. By implication, this claim is asserted to have universal applicability – to all children everywhere, past, present or future. But generalizations are, in themselves, just claims that something is known, not proof that it is known. You may always, appropriately, ask the critical question: is there sufficient evidence to support the degree of generalization adopted (or implied) for this claim?

The broader the range of contexts to which a claim is generalized, the more it may affect the *level of abstraction*. The issue here is the extent to which the intricate details of the specific context that was directly examined can be set aside, so that a greater range of contexts becomes eligible for the generalization. The broader the generalization, the more likely it is to be at a high level of abstraction, glossing over details of individual contexts to make a claim about some quite abstract feature that is supposedly common to them all. The generalization 'learning how to learn is a more effective preparation for adult life than learning lots of facts' glosses over the multiplicity of details that may vary between different contexts. They include learning environments (does it matter if you have a computer-equipped classroom or just an open space?), the characteristics of learners (is the claim equally true of adventurous and quietly reflective learners?), or purposes for promoting learning (can the learning be for its own sake or must it be aiming to contribute to society?)

These two dimensions of variation for claims to knowledge – certainty and generalization – are presented diagrammatically in Figure 7.1. The four cells indicate the degree of vulnerability of a claim, according to whether it is made with more or less certainty and is more or less generalized. The more certainty with which a claim is asserted, the more vulnerable it is to the critical question: is there sufficient evidence to support this degree of certainty? The broader the generalization embodied in a claim, the more vulnerable it is to the critical question: is there sufficient evidence to support this breadth of generalization? The four cells illustrate the four questions that are derived when the degree of certainty and the degree of generalization interact.

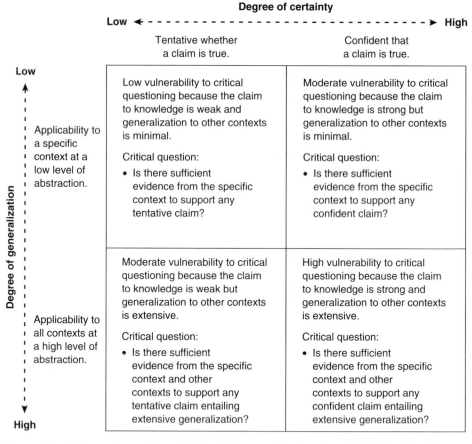

Figure 7.1 **Dimensions of knowledge claims and their vulnerability to critical questioning**

SIGNALLING THE DEGREE OF CERTAINTY AND GENERALIZATION

Wallace (Appendix 2) makes explicit both the level of certainty with which he makes his claims about effective sharing of school leadership and the extent to which he is prepared to generalize beyond the few settings in his research.

Early on, he raises questions about the risks that headteachers face when sharing leadership and about the justifiability of headteachers varying the extent to which they share according to the evolving situation (page 199). He then states: 'The remainder of the paper seeks a tentative answer to these questions.' ... Tentativeness implies a relatively low degree of certainty over his claims to knowledge.

(Continued)

(Continued)

Later, having presented his findings, Wallace refers (pages 206–7) to … 'two features of the real world, at least in Britain'. Further 'The research implies that prescriptions for school leadership should be informed by evidence, and so rest on principles that are context-sensitive: the approach advocated will therefore be contingent on circumstances'. He articulates three such principles for the UK, then claims that: 'These principles would justify British headteachers working toward the most extensive, equal sharing of leadership possible to maximize potential for synergy, while allowing for contingent reversal to hierarchical operation to minimize the risk of disaster'. Wallace generalizes to all schools in the UK but not to those in other countries, nor to any organizations other than schools.

In combination, his claims are tentative and are only moderately generalized beyond his own research settings – to other schools that he judges to be affected by the same contingent circumstances. His assessment about the limit of this generalization reflects his belief that central government reforms affecting all UK schools (but not, of course, non-UK schools or any organizations other than schools) played a critical role in the outcomes he observed. In Figure 7.1 his position might be located between the upper and lower left-hand cells: low certainty, but a moderate degree of generalization.

Claims you should watch out for are those embodying recommendations for improving practice. They tend to make the strongest claims to knowledge, often combining a high degree of certainty with a high degree of implicitly or explicitly expressed generalization, at a high level of abstraction. That is, they fall into the lower right-hand cell of the diagram. Popular 'how to do it' management books typically make high certainty, high generalization claims along the lines of 'effective managers are visionaries who inspire others to go the extra mile to realize corporate objectives'.

Conversely, least vulnerable to critical questioning are those accounts that make the weakest claims to knowledge: tentative assertions about a specific context (represented in the upper left-hand cell of the diagram). Although safe from the criticism of over-ambitious claims, such accounts are naturally limited. How useful is information that cannot reliably be extended beyond its specific domain?

As a critical reader, you will find it helpful to identify the degree of certainty and degree of generalization made about the claims to knowledge you encounter in the literature. Your judgements will provide you with clues about the sorts of critical questions to ask before you are convinced.

As a self-critical writer, you will wish to make your writing robust to the demands and expectations of the critical readers of your work. Be cautious about asserting greater certainty over your claims to knowledge than you have evidence to support and about making broad generalizations – except perhaps at a high level of abstraction.

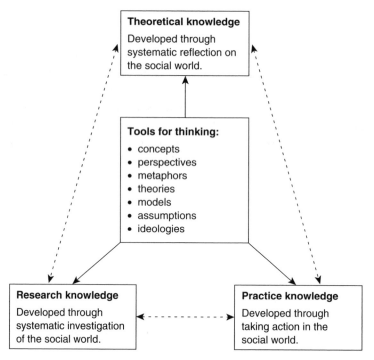

Figure 7.2   Tools for thinking and the creation of three kinds of knowledge about the social world

Three kinds of knowledge

The three kinds of knowledge that we distinguish are *theoretical*, *research* and *practice*. We describe each below and show how they relate to the set of tools for thinking. Figure 7.2 represents that relationship, showing that the tools for thinking play a central role. They are employed both to generate and to question the three kinds of knowledge.

What is theoretical knowledge?

The tools for thinking are most obviously reflected in *theoretical knowledge* – you cannot have a theory without a set of connected concepts. We define theoretical knowledge as deriving from the creation or use of theory, in the following way. On the basis of a theory about the social world, we make claims to knowledge about what the social world is like. The theory itself may or may not be our own and will have been developed on the basis of patterns discerned in that social world, whether through general observation (armchair theorizing), through specific investigations (empirically based theorizing), or a mixture of the two.

For example, in order to provide a warrant for the claim that all children should be given the chance to learn a foreign language before the age of eight, an author might offer as evidence the theoretical knowledge that there is a 'critical period' for language acquisition. The theory upon which the author is drawing for this knowledge has been built up over the years by various theorists (beginning with Eric Lenneberg). The theorists have used both general observation about what happens when people of different ages learn a language and a range of empirical studies that have sought to establish what the critical age and determining factors are. Bundled up in the theory are potential claims about roles for biology, environment and motivation. The author would need to unpack these roles if the fundamental claim were to be developed into an empirical research study (to see how well it worked to offer foreign language tuition to eight-year olds) or into practice or policy-based recommendations (about whether, and how, foreign language teaching should be introduced into schools).

So-called armchair theorizing can involve reflecting on personal experience in an area of practice. Normally one would also expect it to be supported by reflection on what the author has read in the literature, so that it draws on others' theoretical, research or practice knowledge. Where the links with other kinds of knowledge are weak, armchair theorizing can lead to explanations or prescriptions for practice that are not backed by evidence. Anyone can dream up a theory. However, without the support of evidence, why should others accept it?

Empirically based theorizing entails the abstraction of generalities from specific evidence. Characteristically, existing theory is used to make predictions. The predictions are tested through experimentation, survey or observation. If the results fail to support the predictions and are considered robust enough, adjustments may be made to the theory (see Figure 2.1). Empirically based theoretical knowledge is thus knowledge that, potentially, can be critically evaluated by returning to the studies upon which it was based. However, theorizing necessarily entails abstraction. Some aspects of a claim to theoretical knowledge may be weak, not because of the original evidence but because of the level of generalization that has been made from it.

Theoretical knowledge needs to be conceived of in the same terms as other kinds of knowledge. It is a form of evidence that is used by authors to justify their claims. Therefore, it can be critically questioned in the same way. How might you engage with a claim such as: 'Lenneberg's theory holds that there is a critical period for language acquisition, therefore children should receive foreign language teaching before the age of eight'? There are two basic approaches. One is to question the validity of the theory itself, by finding reasons why you believe that the 'critical period' hypothesis is illogical or ill-founded. The other is to challenge the claim to theoretical knowledge that has been derived from the theory, by offering counter-evidence from other domains: empirical studies and practice. Thus, one might ask: 'what evidence is there that teaching foreign languages to eight-year-olds matches the predictions of the critical period hypothesis?' and 'what do foreign language teaching initiatives introduced in primary schools around the world tell us about what can be done?'

What is research knowledge?

Research in the social world entails the focused and systematic empirical investigation of an area of experience or practice to answer an explicit or implicit central question about what happens and why. Sometimes the domain is extended to normative questions about how to improve practice. *Research knowledge* consists of claims about what happens, supported by empirical evidence gathered through data collection and analysis in the course of an investigation. As described in the previous section, research is often based on predictions made by a theory. However, it can also be atheoretical, where it is not explicitly linked with any perspective, theory or model. In either event, because research cannot be conducted without using tools for thinking, it is inevitable that some concepts will be employed. They may be undefined and used unsystematically, but concepts are bound to inform choices about what evidence to gather and how to interpret findings.

The research approach may vary, from an investigation by professional researchers who do not attempt to intervene in the phenomenon they study, through an intervention study where researchers work in partnership with those they study to help them improve their practice, to practitioners' action research where they investigate their own practice.

The research process proceeds through the application of particular *methods* or techniques for focusing the investigation, collecting data as the basis of evidence, analyzing and reporting the results, and drawing conclusions about what they mean. These detailed methods tend to reflect a particular *methodology*, that is, the researchers' philosophical assumptions about the nature of the social world and how it can be investigated (including whether social phenomena are or are not subject to universal laws).

The conclusions drawn, based on the results of an investigation, embody the researchers' claims about what happens and why, and possibly about how to make improvements. These claims are typically made public by publishing an account of the research in the literature. The account may be more or less descriptive, explanatory or evaluative, depending on what explicit or implicit central question the researchers were attempting to answer.

What is practice knowledge?

You know a great deal about practice in your domain of the social world, but you may not be aware of just how much you know. We define 'practice' to mean 'everyday activity'. Those engaging with *practice knowledge* interpret and evaluate their practice, guided knowingly or unknowingly by tools for thinking that are related – however loosely – to theoretical knowledge. Part of practice knowledge is largely unconscious: the know-how entailed in the skilful performance of practical tasks. Some of this know-how can be raised to consciousness by reflecting on practice, informed either by theories or by investigating and challenging habitual activity, as in some versions of action research. Practice knowledge that is made explicit embodies claims about what does or should happen in the practical domain concerned. Some of this explicit practice knowledge is summarized in the literature, as when experienced practitioners write an account of their practice, or where informed professionals (such as inspectors) report on their work in evaluating practice.

Practice knowledge claims in the literature are open to critical questioning for the same reasons as the other kinds of knowledge. Anyone can hold a view about good practice. However, you can always question what meaning is being given to the concepts used, whether the concepts are used coherently and whether the claims are supported by evidence.

A HIERARCHICAL MIX OF DIFFERENT KINDS OF KNOWLEDGE

Any piece of literature may relate to one or more kinds of knowledge. Wallace's article (Appendix 2) is clearly concerned with research knowledge generated by his empirical investigation as a professional researcher. Early on he states (page 195): 'I wish to explore empirical factors connected with the contexts of schools and consequent risks – especially for headteachers – that may inhere in their endeavour to share leadership.'

But his research focus is also informed by his combined cultural and political perspective, which channels his attention towards those empirical factors connected with uses of power as determined by different cultural allegiances. He both draws on theoretical knowledge and generates a model of his own to synthesize his findings. Further, his explicitly normative argument culminates in practical prescriptions, designed to influence the development of practice knowledge by school managers and trainers.

So this example of academic literature relates unequally to all three kinds of knowledge. At the top of the hierarchy is research knowledge. But theoretical knowledge is both drawn on and developed, and profitable directions are advocated for practitioners to develop more effective practice knowledge.

Four types of literature

It is theoretical, research and practice knowledge, written down and published, that constitutes the bulk of front-line literature. As you would expect, each kind of knowledge is commonly expressed through its associated type of literature. You will recall, however, that in Chapter 2 we distinguished four types of front-line literature, not three. The fourth type is policy literature. The different types of literature are characterized as follows:

1 Theoretical – presents models and theories for interpreting and explaining patterns in practice.

2 Research – describes systematic enquiries into policy and practice.

3 Practice – written by informed professionals who evaluate others' practice and by practitioners who evaluate their own practice.

4 Policy – proposes changes in practice that are desired by policy-makers, thereby implying a negative evaluation of present practice.

Policy literature tends to emphasize practice knowledge, since policy-makers are essentially concerned with improving some practical domain. To a varying extent, policy literature may also draw on research knowledge and theoretical knowledge. A frequent point of discussion in professional groups is whether policy should be built upon, or at least informed by, these types of knowledge. In policy literature, authors will tend to base their vision for improvement on their evaluation of the present situation and this evaluation will be according to the values and assumptions underlying their political ideology. (Their evaluation of what is wrong with the present situation, and predictions about what will work better, may or may not be warranted by research knowledge.)

When you first come across a text, it is worth identifying what type of literature it conforms most closely to, because each type tends to emphasize claims to particular kinds of knowledge. Each type of literature is prone to specific limitations affecting the validity of the knowledge claims it contains. By identifying the type of literature at the outset you can alert yourself to what you should look for in the text to help you decide how convincing claims are, including any generalization about the extent of their applicability to different contexts.

Table 7.1 indicates some limitations of the four types of front-line literature. For each type we have included an indicative list of features to look out for, which may affect the extent to which you find the claims convincing.

These potential limitations underline how open to challenge and alternative interpretation our knowledge of the social world can be. Becoming a critical reader entails developing the habit of questioning whether such limitations have a bearing on claims made in the literature you encounter. (In the next chapter we explain how you might react to these limitations when developing a Critical Analysis of a text.)

Table 7.1 Types of literature and indicative limitations of claims to knowledge expressed in them

Type of literature	Common features	Some potential limitations of claims to knowledge
Theoretical (emphasizes theoretical knowledge)	Academic theorists develop a system of related concepts and apply them, in order to understand an aspect of the social world and sometimes to advocate improvement in practice.	• Key concepts may not be defined. • Concepts may not be mutually compatible. • Assumptions about the social world may be false. • Attention may be drawn away from important features of the social world. • A supposedly impartial theory may be affected by implicit values reflecting a particular ideology. • Explicit values underlying any advocated improvement may be unacceptable. • Evidence from the social world may not support the theory.
Research (emphasizes research knowledge)	Academic researchers or practitioners (including postgraduate students) report on the conduct and outcomes of a systematic investigation into an aspect of the social world and sometimes make recommendations for improving practice and policy.	• The focus of the research may be diffuse. • The research may be atheoretical or employ theoretical ideas unsystematically. • Any conceptual framework may not be rigorously applied to inform data collection and analysis. • The design and methods may not be given in sufficient detail to check the rigour of the investigation. • The design and methods may be flawed. • Generalizations about the applicability of the findings to other contexts may lack sufficient supporting evidence. • The findings may contradict those of other research investigations. • Recommendations for improving practice and policy may not be adequately supported by the findings. • Values connected with an ideology about the aspect of the social world under investigation may affect the choice of topic for investigation and the findings.
Practice (emphasizes practice knowledge)	Academic tutors, informed professionals, trainers or experienced	• Significant factors affecting the capacity to improve practice may be ignored. • Criteria for judging the quality of practice may be implicit and unjustified.

(Continued)

Table 7.1 (Continued)

Type of literature	Common features	Some potential limitations of claims to knowledge
	practitioners offer an account of lessons for good practice in an aspect of the social world, based on personal experience or on the evaluation of others' practice.	• Generalizations about the applicability of any advocated practice and means of improvement to other contexts may lack sufficient supporting evidence. • Values connected with an ideology about good practice and how most effectively to improve it may influence recommendations for practice and how to improve it. • The evidence base may be flimsy, narrow and impressionistic.
Policy (emphasizes practice knowledge)	Policy-makers and their agents articulate a vision of improved practice in an aspect of the social world and the means of achieving their vision.	• Implicit or explicit assumptions about the need for improvement and the content of the vision may be based on values connected with a political ideology which is open to challenge. • Any analysis of the current situation, the vision and means of achieving it may be uninformed by research and may contradict research findings.

A HIERARCHICAL MIX OF DIFFERENT TYPES OF LITERATURE

Just as the three kinds of knowledge relate to each other, so do the four types of literature. Our distinctions between types of literature are crude and many texts actually give unequal emphasis to more than one kind of knowledge. Combinations include:

1   *Theoretical literature* illustrated by examples drawn from *practice literature* (e.g., an account of systems theory using the authors' experience of higher education organizations to illustrate its application to practice).
2   *Research literature* based on data drawn from *practice literature* (e.g., research to see if there is a correlation between different hospitals' bed-occupation turn-over and readmission of discharged patients).
3   *Research* interpreted through *theory* (e.g., research using a political perspective as a theoretical framework).

(Continued)

(Continued)

4   *Research* into practitioners' informal *theories* of *practice* (e.g., research into the beliefs and values that guide senior managers' leadership practice).
5   *Research* reports commissioned by policy-makers to inform *policy* designed, in turn, to change *practice* (e.g., systematic reviews of research commissioned by a central government agency).
6   *Policy* statements developed in consultation with representatives of *practitioner* groups (e.g., documents outlining national standards for patient care).

There are often sufficient clues in the title of a text alone for you to work out which type of literature you are dealing with (italicized in these fictional examples):

*   Theoretical literature – 'An Ironic *Perspective* on Organizational Life'.

*   Research literature – 'The Impact of Marketing on Consumer Decision-Making: A *Large-Scale Survey* of English Householders'.

*   Practice literature – 'Effective Hospital Management: the Evidence from *Inspection*'.

*   Policy literature – 'Delivering Better Public Services: *the Way Forward*'.

A SHORTCUT FOR IDENTIFYING THE TYPE OF LITERATURE

Look at the abstract for Wallace's article (Appendix 2). Within it, certain key words indicate what type of literature it is: *empirically backed … findings … research … model*.

Wallace is developing an argument about how leadership should be shared. His conclusion about sharing is backed by a warrant consisting of findings from empirical research, which he reports. In the light of the research, he develops a model which uses patterns in the findings as a means of supporting his argument about the value of a contingent approach to sharing school leadership. This piece of research literature is therefore providing evidence to support a model, which itself legitimizes a conclusion. By this means, Wallace aims to convince the target readers of the paper that his conclusion is valid.

Elements of research and theoretical literature are being combined here. But this is *research* literature because the empirical investigation underpinning the model is the central feature of the author's work. Whether the conclusion is convincing rests on the adequacy of the claims made possible by the investigation.

Failing that, you may get clues from an abstract, the blurb on the cover of a book, or the introduction and conclusion of the text. Theoretical literature will have a strong emphasis on one or more tools for thinking. Research literature will include a report or discussion of empirical evidence, whether gathered by professional researchers or by practitioners investigating their own work. Practice literature will focus on experience in some practical domain. Policy literature will tend to assert that existing practice needs improving or that a new practice should be implemented.

Five sorts of intellectual project for studying

An author's *intellectual project* is the nature of the enquiry that she or he undertakes in order to generate the desired kind of knowledge and resultant type of literature. We identify five sorts of intellectual project, named for the outcome that they offer:

- *Knowledge-for-understanding* – attempting to develop theoretical and research knowledge from a relatively impartial standpoint. The rationale is to understand (rather than change) practice and policy or underlying ideologies.

- *Knowledge-for-critical evaluation* – attempting to develop theoretical and research knowledge from an explicitly negative standpoint towards existing practice and policy. The rationale is to criticize and expose the prevailing ideology, arguing why it should be rejected and sometimes advocating improvement according to an alternative ideology.

- *Knowledge-for-action* – attempting to develop practice-relevant theoretical and research knowledge, taking a positive standpoint towards practice and policy. The rationale is to inform efforts to bring about improvement within the prevailing ideology.

- *Instrumentalism* – attempting, through training and consultancy, to impart practice knowledge and associated skills, taking a positive standpoint towards practice and policy. The rationale is directly to improve practice within the prevailing ideology.

- *Reflexive action* – practitioners attempting to develop and share their own practice knowledge, taking a constructively self-critical standpoint. The rationale is to improve their practice, either within the prevailing ideology or according to an alternative ideology.

As a critical reader, identifying the sort of intellectual project that authors have undertaken gives you an overview of what they are trying to do and how they are trying to convince their target audience. It provides clues about how they are likely to go about achieving their purpose and what the strengths and limitations of their approach may be. The type of literature that they have produced, the kind of knowledge claims they are making and the assumptions and values that lie behind these claims will all be linked to their intellectual project for studying. So once you are clear about the authors' intellectual project, you will be in a strong position critically to assess the extent to which the claims are convincing.

INHERENT VALUES IN INTELLECTUAL PROJECTS

Is the investigator relatively impartial, positive or negative about the issues under investigation?

- *Knowledge-for-understanding* typically reflects a **relatively impartial** stance. The author is seeking to understand without wishing to try and improve what happens.
- *Knowledge-for-critical evaluation* typically reflects a **negative** stance. The author is seeking to demonstrate what is wrong with what happens and may suggest a better alternative way of doing things.
- *Knowledge-for-action*, *Instrumentalism* and *Reflexive Action* typically reflect a **positive** stance. The author seeks to justify and improve what happens, though there may be some measure of implicit negative evaluation of particular aspects of the current situation.

Postgraduate students are themselves engaged in an intellectual project as they develop work for assessment or publication. Their training commonly emphasizes *knowledge-for-understanding, knowledge-for-critical evaluation* and *knowledge-for-action*. In all three of these intellectual projects, critically reviewing the literature plays a central part in supporting or challenging claims to knowledge.

Whichever intellectual project you identify in a text, certain features should be discernible: the author's rationale for undertaking the study, the typical mode of working, the value stance that the author takes, the questions that are typically asked, the way that theoretical knowledge is viewed, the type of literature that is character-istically produced and the typical target audience. In Table 7.2 the five intellectual projects head the columns. Each row indicates one feature and shows how it is man-ifested in that particular intellectual project. When reading literature, you can iden-tify an author's intellectual project by considering each feature in turn to check which project it best fits. In other words, the realization of these features can be used as an indicator:

Table 7.2 Five intellectual projects for studying aspects of the social world

	Intellectual project for studying an aspect of the social world				
	knowledge-for-understanding	knowledge-for-critical evaluation	knowledge-for-action	instrumentalism	reflexive action
Rationale	To understand policy and practice through theory and research.	Critically to evaluate policy and practice through theory and research.	To inform policy-makers' efforts to improve practice through research and evaluation.	To improve practitioners' practice through training and consultancy.	To improve practitioners' own practice through evaluation and action for improvement.
Typical mode of working	Social science-based basic research and theory.	Social science-based basic research and theory.	Applied research, evaluation and development activity.	Designing and offering training and consultancy programmes.	Action research, basing practice on evidence.
Value stance towards an aspect of the social world	Relatively impartial towards policy and practice.	Critical about policy and practice.	Positive towards policy and the possibility of improving practice.	Positive towards policy and the possibility of improving practice.	Critical of practitioners' own practice and positive about improving it.
Typical question about the social world	What happens and why?	What is wrong with what happens and why?	How may what happens be improved?	How may this programme improve practice?	How effective is my practice and how may I improve it?

(Continued)

Table 7.2   (Continued)

| | Intellectual project for studying an aspect of the social world | | | | |
	knowledge-for-understanding	knowledge-for-critical evaluation	knowledge-for-action	instrumentalism	reflexive action
Place of theoretical knowledge in the study	Informed by and generates social science theory.	Informed by and generates social science theory.	Informed by and generates practical theory.	Largely atheoretical, informed by a practical theory of training.	Variably atheoretical and developing a practical theory.
Common types of published literature produced	Academics' social science-based theory and research (reference may be made in associated policy literature).	Academics' critical social science-based theory and research.	Informed professionals' practice and academics' applied research (reference may be made in associated policy literature).	Trainers' and consultants' practice literature (reference may be made in associated policy literature).	Practitioners' practice literature.
Main target audience for published literature.	Policy-makers, academics, practitioners on advanced education programmes.	Policy-makers, academics, practitioners on advanced education programmes.	Policy-makers, academics, trainers, practitioners on advanced education programmes.	Practitioners, other trainers, those practitioners on education and training programmes.	Practitioners themselves.

- *Rationale for undertaking the study* – indicates how authors' explicit or implicit values about some aspect of the social world, their theorizing, research methodology and methods may affect their focus and the nature of the knowledge claims they make.

- *Typical mode of working* – indicates which kinds of knowledge authors are attempting to develop and how they make use of different types of literature.

- *Value stance* towards the aspect of the social world they are studying – indicates authors' attitudes towards policy and practice and towards attempts to improve them.

- *Typical question* or questions they ask about the social world – indicates which aspects authors are attending to or ignoring and the focus of the answers they are offering.

- *Assumptions about the place of theoretical knowledge* in the study – indicates how authors employ any explicit definition of concepts and the extent to which they are drawing ideas from the social sciences or from practical experience.

- *Types of literature produced* – indicates the kinds of knowledge authors are attempting to create, and where they publish.

- *Target audience* – indicates the people whose understanding or practice authors wish to inform.

Bear in mind that these categories are simplistic and that, in reality, intellectual projects are not always pursued separately. You may expect to come across authors whose activity spans more than one intellectual project. For instance, an account of social science-based research, designed mainly to generate knowledge-for-understanding, may include in the conclusion some recommendations for improving policy and practice (reflecting a knowledge-for-action agenda). However, even in such cases, you will probably be able to identify a study as being primarily connected with a single intellectual project.

A SHORTCUT FOR IDENTIFYING THE INTELLECTUAL PROJECT BEING PURSUED

The title and abstract of Wallace's article (Appendix 2) offer indications of the sort of intellectual project that he is undertaking. The following words suggest to us that Wallace is pursuing *knowledge-for-action*: *Justifiable … normative … should … risks … implications for training.*

(Continued)

(Continued)

We judge that Wallace's research and model-building are explicitly value-laden: developing a normative argument to justify a claim to knowledge about how leadership should be shared, on the basis of a study of what happens in British primary schools. His knowledge claim is directed towards informing senior school staff, trainers who design training programmes on school leadership and possibly policy-makers who commission them. Wallace points to the implications of his research, along with the model for improving training that he presents, as relevant to the improvement of school leadership practice. The centrality of his explicitly stated values about practice, his focus on implications for training and the absence of a critique of related policy and practice, all point towards a *knowledge-for-action* intellectual project.

Using Table 7.2 as a checklist, here is the emerging evidence for this conclusion, using just the title and abstract of Wallace's paper:

1 What is the *rationale*? To use the research findings to support an argument that may inform senior school staff, trainers and policy-makers about improving practice and related training.
2 What is the *mode of working*? Evaluative research, where judgements are made about what happens and then used as a basis for model-building and, in turn, as a basis for identifying implications for training.
3 What is the *value stance*? Positive towards sharing school leadership through teamwork.
4 What is the *question* being addressed? Implicitly, something like 'how effective are attempts to share school leadership through teamwork and how may they be improved?'
5 What is the *place of theoretical knowledge* in the work? The author generates practical theory from his research findings.
6 What *type of literature* is this? Primarily research literature because it hinges on data.
7 What is the *main target audience*? Implicitly those who might be in a position to do something about addressing the training needs that are identified – senior school staff, trainers, and policy-makers.

Four map components and a key to help you explore the literature

Approaching the reading of the published literature with a mental map will help you identify landmarks that indicate the purpose and nature of the material. Understanding what authors are trying to do, why and how, is a necessary prerequisite for making a fair critical assessment of their success in doing it. Selecting and commenting on arguments out of context can easily distort one's view. A responsible critical reader aims to consider not only what is said but also the authors' purposes, assumptions and intentions in saying it, along with an appreciation of whom the authors are primarily saying it to. Where you detect, by this means, that you are not a typical member of the authors' target audience, it is still legitimate to indicate what information you would require in order to be satisfied (e.g., a stronger line of evidence to back up claims). You will be able to make this assertion in a manner appropriate to your understanding that the authors made choices on the basis of a different readership.

Let us, finally, recap on the relationship between the key to the mental map (the tools for thinking introduced in Chapter 6) and the four map components:

- *ONE set of tools for thinking* (concepts, perspectives, metaphors, theories, models, assumptions and ideologies) is employed in creating authors' claims to knowledge. These claims to knowledge are subject to …

- *TWO dimensions of variation* – the degree of certainty authors have that a claim is true, and the degree of generalization that it is legitimate to make, beyond the context from which the claim was derived. Independently of the degrees of certainty and generalization, the claims made fall into one of …

- *THREE kinds of knowledge* – theoretical knowledge, research knowledge and practical knowledge. Each kind of knowledge is related to the others. When these kinds of knowledge are written down, they are embodied in …

- *FOUR types of literature*. Theoretical, research and practice literature relate directly to each kind of knowledge. Policy literature reflects policy-makers' evaluation of present practice and their vision for improvement according to their values. It may draw on practice and the other kinds of knowledge. Authors may produce these types of literature as an outcome of pursuing …

- *FIVE sorts of intellectual project* for study – knowledge-for-understanding, knowledge-for-critical evaluation, knowledge-for-action, instrumentalism and reflexive action. The authors' intellectual project governs the type of literature most suited to their purpose, the kinds of knowledge reflected and the degree of certainty and generalization with which knowledge claims are made, reflecting the way the tools for thinking have been used.

You are now ready to employ the mental map as an aid to becoming a more critical reader of the literature. To demonstrate how this is done, we offer next a structured approach that can be used to conduct a Critical Analysis of a text.

8 Developing a Critical Analysis of a Text

This chapter focuses on how you can use your mental map in developing an in-depth analysis of any text from the front-line literature. The framework we put forward and exemplify in use is an elaboration of the Critical Summary based on the five Critical Synopsis Questions that you met in Part One. Completing a Critical Analysis of a text takes a lot of effort. But you will reap some very valuable rewards if you make that effort for the texts that are of most central significance for your work. First, you will get to know the texts extremely well and will have quite comprehensively evaluated them. Second, you will have assembled, in a structured format, the basis for writing an incisive Critical Review of each text individually, or a Comparative Critical Review of multiple texts (to be discussed in a subsequent chapter). Most importantly, the more Critical Analyses you do, the more familiar you will become with the key and components of your mental map, and with the Critical Analysis Questions that can be asked of a text. Eventually, using the map and asking the Critical Analysis Questions will become automatic. Then you will be in a position to use your mental map and Critical Analysis Questions selectively, without necessarily having to check whether you have forgotten to ask any questions, or needing to write your responses down.

We now introduce our structured approach for undertaking a Critical Analysis of a text. At the end of the chapter, once you have read through these ideas, we invite you to conduct your own full Critical Analysis of Wallace's article in Appendix 2, referring as you go along to the various sources of guidance we have provided. (In the following chapter we will offer our own Critical Analysis along with comments on our reasoning at each step, so that you can compare your responses with ours.)

From five Critical Synopsis Questions to ten Critical Analysis Questions

The five Critical Synopsis Questions introduced in Chapter 3 encouraged you to:

- think why you are investing your time in reading a particular text;

- get a sense of what the authors have done to convince their target audience;

- summarize what they have to say that is of relevance to you;

- consider how convincing their account is and ...

- draw a conclusion about how you might use the text for your purposes, in the light of its content and your evaluation of the authors' argument.

Table 8.1   Linking Critical Synopsis Questions with Critical Analysis Questions

Critical Synopsis Question	Associated Critical Analysis Question(s)
A Why am I reading this?	1 What review question am I asking of this text?
B What are the authors trying to do in writing this?	2 What type of literature is this? 3 What sort of intellectual project is being undertaken?
C What are the authors saying that is relevant to what I want to find out?	4 What is being claimed that is relevant to answering my review question?
D How convincing is what the authors are saying?	5 To what extent is there backing for claims? 6 How adequately does any theoretical orientation support claims? 7 To what extent does any value stance affect claims? 8 To what extent are claims supported or challenged by others' work? 9 To what extent are claims consistent with my experience?
E In conclusion, what use can I make of this?	10 What is my summary evaluation of the text in relation to my review question?

The ten Critical Analysis Questions do the same job (Table 8.1), but in more detail. The first expansion, in Critical Analysis Questions 2 and 3, helps you analyze what the authors are doing (and so alerts you to potential limitations of their work that might affect how convincing you find their claims). The second expansion, in Critical Analysis Questions 5 to 9, helps you evaluate the claims in a more sophisticated way.

We will presently introduce a form that is completed as part of the process of conducting the structured Critical Analysis. The form contains ideas to guide your critical thinking at three levels:

1   The *Critical Analysis Questions*, numbered 1–10, to ask yourself when reading and analysing a text.

2   For most of these Critical Analysis Questions, one or more *sub-questions*, lettered (a), (b) and so on, that help to highlight aspects of the question.

3   *Prompts*, enclosed in brackets, to draw your attention to possible details you could look out for in working towards your answer to any Critical Analysis Question or sub-question.

We suggest you carry out your Critical Analysis at the same time as you read a text, rather than afterwards. The Critical Analysis Questions are grouped to form a sequence:

- Critical Analysis Question 1 encourages you to think about why you have selected the text and how your Critical Analysis of it may contribute to your enquiry.

- Critical Analysis Questions 2 and 3 guide you in determining what the authors are attempting to do and alert you to potentially fruitful lines of critical questioning.

- Critical Analysis Question 4 encourages you to summarize whatever content of the text is of significance to you.

- Critical Analysis Questions 5, 6, 7, 8 and 9 are complementary. Together they help you critically to examine different aspects of this content to see to what extent you find it convincing.

- Critical Analysis Question 10 invites you to form a conclusion, in the light of your Critical Analysis, based on your informed judgement about the extent to which any claims relating to the focus of your enquiry are convincing, and why.

Below, we set out all the Critical Analysis Questions, sub-questions and prompts in the order that they appear on the blank Critical Analysis form. Beneath each of the ten Critical Analysis Questions we have offered our rationale (boxed) for why we consider it important to ask this question of the text.

We suggest you now read carefully through the explanations, checking that you understand the rationale for each Critical Analysis Question.

Advice on making effective use of critical analysis questions

1   **What review question am I asking of this text?**
(e.g., What is my central question? Why select this text? Does the Critical Analysis of this text fit into my investigation with a wider focus? What is my constructive purpose in undertaking a Critical Analysis of this text?)

Rationale for Critical Analysis Question 1. It is crucial to begin by identifying a review question. In an essay, this question may map onto a central question, while in a longer piece of work it will probably reflect one aspect of the central question. The review question provides you with a rationale for selecting a particular text and a constructive purpose for reading it critically. Any text you select should potentially contribute to addressing your review question.

2 **What type of literature is this?**

(e.g., Theoretical, research, practice, policy? Are there links with other types of literature?)

Rationale for Critical Analysis Question 2. Identifying the main type of literature that the text belongs to will help you to predict what its features are likely to be. The type of literature will indicate the main kind of knowledge embodied in any claim, enabling you to check whether typical limitations of claims to this kind of knowledge may apply. (See the section in Chapter 7 on types of literature, including Table 7.1.)

3 **What sort of intellectual project for study is being undertaken?**

Rationale for Critical Analysis Question 3. Establishing the authors' intellectual project will clue you in to what they are trying to achieve, why and how. You will be aware of whom they are seeking to convince of their argument and associated claims to knowledge. You will then be in a good position to evaluate what they have done. (See the section in Chapter 7 on different sorts of intellectual project, including Table 7.2.)

Sub-questions

(a) How clear is it which intellectual project the authors are undertaking? (i.e., Knowledge-for-understanding, knowledge-for-critical evaluation, knowledge-for-action, instrumentalism, reflexive action?)

(b) How is the intellectual project reflected in the authors' mode of working? (e.g., A social science or a practical orientation? Choice of methodology and methods? An interest in understanding or in improving practice?)

(c) What value stance is adopted towards the practice or policy investigated? (e.g., Relatively impartial, critical, positive, unclear? What assumptions are made about the possibility of improvement? Whose practice or policy is the focus of interest?)

(d) How does the sort of intellectual project being undertaken affect the research questions addressed? (e.g., Investigation of what happens? What is wrong? How well a particular policy or intervention works in practice?)

(e) How does the sort of intellectual project being undertaken affect the place of theory? (e.g., Is the Investigation informed by theory? Generating theory? Atheoretical? Developing social science theory or a practical theory?)

(f)   How does the authors' target audience affect the reporting of research? (e.g., Do the authors assume academic knowledge of methods? Criticize policy? Offer recommendations for action?)

4   What is being claimed that is relevant to answering my review question?

Rationale for Critical Analysis Question 4. As a basis for considering whether what the authors have written is convincing, you will need to identify any argument that they are putting forward in the text and establish what main claims to particular kinds of knowledge underlie it. Concentrate on identifying a small number of major ideas by summarizing the content of the text. Try to avoid getting distracted by minor details. (See the section in Chapter 7 on kinds of knowledge, including Figure 7.2.) As further preparation for a critical consideration of the authors' claims, it is helpful to work out the degree of certainty with which any knowledge claim is asserted and the degree to which the authors generalize beyond the context from which the claim to knowledge was derived. (See the section in Chapter 7 on dimensions of variation among knowledge claims, including Figure 7.1.)

Sub-questions

(a)   What are the main kinds of knowledge claim that the authors are making? (e.g., Theoretical knowledge, research knowledge, practice knowledge?)

(b)   What is the content of each of the main claims to knowledge and of the overall argument? (e.g., What, in a sentence, is being argued? What are the three to five most significant claims that encompass much of the detail? Are there key prescriptions for improving policy or practice?)

(c)   How clear are the authors' claims and overall argument? (e.g., Stated in an abstract, introduction or conclusion? Unclear?)

(d)   With what degree of certainty do the authors make their claims? (e.g., Do they indicate tentativeness? Qualify their claims by acknowledging limitations of their evidence? Acknowledge others' counter-evidence? Acknowledge that the situation may have changed since data collection?)

(e)   How generalized are the authors' claims – to what range of phenomena are they claimed to apply? (e.g., The specific context from which the claims were derived? Other similar contexts? A national system? A culture? Universal? Is the degree of generalization implicit? Unspecified?)

(f)   How consistent are the authors' claims with each other? (e.g., Do all claims fit together in supporting an argument? Do any claims contradict each other?)

5 To what extent is there backing for claims?

Rationale for Critical Analysis Question 5. It is important to check the extent to which the main claims to knowledge upon which any argument rests are sufficiently well supported to convince you, whether through evidence provided by the authors or through other sources of backing. (See the section in Chapter 7 on dimensions of variation amongst knowledge claims, including Figure 7.1, and the section on types of literature, including the potential limitations of claims to knowledge listed in Table 7.1.)

Sub-questions

(a) How transparent are any sources used to back the claims? (e.g., Is there any statement of the basis for assertions? Are sources unspecified?)

(b) What, if any, range of sources is used to back the claims? (e.g., First-hand experience? The authors' own practice knowledge or research? Literature about others' practice knowledge or research? Literature about reviews of practice knowledge or research? Literature about others' polemic? Is the range of sources adequate?)

(c) If claims are at least partly based on the authors' own research, how robust is the evidence? (e.g., Are there methodological limitations or flaws in the methods employed? Do the methods include cross-checking or 'triangulation' of accounts? What is the sample size and is it large enough to support the claims being made? Is there an adequately detailed account of data collection and analysis? Is there a summary of all data that is reported?)

(d) Are sources of backing for claims consistent with the degree of certainty and the degree of generalization? (e.g., Is there sufficient evidence to support claims made with a high degree of certainty? Is there sufficient evidence from other contexts to support claims entailing extensive generalization?)

6 How adequately does any theoretical orientation support claims?

Rationale for Critical Analysis Question 6. Any text must employ certain concepts to make sense of whatever aspect of the social world is being discussed. Many texts will feature an explicit theoretical orientation as a framework for understanding and possibly as a basis for the authors' recommendations for improvement. You will need to decide whether the claims being made are clear and coherent, and whether you accept the assumptions on which they rest. To assist your critical reflection, check which concepts and other tools for thinking have been used, what they are taken to mean and how they frame the claims being made. (See the section in Chapter 7 on tools for thinking, the section on types of literature, including the potential limitations of claims to knowledge listed in Table 7.1, and the section on different sorts of intellectual project, including Table 7.2.)

Sub-questions

(a) How explicit are the authors about any theoretical orientation or conceptual frame-work? (e.g., Is there a conceptual framework guiding the data collection? Is a con-ceptual framework selected after the data collection to guide analysis? Is there a largely implicit theoretical orientation?)

(b) What assumptions does any explicit or implicit theoretical orientation make that may affect the authors' claims? (e.g., Does a particular perspective focus attention on some aspects and under-emphasize others? If more than one perspective is used, how coherently do the different perspectives relate to each other?)

(c) What are the key concepts underpinning any explicit or implicit theoretical orientation? (e.g., Are they listed? Are they stipulatively defined? Are concepts mutu-ally compatible? Is the use of concepts consistent? Is the use of concepts congruent with others' use of the same concepts?)

7 To what extent does any value stance adopted affect claims?

Rationale for Critical Analysis Question 7. Since no investigation of the social world can be completely value-free, all claims to knowledge will reflect the value stance that has been adopted. So it is important to check what values have guided the authors of a text, how these values affect their claims and the extent to which the value stance makes the claims more or less convincing. (See the section in Chapter 7 on tools for thinking, the section on types of literature, including the potential limitations of claims to knowledge listed in Table 7.1, and the section on different sorts of intellectual project, including Table 7.2.)

Sub-questions

(a) How explicit are the authors about any value stance connected with the phenomena? (e.g., A relatively impartial, critical or positive stance? Is this stance informed by a par-ticular ideology? Is it adopted before or after data collection?)

(b) How might any explicit or implicit value stance adopted by the authors be affecting their claims? (e.g., Have they pre-judged the phenomena discussed? Are they biased? Is it legitimate for the authors to adopt their particular value stance? Have they over-empha-sized some aspects of the phenomenon while under-emphasizing others?)

8 To what extent are claims supported or challenged by others' work?

Rationale for Critical Analysis Question 8. It is unlikely that any study of an aspect of the social world will be wholly unrelated to others' work. One valuable check is therefore to examine whether authors make links with other studies. Another is to consider, from your knowledge of other literature, how far the claims being made are supported by work that others have done. So you may wish to refer to other texts that address phenomena related to the text you are analyzing.

Sub-questions

(a) Do the authors relate their claims to others' work? (e.g., Do the authors refer to others' published evidence, theoretical orientations or value stances to support their claims? Do they acknowledge others' counter-evidence?)

(b) If the authors use evidence from others' work to support their claims, how robust is it? (e.g., As for 5(c).)

(c) Is there any evidence from others' work that challenges the authors' claims and, if so, how robust is it? (e.g., Is there relevant research or practice literature? Check any as for 5(c).)

9 To what extent are claims consistent with my experience?

Rationale for Critical Analysis Question 9. Your own experience of the social world will probably not be identical to that being studied in the text but it is still relevant. In considering how convincing the claims made in a text may be, it is worth checking whether these claims have significant similarities with your experience and evaluating whether they sound feasible or unrealistic, given what you know from experience.

10 What is my summary evaluation of the text in relation to my review question?

Rationale for Critical Analysis Question 10. What you have learned from your answers to Critical Analysis Questions 2–9 provides the basis for your overall, well-informed and balanced judgement about how convincing are the claims being made that relate to your review question (Critical Analysis Question 1). All your answers will now be available for you to draw upon selectively as you write an account of the text when addressing the review question that has driven your critical reading activity.

Sub-questions

(a) How convincing are the authors' claims and why?

(b) How, if at all, could the authors have provided stronger backing for their claims?

Appendix 3 is a blank Critical Analysis form. You may wish to photocopy it and then complete one form for each text that you analyze in detail. If you have access to a computer, you may prefer to create a master file by typing in the content of the blank form, then using it as a template. (You can also download a Critical Analysis template from the Sage website www.sagepub.co.uk/wallace) You will find it useful to save each completed Critical Analysis form as a separate file on your computer. Computerizing the form enables you to write as much as you like in answering each question. If you print out a completed Critical Analysis form, keep it with the original text if possible. Then you can quickly refer back to the text if necessary.

Your Critical Analysis of an article reporting research

To make the exercise work, we will specify the two review questions that you should ask of Wallace's text. (We have done this so that you can compare your responses with ours, which we will provide in the next chapter.) The review questions are:

1   What does this text suggest may be key factors promoting or inhibiting the effectiveness of a particular aspect of educational leadership and management practice?

2   To what extent are the factors identified applicable to the leadership and management of my organization or one known to me?

Remember that you can refer, as necessary, to:

- the discussion in Chapters 6–7 relating to the key and components of your mental map;

- Table 7.1 for a list of potential limitations of each type of literature that you can look out for;

- the advice in this chapter on making effective use of each Critical Analysis Question.

(We have indicated above that knowledge of other relevant literature is needed to complete Critical Analysis Question 8, sub-question (c). However, if our example paper is not within your subject area, you do not need to refer to other texts in this exercise.)

Students embarking on a detailed Critical Analysis like this for the first time often encounter difficulties in finding answers to one or more questions but it is important not to give up too soon. Always think carefully about how the text might, in fact, contain the information, perhaps implicitly, that you need. Expect to read the text with great attention in order to detect some of the indicators that you are looking for. Now complete your own Critical Analysis of Wallace's article in Appendix 2 (for which you may wish to use the blank form in Appendix 3).

Once you have completed your Critical Analysis, turn to the next chapter. You will be able to check your responses to each Critical Analysis Question or sub-question against ours, to see what our rationale was for each of our responses and to decide whether you agree or not.

9 A Worked Example of a Critical Analysis

We further develop our ideas on constructing a Critical Analysis in this chapter by taking you step-by-step through our completed Critical Analysis of Wallace's article (Appendix 2). Hopefully, you will already have completed your own Critical Analysis of this text to answer the two review questions that we set, as suggested at the end of the last chapter. If you can compare your responses with ours as you read through the present chapter, it will enable you to consolidate your learning.

After each of our responses to a question or sub-question we have provided a comment (boxed). It explains our reasons for making this response. We have sometimes given further information about the nature of Wallace's text and suggested what you might look out for in any text when conducting a critical analysis. (To keep the example as simple and clear as possible, in our response to Critical Analysis Question 8, sub-question (c) we have not made direct reference to other literature. Normally, however, you would do so.)

When you examine your responses alongside ours, do not expect them to be identical. In particular, your answer to Critical Analysis Question 9 (and hence the second review question) will naturally be different because you will be referring to your knowledge of a different organization. More generally, however, bear in mind that we have taken charge of our Critical Analysis, so it is as personal to us as yours is to you. Our answers are based on our perceptions and values, which we have supported through our explanatory commentary. Your answers may be different. Indeed, you may wish to challenge our analysis and the reasoning behind our answers. The article happens to relate to an applied field of enquiry and, since applied fields tend to be value-laden, people will differ in what they regard as significant, good or bad. The important point to note is that, like us, you should be able to justify why you respond as you do when conducting a Critical Analysis of a text. (Of course, you do not need to write a commentary on each response. We have provided the commentaries here to help you understand the process.)

You will find that some of our answers are already familiar to you, where we introduced the ideas in Chapter 7 when referring to Wallace's article to illustrate components of the mental map.

An illustrative Critical Analysis of a text

Wallace, M. (2001) 'Sharing leadership of schools through teamwork: a justifiable risk?' *Educational Management and Administration* 29 (2): pp. 153–167, [abridged as Appendix 2 of Wallace, M. and Wray, A. (2006) *Critical Reading and Writing for Postgraduates*. London: Sage.]

1   What review question am I asking of this text?

(e.g., What is my central question? Why select this text? Does the Critical Analysis of this text fit into my investigation with a wider focus? What is my constructive purpose in undertaking a Critical Analysis of this text?)

Review Question 1: What does this text suggest may be key factors promoting or inhibiting the effectiveness of team approaches to the leadership and management of educational organizations?

Review Question 2: To what extent are the factors identified applicable to leadership and management in Universities in which we have worked?

> *Comment.* We are imagining that our purpose in reading the text by Wallace is to prepare for writing a critical review of it, to answer two review questions. Review Question 1 reflects our interest in team approaches to educational management. Review Question 2 reflects the organizational situation in which we work – the university.

2   What type of literature is this?

(e.g., Theoretical, research, practice, policy? Are there links with other types of literature?)

This is primarily research literature based on Wallace's own investigation but Wallace is informed by theory, puts forward practical prescriptions and is critical of British central government policy.

> *Comment.* Our response to Critical Analysis Question 2 is derived from the following observations. Wallace's argument rests for its backing on the evidence of his empirical research in four British primary schools. However, the focus of his investigation was guided by a cultural and political perspective, his argument and the model he develops are explicitly concerned with improving teamwork practice in schools, and he criticizes relevant British central government policies on the training of headteachers for failing to focus on sharing leadership through a team approach.

3   What sort of intellectual project for study is being undertaken?

(a)   How clear is it which project the authors are undertaking? (e.g., Knowledge-for-understanding, knowledge-for-critical evaluation, knowledge-for-action, instrumentalism, reflexive action?)

This is clearly a knowledge-for-action intellectual project for study, but Wallace's argument is informed by research that appears to have had a strong knowledge-for-understanding emphasis.

Comment. How do we know? Wallace states (page 195) that his purpose is to develop a normative argument about the extent to which he believes school leadership should be shared. This purpose implies that the rationale for his study of teamwork was to inform efforts to improve practice. In his conclusion his criticism of central government training policy appears to be intended to convince policy-makers and trainers of the need to develop a stronger emphasis on teams. However, the research itself seems to have been driven partly by a wider concern to understand the phenomenon of team approaches.

(b)   How is the intellectual project reflected in the authors' mode of working? (e.g., A social science or a practical orientation? Choice of methodology and methods? An interest in understanding or in improving practice?)

The knowledge-for-action project is reflected in the explicitly practical use of the research findings to support the development of a normative model and linked claims about what constitutes effective teamwork practice.

Comment. We made this judgement because even though the research approach may have had a strong social science orientation, it contained a major element of evaluation. Wallace made judgements about his findings on teamwork in terms of different degrees of synergy (pages 206–7).

(c)   What value stance is adopted towards the practice or policy investigated? (e.g., Relatively impartial, positive, unclear? What assumptions are made about the possibility of improvement? Whose practice or policy is the focus of interest?)

A positive value stance is adopted towards teamwork as a way of sharing school leadership, especially where it is shared relatively equally. This stance is indicative of a knowledge-for-action project.

Comment. How did we reach this conclusion? Wallace evaluates relatively equal sharing of leadership more positively than relatively hierarchical sharing. But he does not claim that the latter approach is ineffective or wrong. Indeed, though he advocates relatively equal sharing (page 207), he also implies that a contingent return to relatively hierarchical sharing may carry less negative risk for headteachers in certain circumstances. While Wallace makes negative claims about central government training policy (page 207), he is not claiming that training is wrong, just that it could be improved. Therefore this is not a knowledge-for-critical evaluation project, as Wallace is positive towards the educational management practice he investigates.

(d) How does the sort of project being undertaken affect the research questions addressed? (e.g., Investigation of what happens? What is wrong? How well a particular policy or intervention works in practice?)

The research questions are not specified. However, Wallace does ask two questions (page 199) consistent with a knowledge-for-action project, namely, about the extent to which headteachers should be expected to share leadership and about the justifiability of them adopting a contingent approach to sharing. He sets out to answer these questions on the basis of his research findings.

Comment. Constraints on the length of journal articles often mean that research methodology and methods are not fully reported, as may have happened here. The research appears implicitly to have addressed a knowledge-for-understanding research question – perhaps along the lines of 'how do SMTs operate, why and to what effect?' But Wallace uses the findings to address the two normative questions (page 199) and to support the context-sensitive principles that he derives for justifying and prescribing practice (pages 206–7). He clearly wishes to inform action.

(e) How does the sort of intellectual project being undertaken affect the place of theory? (e.g., Is the investigation informed by theory? Generating theory? Atheoretical? Developing social science theory or a practical theory?)

The research was informed by a social science-based cultural and political perspective. It led to the development of a model reflecting this perspective, consistent with a knowledge-for-understanding intellectual project. But the model forms the basis of Wallace's prescription of principles for practice, suggesting that his overall aim is to develop knowledge-for-action.

Comment. We have come to these conclusions because Wallace harnesses social science-based theoretical ideas to focus his research and underpin the development of a model. He employs this model as a practical theory to justify the principles that he prescribes for practice. If he adopts a knowledge-for-understanding element in his intellectual project, it seems to be there to serve his more fundamental intention of developing knowledge-for-action.

(f) How does the authors' target audience affect the reporting of research? (e.g., Do the authors assume academic knowledge of methods? Criticize policy? Offer recommendations for action?)

The target audience is not specified but the concluding section (pages 206–7) asserts implications for British headteachers, trainers and policy makers. The inclusion of trainers, policy makers and practitioners in the projected audience for a publication is typical of a knowledge-for-action project.

> *Comment.* Specifying the audience for an academic journal article is rare. But there were enough clues in Wallace's abstract and conclusion to work out whom he is trying to convince of his argument. We also note that he must have chosen to submit the article to this particular journal, whose international readership consists mainly of academics, trainers and practitioners (including senior school staff), some of whom are undertaking advanced courses of study. So he is likely to have been aware that he would reach an audience beyond the UK, including academics involved in training of senior managers in diverse educational contexts.

4   What is being claimed that is relevant to answering my review question?

(a)   What are the main kinds of knowledge claim that the authors are making? (e.g., Theoretical knowledge, research knowledge, practice knowledge?)

The main kind of claim is to research knowledge.

> *Comment.* How could we tell? Wallace's claims to knowledge about how leadership is shared through different approaches to teamwork are derived from his investigation of practice in schools. His empirical evidence is based partly on observation. It also includes aspects of the practitioners' practice knowledge gathered through interviews. In addition, he draws on and develops theoretical knowledge to frame his research knowledge.

(b)   What is the content of each of the main claims to knowledge and of the overall argument? (e.g., What, in a sentence, is being argued? What are the three to five most significant claims that encompass much of the detail? Are there key prescriptions for improving policy or practice?)

The argument is that school leadership should be shared as widely as possible, contingent on the degree of risk for headteachers of sharing turning out to be ineffective.

The most significant claims relevant to Review Question 1 are:

1   Principles based on staff entitlement and effective leadership outcomes are widely used to justify extensive sharing of school leadership, but theories reflecting these principles tend to rest on assumptions that may not be realistic for particular contexts (pages 196–9).

2   In UK state-funded schools, central government reforms have increased headteachers' dependence on their senior colleagues for support with implementation. However, they simultaneously increase the risk of being held uniquely accountable for sharing leadership if the outcome is judged to be ineffective (page 199).

3   Wallace's research in UK secondary and primary school SMTs implies that the culture of teamwork shared among headteachers and other SMT members includes contradictory beliefs, in both (a) a management hierarchy where the headteacher is top manager and (b) the ability and entitlement of all members to make an equal contribution to the work of the team (pages 198, 201–4).

4   Wallace's UK primary school research suggests that maximum synergy (combining individual energies to achieve shared goals (page 205)) may be achieved where headteachers enable other SMT members to make a relatively equal contribution to the work of the team, and other members are willing to operate inside parameters with which headteachers are comfortable. Maximizing synergy holds most potential for maximum SMT effectiveness but also holds most risk of ineffectiveness (page 207).

5   In a context of high accountability, headteachers should aim to share SMT leadership as widely as they dare risk. However, they and other SMT members should accept that headteachers may pull rank and operate hierarchically to ensure that the work of these teams remains inside parameters with which headteachers are comfortable (page 207).

Comment. How have we singled out these key claims? Wallace gives explicit clues as to his overall argument but does not label his main claims as such. We are reading this article in the hope that its content may contribute to answering our two review questions. So we have used these review questions as criteria in deciding which claims are most relevant. We have concentrated mainly on the first question about factors promoting or inhibiting the effectiveness of team approaches. This is because the second question depends on our judgement when we are in a position to reflect on what we have learned about these factors. (Focusing on the two review questions may, of course, mean that other claims that Wallace makes are not included in the list. This is appropriate because the review must be driven by our own purpose in reading the text, not by its overall content, which might encompass issues that are irrelevant to our current interests.)

(c)   How clear are the authors' claims and overall argument? (e.g., Stated in an abstract, introduction or conclusion? Unclear?)

The overall argument is clear – stated twice on page 195. Claims relating to the first review question are also quite clear, most being put forward and illustrated section by section.

Comment. Few authors explicitly label their overall argument, fewer label their main claims as 'claims to knowledge' and fewer still will happen to have focused directly on answering your review question. So, as a critical reader you will usually have to make your own judgements. But it is worth looking out for clues, as where Wallace states in his abstract and the introduction to the article what his overall argument is. Common locations for statements about main claims include the end of an introductory section or a paragraph labelled as a summary.

(d) With what degree of certainty do the authors make their claims? (e.g., Do they indicate tentativeness? Qualify their claims by acknowledging limitations of their evidence? Acknowledge others' counter-evidence? Acknowledge that the situation may have changed since data collection?)

There is a low degree of certainty – on page 199 Wallace states that he is being tentative in using evidence from his research to back his argument about a contingency approach to sharing leadership.

Comment. Authors rarely state their degree of certainty as explicitly as Wallace did here. Remember to look for clues, for example whether authors qualify the certainty of their claims through devices like asserting that something may be the case rather than something is the case. Wallace uses devices like the word 'arguably', as where he makes the claim that theories of leadership should be elaborated and refined to reduce their cultural relativity (page 207).

(e) How generalized are the authors' claims – to what range of phenomena are they claimed to apply? (e.g., The specific context from which the claims were derived? Other similar contexts? A national system? A culture? Universal? Is the degree of generalization implicit? Unspecified?)

There is a moderate degree of generalization – Wallace makes clear that his source of empirical backing is research in British primary schools, drawing on an earlier study in secondary schools. In the conclusion he claims only that the principles he advocates for school leadership apply to the UK (page 206). He has not specified whether his claims apply to private sector as well as state sector schools.

Comment. The proviso in the final sentence is important. The policy context that Wallace identifies as possibly having raised the risk for headteachers in-sharing leadership might be more directly relevant to state-funded than private-sector schools. It is always worth checking whether authors have taken into account the full range of contexts to which they apparently assume that their claims apply.

(f)   How consistent are the authors' claims with each other? (e.g., Do all claims fit together in supporting an argument? Do any claims contradict each other?)

The main claims do follow logically from each other and are consistent with the overall argument.

> *Comment.* Wallace's argument is quite complex so the article may require reading more than once to check whether the main claims and the overall argument fit together well. (It will probably be easier for you to scrutinize for logical consistency the arguments and claims that relate to your review question if you first identify them and write them down, as this approach to the Critical Analysis of a text encourages you to do.)

5   To what extent is there backing for claims?

(a)   How transparent are any sources used to back the claims? (e.g., Is there any statement of the basis for assertions? Are sources unspecified?)

Sources of research evidence are transparent, specified in the section describing the research design (page 200). Wallace also draws on a small range of relevant international academic literature to support his account of principles for sharing school leadership and his critique of influential leadership theories.

> *Comment.* Wallace provides enough detail of his research design and theoretical orientation to give readers a reasonably clear idea of the scope of his investigation. He also refers to a book (page 200) to which readers could, in principle, refer if they wanted more information.

(b)   What, if any, range of sources is used to back the claims? (e.g., First-hand experience? The authors' own practice knowledge or research? Literature about others' practice knowledge or research? Literature about reviews of practice knowledge or research? Literature about others' polemic? Is the range of sources adequate?)

Most claims are based on Wallace's own modest investigation – case studies of four primary school SMTs, involving observation of meetings, interviews and document survey. Research questions were informed by an initial postal survey and Wallace's previous research in UK secondary schools. Wallace also refers to a small amount of other research and theoretical literature. This range of sources seems adequate for the contextualized claims made.

> *Comment.* Authors reporting their research commonly summarize their design and the scope of data collection. It is always advisable to check whether they have given enough detail to judge whether they have sufficient data to support the claims they make on the basis of their research.

(c)   If claims are at least partly based on the authors' own research, how robust is the evidence? (e.g., Are there methodological limitations or flaws in the methods employed? Do the methods include cross-checking or 'triangulation' of accounts? What is the sample size and is it large enough to support the claims being made? Is there an adequately detailed account of data collection and analysis? Is there a summary of all data that is reported?)

The evidence appears to be moderately robust. Wallace observed primary school SMTs in action in their normal setting. He was in a position to triangulate accounts as he interviewed school staff both inside and outside the teams. A summary is given of findings related to Wallace's argument for each of the four SMTs. However, no outcome indicators of team effectiveness were reported which might have backed Wallace's claims about different degrees of synergy in the four teams. The sample of meetings and informants was small, limiting the extent to which Wallace can support generalization to other primary schools and to secondary schools across the UK.

> *Comment.* Our judgement of robustness of the evidence depended on the amount of information given about how the research was done and on the range of findings reported. We checked the findings section of the article to see if Wallace had reported relevant findings from all four of the SMTs he investigated. Limitations on the length of journal articles can lead authors to report findings from only part of their sample.

(d)   Are sources of backing for claims consistent with the degree of certainty and the degree of generalization? (e.g., Is there sufficient evidence to support claims made with a high degree of certainty? Is there sufficient evidence from other contexts to support claims entailing extensive generalization?)

The sources of backing are consistent with Wallace's tentativeness about his claims. The sample is very small compared with the number of schools in the UK to which Wallace generalizes. However, in all schools that are affected by central government reforms, similar issues regarding the sharing of leadership are likely to ensue. The fact that he found such different approaches to sharing leadership in the four schools suggests that variation in practice across the country may be considerable. A larger sample and the use of outcome indicators for judging teamwork would have made his claims about variation in the degree of synergy and team effectiveness more convincing.

> *Comment.* Part of the knack of answering this sub-question is establishing the inevitable limitations of the study, which derive from the fact that one cannot include everything in a piece of research. All research involves compromise and Wallace's investigation was only of moderate scope. The design was also qualitative, giving the potential for depth of understanding but not of convincing generalization from his sample to the wider population of SMTs in other schools. We judge that Wallace

was not in a position to have made claims with greater certainty or to have generalized more widely than he does.

6 How adequately does any theoretical orientation support claims?

(a) How explicit are the authors about any theoretical orientation or conceptual framework? (e.g., Is there a conceptual framework guiding the data collection? Is a conceptual framework selected after the data collection to guide analysis? Is there a largely implicit theoretical orientation?)

Wallace is explicit about the theoretical orientation guiding his data collection, defining the concepts he uses within his cultural and political perspective in the research design section (pages 200–1). He makes extensive use of these concepts in reporting findings and he develops a model to explain the variation in practice that he found.

Comment. Since Wallace claims to have adopted an explicit theoretical orientation, we checked the research design section for his account of it, to see if he defined the key concepts he used. We also examined the report of his findings and his model to determine whether he actually employed these ideas in framing his analysis.

(b) What assumptions does any explicit or implicit theoretical orientation make that may affect the authors' claims? (e.g., Does a particular perspective focus attention on some aspects and under-emphasize others? If more than one perspective is used, how coherently do the different perspectives relate to each other?)

The cultural and political perspective focuses on beliefs and values and the extent to which they are shared, in relation to different uses of power. However, it does not deal with other factors that may be relevant to understanding the effectiveness of team approaches to sharing leadership, such as individuals' psychological needs or responses to stress. So Wallace's claims are restricted to (a) those social factors connected with the cultural factors affecting uses of power in SMTs and (b) ways in which power is used to try and shape the culture of teamwork.

Comment. We have identified here some limitations inherent in Wallace's focus. It is impossible to focus at the same time on all aspects of complex phenomena like team approaches. From our own experience of teams, we are aware that the cultural and political factors Wallace identifies are not the only ones that are relevant to our review questions. Therefore, even if we became convinced of his claims, we judge that there will probably be other important factors too.

(c) What are the key concepts underpinning any explicit or implicit theoretical orientation? (e.g., Are they listed? Are they stipulatively defined? Are concepts mutually compatible? Is the use of concepts consistent? Is the use of concepts congruent with others' use of the same concepts?)

Key concepts are listed (pages 200–1) and stipulative definitions offered. We are aware that some other academics define culture and power differently, but Wallace is consistent in his use of the concepts as he defines them.

> Comment. The statement in the introduction (page 196) that a combined cultural and political perspective was used alerted us to look in the research design section for stipulative definitions of key concepts, to check whether they were used to interpret the findings, and, if so, how.

7 To what extent does any value stance adopted affect claims?

(a) How explicit are the authors about any value stance connected with the phenomena? (e.g., A relatively impartial, critical or positive stance? Is this stance informed by a particular ideology? Is it adopted before or after data collection?)

Wallace explicitly develops a normative argument about the degree to which school leadership should be shared in particular circumstances, and so is generally positive about team approaches as a way of doing so. He may have been relatively impartial prior to data collection. But, if so, he clearly made judgements about his data, because he uses his model of degrees of synergy to assert principles for effective team approaches in the UK political context.

> Comment. Wallace tells us in the introductory section that his purpose is to develop a normative argument (page 195). So we checked that he actually does this, especially in his conclusion (pages 206–7).

(b) How might any explicit or implicit value stance adopted by the authors be affecting their claims? (e.g., Have they pre-judged the phenomena discussed? Are they biased? Is it legitimate for the authors to adopt their particular value stance? Have they over-emphasized some aspects of the phenomenon while under-emphasizing others?)

Given the central importance for Wallace of developing knowledge-for-action, it is legitimate for him to take a positive stance towards team approaches to sharing school leadership in general. However, his narrow focus on teamwork in practice means that he has taken for granted the policy context that so deeply affected this practice. It would have been legitimate for him also to question the managerial and educational values underlying central government educational reform policies – especially in the light of the consequence that he identifies, namely that the sharing of leadership is simultaneously necessary and risky for headteachers.

Comment. Identifying Wallace's main intellectual project for study alerted us to consider what investigators following different intellectual projects might have attended to, which Wallace did not. We noted how he was critical of UK central government training policy (page 207) for failing to offer support with developing team approaches in the UK policy context. But he scarcely challenged the reform thrust and the acceptability of its consequences.

8   To what extent are claims supported or challenged by others' work?

(a)   Do the authors relate their claims to others' work? (e.g., Do the authors refer to others' published evidence, theoretical orientations or value stances to support their claims? Do they acknowledge others' counter-evidence?)

No reference is made to other research or theories that might support Wallace's claims about effective team approaches in the UK political context. Nor is any counter-evidence discussed. His claims would be more convincing if he had related them to others' work. It is notable that he questions the orthodox view that extensive sharing of leadership is always effective. If most of the existing research supported the orthodoxy that he sets out to challenge, when Wallace wrote his article there may have been little published evidence from elsewhere to support his view.

Comment. We looked out for references to other research, but we found only that Wallace criticizes leadership theories and associated prescriptions implying that school leadership should always be shared relatively equally. To the extent that such literature is based on research evidence, Wallace is implicitly rejecting the applicability of that evidence to the contexts he investigated. If we were conducting a literature review, we would expect to search for other literature supporting or countering Wallace's claims relating to our review questions.

(b)   If the authors use evidence from others' work to support their claims, how robust is it? (e.g., As for 5(c).)

Wallace refers to no other evidence to support his claims.

Comment. If Wallace had referred to other research to support his claims, we would have tried to find out how strong that evidence was by looking for information about the research design, sample size and methods of data collection and analysis. If we were conducting a literature review, we might have checked by following up the references and reading the original accounts of this work.

(c)   Is there any evidence from others' work that challenges the authors' claims and, if so, how robust is it? (e.g., Is there relevant research or practice literature? Check any as for 5(c).)

The research that has led to the orthodox normative theories of educational leadership may be extensive. It seems likely that its findings would challenge Wallace's claims, just as he challenges the orthodox view.

> Comment. If we were conducting a literature review we might follow up Wallace's references, for example to transformational leadership (page 197), and assess how strong the counter-evidence was.

9   To what extent are claims consistent with my experience?

Wallace's account of the policy context is broadly consistent with our recent experience in UK universities. Reforms have similarly included strong accountability measures, though there is less direct external scrutiny of those with major management responsibility compared with the schools sector. Reforms do require more sharing of leadership but less extensively than in schools. Academics still enjoy greater personal autonomy than state school staff. Within academic departments and across our universities, committees rather than fixed management teams are a central mechanism in leadership and management. Wallace's claims are applicable to our contexts but only at a high level of abstraction. The individual autonomy that academics in our universities are given means that there is less need for maximizing synergy in managing their everyday work across departments or across an entire university. Maximizing synergy for effective teamwork is most important for individual teaching programme and research project teams. Here the claim does apply about sharing as equally as possible, while simultaneously allowing for the academic who is accountable to operate hierarchically where necessary to keep activity within parameters that are comfortable to him or her.

> Comment. Critical Analysis Question 9 is directly relevant to answering our second review question in the light of the earlier analysis. Our reflection focused on considering the extent to which the primary school context that Wallace investigates is similar to the university contexts in which we work, and which of the factors that Wallace identifies as affecting teamwork effectiveness in his school context also apply to that situation.

10   What is my summary evaluation of the text in relation to my review question?

(a)   How convincing are the authors' claims and why?

Review Question 1. Wallace's conclusions are that school leadership should be shared as widely as possible, contingent on the degree of risk for headteachers, and that relatively equal sharing, subject to a contingent reversal to hierarchical operation, promotes effective teamwork. These conclusions are fairly convincing for the context of state-funded primary schools in the UK. He backs his claims with a coherent piece of research that is, however, modest in scope. We share his overall positive stance towards team approaches. Wallace himself restricts the asserted applicability of his claims to UK schools and we are uncertain how far these claims might apply beyond this context. Our university experience suggests that they apply at only a high level of abstraction because of significant contextual differences.

Review question 2. Equal sharing with a contingent reversal to hierarchical operation does appear to be applicable to teaching programme and research project teams in our experience. But important features of the primary school context from which his evidence was derived are only partially applicable to our universities, where there is less reliance on fixed SMTs as a way of managing either departments or the institution as a whole.

> *Comment.* Completing all the earlier Critical Analysis Questions with our two review questions in mind meant that we had already evaluated Wallace's claims in detail. Here we were soon able to compose a summative view by looking back at what we had already written in response to Critical Analysis Questions 5–9.

(b)   How, if at all, could the authors have provided stronger backing for their claims?

Wallace could in principle have provided stronger backing for his claims if he had drawn on a wider range of research literature on team approaches to leadership in schools and elsewhere, had investigated a wider range of organizational and national contexts, and included outcome measures in assessing the degree of synergy achieved in the four SMTs. However, given the modest scope of his research, he appropriately states that his claims are tentative. He avoids gross overgeneralization by indicating that he is making claims only about UK schools.

> *Comment.* By not expressing great certainty or generalizing beyond the UK schools context, Wallace has actually avoided claiming very much. Rather, he has put forward a strong, coherent argument with limited but sound empirical backing, offering a potent stimulus for readers' reflection rather than implying that his argument is fully proven or that his claims will necessarily apply to the readers' situation.

Taking charge of your Critical Analysis of texts

The Critical Analysis form is designed to apply to most types of front-line literature that you are likely to meet in the course of your studies, including material that you may download from the Internet. It is less useful for textbooks or other support literature. (As discussed in Chapter 2, textbooks are an excellent resource for identifying the front-line literature that you need to read and analyze, rather than key sources in their own right.)

Remember that when conducting a Critical Analysis, it is up to you to decide which Critical Analysis Questions are most important for any individual text and what your answers to them must include. Conducting a Critical Analysis prepares you for writing about texts in depth. In the next chapter we will offer ideas about how to develop a Critical Review of one text or a Comparative Critical Review of several texts, structured according to the answers given to each of the Critical Analysis Questions.

10 Developing your Argument in Writing a Critical Review of a Text

By now, especially if you tried doing your own Critical Analysis, you will probably feel quite familiar with our structured approach to critical reading. We hope you are beginning to sense how all this structuring gives you scope to:

- Drive the Critical Analysis according to your review question (or questions), restricting your concern with the content to searching for relevant material.

- Alert yourself to how the authors attempt to convince their target audience.

- Evaluate the authors' claims to knowledge thoroughly in assessing how far they are convincing to you.

- Draw a strong conclusion where you summarize how far the relevant content of the text contributes to answering your review question.

So far, so good. If your critical reading is in preparation for writing for assessment, you will now have to develop a convincing argument of your own, as commentator, about what you have read. In a Critical Review of a front-line text, your conclusion will consist of evaluatory claims about what the authors reported, for which you must provide an adequate warrant. The basis for this is the evidence you have gathered, through your Critical Analysis, about what the authors were doing, their claims that are relevant to your review question and your evaluation of those claims.

In this chapter we show you how you can use a completed Critical Analysis of a text as the platform for a Critical Review. We will invite you to write your own Critical Review of the article by Wallace in Appendix 2, drawing on your completed Critical Analysis from Chapter 8. We will then offer our illustrative Critical Review of Wallace's article, based on our own completed Critical Analysis from Chapter 9. Finally, we will suggest how you can use the completed Critical Analyses of two or more front-line texts as the basis for constructing a Comparative Critical Review.

A Critical Review may be something you are required to produce for a coursework assessment, or for a component of an essay or a dissertation. But they also exist in the published literature. If you browse academic journals in your field, you will probably find reviews of single books and longer, comparative reviews of two or more books or articles on the same topic. In due course you might wish to consider writing such a review, based on our approach, and submitting it for publication in an academic journal.

Structuring a Critical Review of a text

You have already seen in Part One the mechanisms for structuring a Critical Summary of a text. A Critical Review operates on the same principle but goes into more depth. A review can be structured in various ways, depending on its scope and purpose and on the nature of the text under scrutiny. But in all cases it will have to develop an argument that is designed to convince the target audience. The review should therefore introduce the reader to the topic, develop a warrant and provide a conclusion that is backed-up by the warrant. You will probably notice, as you read a wider range of literature, that these three components (introduction, development of warrant, conclusion) underpin the structure of most texts. Frequently the development of the warrant is subdivided into a sequence of sections. The basic structure is flexible, enabling you to design your own text so that each component builds on the previous one, as best suits the material you want to cover. Every part of the text, from the title at the beginning to the reference list at the end, has its place in helping you to build up a convincing argument.

We offer here an adaptation of this basic structure that is appropriate for a Critical Review of an article or book chapter reporting research. The component on developing the warrant will be divided into a sequence of three linked sections, covering:

- what the authors were doing;

- the main claims about findings relevant to the review questions;

- your evaluation of their claims.

You will see that your answers to particular Critical Analysis Questions on your completed form relate to particular sections within the structure. So you can draw on your responses when writing and also refer back to the text that you are reviewing. If you mention any additional literature, follow the normal conventions, referring to the publication by the author's surname and date in the text, with a full reference list at the end.

Note that the projected length of our illustrative Critical Review structure is up to 1,000 words (plus references). We have indicated the approximate number of words that each section should contain. These suggestions may be altered to suit your purpose within the limits imposed by the necessity of developing a convincing argument. (If you were writing a longer or shorter review, you could adjust the length of each section proportionately.)

Structure for a Critical Review of an article or chapter reporting research (1,000 words)

Title

- Your choice of title should include the keywords that will indicate to the reader what you are doing (a Critical Review of a selected piece of literature) and the aspect of the social world that forms your focus.

Introducing the Critical Review (50–150 words)

- A statement of your purpose – critically to review the selected text (give the names of the authors, the title of the chapter or article and the date of publication) as a contribution to answering your review question or questions (Critical Analysis Question 1). You should list the review questions to give the reader an indication of the focus for your review. (For this exercise, we will use the same review questions as those for the Critical Analysis of Wallace's article that you were invited to try out earlier:

  1 What does the text suggest may be key factors promoting or inhibiting the effectiveness of a particular aspect of educational leadership and management practice?

  2 To what extent are the factors identified applicable to the leadership and management of my organization or one known to me?)

Introducing the text being critically reviewed – what the authors were trying to find out and what they did (150–250 words, beginning to build the warrant of your argument)

- A summary of the authors' purposes for the text and the kind of enquiry they engaged in, including an indication of the type of literature they produced (use your answer to Critical Analysis Question 2) and their intellectual project (use your answer to Critical Analysis Question 3).

- A brief indication of why this text is relevant to the review questions guiding your Critical Review (Critical Analysis Question 1).

- A brief summary of how they went about their investigation (e.g., the research design, methodology, sample, methods of data collection and analysis).

The authors' main claims relating to the review questions (150–250 words, continuing to build the warrant of your argument)

- A summary of the main claims made by the authors of the text, as relevant to answering your review questions (use your answer to Critical Analysis Question 4) – a synthesis of, say, up to five main points.

- An indication of the range of contexts to which the authors claim, explicitly or implicitly, that their findings may apply (e.g., they imply that their claims apply to all contexts or do not specify any limits on the extent to which they may be universally applicable).

Evaluating the authors' main claims relating to the review questions (200–400 words, continuing to build the warrant of your argument)

- Your evaluation of these findings and any broader claims, critically assessing the extent to which they are convincing *for the context from which these claims were derived.* (Use your answers to Critical Analysis Questions 5–8, possibly referring to additional literature to support your judgement in relation to Critical Analysis Question 8.) In your critique, you may wish to refer back to your earlier account of the authors' purpose, intellectual project and how they went about their enquiry (e.g., you may wish to assert that the value stance of particular authors led to bias which affected their findings).

- Your critical assessment of how far the claims made by the authors of the text may be applicable *to other contexts, including those in your own experience* (Critical Analysis Questions 5–9, possibly referring to additional literature to support your judgement in relation to Critical Analysis Question 8). In your critique you may wish to refer back to your earlier account of how the authors went about their enquiry (e.g., you may wish to assert that the findings from a particular intellectual project were derived from a context which is so different from yours that you consider the prescriptions for practice emerging from this work are unlikely to apply directly to your context).

Conclusion (150–250 words)

- Your brief overall evaluation of the text, to assess its contribution to answering your review questions (use your answer to Critical Analysis Question 10).

- For this exercise, your summary answer to the first review question. This will include a statement of your judgement, with reasons, about how far the findings and any broader claims are convincing for the context from which they were derived.

- For this exercise, your summary answer to the second review question. This will include a statement of your judgement, with reasons, about how far the findings and any broader claims are applicable (e.g., at how high a level of abstraction?) to your professional context or one known to you.)

References

- Give the full reference for the text you have reviewed.

- If you refer to any additional literature, list the texts to which you have referred, following the normal conventions for compiling a reference list.

Your Critical Review of an article reporting research

When deciding the length of each section in a Critical Review, it is important to ensure there is enough space to develop your argument effectively. Whatever the word length that you must, or wish, to adhere to, you need to decide what proportion of the overall account should be given to each section. You will wish to avoid the common error of giving too much space to describing the authors' claims and leaving too little space for the evaluation of them and the conclusion – offering only half of the warrant and a minimal conclusion will not make for a convincing argument. Now write a Critical Review of Wallace's article in Appendix 2, of up to 1,000 words (plus references). Try to keep to the word length suggestions in the outline for the structure above, and draw on your completed Critical Analysis from the earlier chapter.

Your answer to each Critical Analysis Question will form the starting point for writing the text for each section. You will need to provide your own title and devise your own section headings. When you have written your Critical Review, you will be able to compare what you wrote with our effort below. (We strongly recommend that you write your own Critical Review before looking at ours, to maximize your learning.)

Our Critical Review of Wallace's article

Here is our illustrative Critical Review of Wallace's article, based on the structure we have outlined in this chapter and on our completed Critical Analysis from Chapter 9. As with the Critical Analysis material itself, our review will reflect our responses to the article, our particular experience of organizations and our choice of headings. So it will differ from your review in some details. But we hope that you will find it easy to see both how we have drawn on our Critical Analysis and how we have developed our argument in attempting to convince our critical readers (including you).

Review of an empirical study of leadership in UK school senior management teams

Introduction   The purpose of this review is critically to analyze the article 'Sharing Leadership of Schools through Teamwork: a Justifiable Risk?' by Mike Wallace (abridged from a paper originally published in *Educational Management and Administration* in 2001). Two review questions are addressed:

1 What does the text suggest may be key factors promoting or inhibiting the effectiveness of team approaches to the leadership and management of educational organizations?

2 To what extent are the factors identified applicable to leadership and management in our universities?

Purpose and design Wallace researched the extent to which headteachers of senior management teams (SMTs) in UK primary schools shared leadership with SMT colleagues. SMTs consisted of the headteacher, deputy head and other senior teachers. Their role was to support the headteacher in leading and managing the school.

Wallace sets out to inform the training and practice of senior school staff within the UK policy context. Central government education reforms had rendered the sharing of leadership as risky for headteachers as it was necessary. The obligation to implement reforms meant that headteachers depended on SMT colleagues' contributions. But, as team leaders, they alone were accountable for the SMT's effectiveness in managing the school.

This research relates clearly to the review questions because it highlights factors affecting team effectiveness that could have implications for practice elsewhere. Wallace was informed by research and theoretical literature on school leadership, including his study of secondary school SMTs. His case studies of four SMTs in large primary schools involved interviews and observation and were guided by a cultural and political perspective.

Findings relating to team effectiveness Wallace claims, first, that principles based on staff entitlement and effective leadership outcomes are widely offered to justify extensive sharing of school leadership. But, theories reflecting these principles are unrealistic for the UK context. Second, in UK schools, central government reforms have increased headteachers' dependence on SMT colleagues to support implementation, while increasing the risk of their being blamed for sharing leadership where doing so is judged negatively. Third, his secondary and primary school SMT research implies that headteachers' and other SMT members' culture of teamwork includes contradictory beliefs: in a management hierarchy led by the headteacher and in all members contributing equally to teamwork. Fourth, the primary school research suggests that maximum synergy is achieved where headteachers enable SMT colleagues to contribute equally to teamwork, and other members willingly operate inside parameters set by the headteacher. This approach is most effective but carries most risk of ineffectiveness. Fifth, in a context of high accountability, UK headteachers should share SMT leadership as widely as they dare, while all members should accept that headteachers must sometimes operate hierarchically to keep the SMT's work inside parameters they set.

Wallace suggests that these findings apply to all UK schools because of the system-wide impact of central government reforms. The findings imply that the generic leadership theories he criticizes should embrace contextual factors to extend their generalizability.

Evaluation of claims about team effectiveness   Wallace's findings appear quite robust. He is appropriately tentative, given the limitations of his research. His claims are backed by observation of SMTs at work and triangulation of individual informants' accounts. His generalization that headteachers of all UK schools face a dilemma over sharing SMT leadership is backed by reference to the UK policy context: central government reforms were clearly designed to impact on all schools. But he reports no evidence of teamwork outcomes, so his claims about varying SMT synergy within the four case study teams are only moderately convincing. The sample of informants and SMT meetings is small, so the generalizability of the findings to other schools within the UK remains uncertain. Wallace's research does not address the possibility that diverse local contextual factors may contribute to team effectiveness elsewhere.

Use of the cultural and political perspective to guide data collection is convincing. Wallace defines key concepts and employs the perspective extensively in reporting findings, leading to the generation of a model to explain the variations in SMT practice that he found. However, this perspective does not embrace other factors that might significantly affect team effectiveness, including members' psychological motivations.

Wallace explicitly develops a normative argument and clearly values teamwork. However, he does not question the existence of a management hierarchy entailing unequal sharing of leadership. Equally, he does not challenge the central government reforms despite claiming that they caused the headteachers' dilemma over sharing leadership.

Wallace does not relate his findings to other researchers' work. Therefore they remain untested against other research or theories that might support or challenge them.

Wallace's claims apply to our higher education context at only a high level of abstraction because academics enjoy greater individual autonomy than school staff. In our experience, teamwork is most significant within teaching or research groups, rather than amongst central university leaders.

Conclusion   Wallace identifies a key factor promoting or inhibiting the effectiveness of team approaches to school management, at least in the UK. His conclusions, fairly convincing for this context, are that school leadership should be shared as widely as possible, contingent on the degree of risk for headteachers, and that relatively equal sharing coupled with a contingent reversal to hierarchical operation promotes effective teamwork. His claims are backed by coherent research, though of modest scope. It remains uncertain how far these claims might apply beyond the UK.

Equal sharing with a contingent reversal to hierarchical operation is applicable to teaching-programme and research-project teams in our university contexts. However, important features of the primary school context from which his evidence was derived are only partially applicable to our higher education institution, where there is less reliance on fixed SMTs as a way of managing either departments or the university as a whole.

This study bears testing against a wider range of research and theoretical literature. Further research is needed on team approaches to leadership in schools and other organizations in different contexts, and should include leadership outcome measures.

Reference   Wallace, M. (2001) 'Sharing leadership through teamwork: a justifiable risk?' *Educational Management and Administration* 29(2): pp. 153–167 [abridged as Appendix 2 of Wallace, M. and Wray, A. (2006) *Critical Reading and Writing for Postgraduates*. London: Sage.]

DID WE WRITE THE PERFECT REVIEW?

No – we hope we have convinced you by now that there is no single best outcome in critical reading or self-critical writing. Much depends on the authors' insights, values and capacity to argue convincingly, and on the readers' assessment criteria and values. But there are good and not-so-good practices. We have attempted to follow what we believe to be good practice: taking charge by asking review questions and developing our own argument about how the literature contributes to answering them.

If you were to count up the number of words in each section, you would find that it lies within our recommended range and so contributes proportionately to the review. The entire review (excluding the reference) comes close to our target of 1,000 words.

You may have noticed how we have sometimes taken material direct from our Critical Analysis of the article in Chapter 9, then edited it to fulfil our slightly different purpose in writing that part of our Critical Review. An electronically-stored Critical Analysis of a text will enable you to 'cut and paste' material into any Critical Review that you write. However, avoid the mistake of just moving chunks of material around – a Critical Analysis of a text is not identical to a Critical Review of it and editing will be required. Ensure that everything you write in your Critical Review is doing its job in contributing to the answering of your review questions.

Structuring a Comparative Critical Review of several texts

The structure for reviewing a single text can be adapted for reviewing several texts in depth. Rather than writing a sequential review of one text after another, a comparative approach requires you to review the texts *together* by grouping and synthesizing your answers to the same Critical Analysis Question across some or all of the texts at the same time. (Recall that we exemplified doing this at a less in-depth level in Chapter 5.) As with the single text structure, the Comparative Review structure may be modified to suit the nature of the literature.

Our suggested structure below has been adapted for reviewing several (up to maybe five) front-line texts reporting research – typically, published journal articles, book chapters or books. The projected length of the review is around 4,000 words, excluding references. We have used the same two illustrative review questions as in the single-text review, leaving the field of enquiry unspecified. Obviously, you can modify it for the types of literature you are reviewing and identify your own review questions to address. To write a Comparative Critical Review, your first step will be to complete a Critical Analysis for each of the texts. Putting them side-by-side, your Comparative Critical Review will be relatively simple to construct, because parallel information about each text will be located in the corresponding place on each form.

Although we have not expanded this structure into a full 4,000 word review, you will find that our example Critical Review for one text above, along with the less detailed one- and three-text Critical Summaries that we exemplified in Part One, will provide you with indications of how the structure below can be fleshed out.

Structure for a Comparative Critical Review of several texts reporting research (4,000 words)

Title

- Your choice of title should include the keywords that will indicate to the reader what you are doing (a Comparative Critical Review) and the aspect of practice that forms your focus.

Introducing the Comparative Critical Review (250–750 words)

- A statement of your purpose – critically to review the selected texts in depth as a contribution to answering your review question or questions (Critical Analysis Question 1).

- Your justification for selecting this focus (e.g., its significance for improving the aspect of practice) perhaps referring to other literature to support your argument.

- Your acknowledgement of the scope of your review (e.g., an indication of the texts you will analyze in depth, giving the names of the authors, title and date of publication for each, and the reasons why you selected them for in-depth review).

- Your acknowledgement of the limitations of your review (e.g., that your focus is confined to these few texts and there may be others relating to this focus which you will not be examining in depth).

- An indication of the topics to be covered in each of the remaining sections of your review, so that the reader can see how you will develop your argument.

Introducing the texts being critically reviewed (250–750 words)

- A cross-comparative summary of the authors' purposes and of the kind or kinds of enquiry they engaged in, including an indication of the type or types of literature they produced (use your answers to Critical Analysis Question 2) and their intellectual projects (use your answers to Critical Analysis Question 3).

- A brief indication of why these texts are relevant to the review questions guiding your Comparative Critical Review (Critical Analysis Question 1).

- A brief summary of how the authors went about their enquiry (for example:

  - for a research report, the research design, sample, methods of data collection and analysis;

  - for a research synthesis, the sequence of topics addressed and range of sources employed;

  - for a theoretical work, the main theoretical ideas, the sequence of topics and any use of evidence;

  - for a practical handbook, the sequence of topics addressed and any use of evidence).

(You may either present this summary in cross-comparative form, or outline each text separately, according to the nature of the texts and your judgement about which approach will be clearer for the reader.)

The authors' main claims relating to the review questions (500–1,000 words)

- A comparative summary of the main claims made by the authors of each text, as they are relevant to your review questions (use your answers to Critical Analysis Question 4) – a synthesis of, say, up to five main points for each text reviewed, indicating the extent to which there is overlap between texts (e.g., a particular claim was common to all the texts, or to three out of the four, etc.).

- An indication of the range of contexts to which the authors claim explicitly or implicitly that their findings may apply, paying attention to how two authors might ascribe different scopes of application to similar claims.

Evaluating the authors' main claims relating to the review questions (1,500–2,000 words)

- Your comparative evaluation of these claims, critically assessing the extent to which claims made by the authors of each text are convincing. (Use your answers to Critical Analysis Questions 5–9, possibly referring to additional literature to support your judgement in relation to Critical Analysis Question 8.) In your critique, you may wish to refer back to your earlier account of the authors' purpose, intellectual project and how they went about their enquiry.

Conclusion (250–750 words)

- Your brief overall evaluation of each of the texts reviewed, to assess their combined contribution to answering your review questions (use your answers to Critical Analysis Question 10).

- The summary answer to each review question, in turn, offered by all the texts reviewed. Each summary answer should include a statement of your judgement, with reasons, about the extent to which the claims across all the texts provide a convincing warrant for the relevant conclusions drawn by the authors.

- If appropriate, any reasons why you think, in the light of your Comparative Critical Review, that there may be difficulties in finding definitive answers to your review questions.

References
- The list of texts to which you have referred, including those you have analyzed in depth, following the normal conventions for compiling a reference list.

Gearing up for writing Critical Reviews of texts

The structures we have presented offer you a template which you can modify, whether by adding or subdividing sections or by changing their content, for in-depth reviews that are freestanding or part of something bigger. The length of each section can be adjusted according to the amount you need, or want, to write in total.

In Part Two we have outlined a mental map for exploring the literature and indicated how you can apply it as part of a structured approach for the Critical Analysis of texts. We have shown that, in turn, Critical Analyses offer a platform for structuring a Critical Review of one text or a Comparative Critical Review of several texts. The more you practice by using the mental map, completing Critical Analysis forms and writing Critical Reviews of texts, the more the ideas underlying these structures will become integral to your critical reading and self-critical writing. You will be able to employ the ideas flexibly and discard any props that you no longer need.

So far we have concentrated on helping you learn how to engage critically with a few texts: in summary in Part One and in depth in Part Two. In Part Three we expand the focus to consider how to engage critically with a potentially unlimited number of texts in developing a Critical Literature Review.

Part III   Constructing a Critical Review of the Literature

11 Focusing and Building up Your Critical Literature Review

Part Three brings together the ideas from Parts One and Two. We will show how you can extend the scope of your critical reading and self-critical writing by using Critical Analyses and Critical Synopses together in constructing a larger-scale Critical Literature Review.

A Critical Literature Review addresses a potentially unlimited number of texts. Unless you have been set the task of writing about one or more specified texts, your exploration of a topic is sure to engage with a range of material. Our techniques will help you decide what is most important. Applying the techniques will enable you to see whether to foreground or background the different texts that you want to mention. In other words, a good Critical Literature Review combines in-depth Critical Analyses of single and multiple texts, with more passing reference to Critical Synopses of other texts. These different levels of engagement must flow naturally as you build up your argument. It takes some skill to create a seamless account that brings in the appropriate amount of detail to achieve your objectives.

Literature reviews form the basis of some postgraduate assignments and are expected as part of a dissertation. A common assessment criterion at doctorate level is that your investigation must generate new knowledge in the field of enquiry. So you may wish to demonstrate through Critical Literature Reviews that your research and theorizing step significantly beyond the boundaries of existing academic knowledge. In due course, you may wish to try getting a Critical Literature Review published as a paper in an academic journal, especially if you are set on an academic career. Similarly, you may be interested in writing a research grant proposal, where a Critical Literature Review supports your case for funding.

Whatever your reason for reviewing literature, you will find that a focused and constructively Critical Literature Review is more manageable than one that is merely descriptive. If you take charge, the literature is then available to serve your purposes. You make your own critical choice of what literature to seek and suit yourself in how you use it. If you let yourself become a servant of the literature, you will rapidly become overwhelmed by trying to read and describe everything written in the field. Conversely, a Critical Literature Review will enable you to develop a strong argument that maximizes your chances of convincing the critical readers who are your assessors (whether in the role of tutor, supervisor, examiner, academic journal referee, or member of a committee that allocates research grants).

In this chapter we define what we mean by a Critical Literature Review and propose some criteria that might mark one out as being of high quality, to give you something to aim for. We offer a structured approach to creating a self-contained Critical Literature Review that integrates the Critical Synopsis, Critical Summary, Critical Analysis and Critical Review structures from Parts One and Two. We then suggest how it is possible to start moving away from such heavy reliance on the direct translation of material from your Critical Synopses and Critical Analyses into your Critical Literature Review. You could make more flexible use of them, adapting the basic review structure to suit the development of your argument, and bringing in additional literature as appropriate.

Chapter 12 considers how Critical Literature Reviews contribute to small-scale research for your dissertation. Conducting Critical Literature Reviews before you begin any empirical work will valuably inform what you choose to investigate and how you conduct the enquiry. After completing your investigation you can refer back to your reviews and additional literature to help you interpret your findings and reflect self-critically on the strengths and limitations of your research. We show how, in writing up your account of your investigation, Critical Literature Reviews are often distributed across the dissertation. Each then makes its own contribution to the development of your argument within the component where it is located and of your overall argument across the whole study. Chapter 13 offers some techniques to help you ensure that whatever you are writing, including your Critical Literature Reviews, contribute to the logic of this argument. Finally, in Chapter 14, we explore how you may build on what you have learned from your postgraduate studies about critical reading and self-critical writing, if you pursue an academic career.

What makes a literature review critical?

Critical Literature Reviews are personal. They reflect the intellect of the reviewer, who has decided the focus, selected texts for review, interpreted and engaged critically with them, ordered and synthesized what was found, and written the final account. We define a Critical Literature Review as:

> a reviewer's constructively critical account, developing an argument designed to convince a particular audience about what the published – and possibly also unpublished – literature (theory, research, practice or policy) indicates is and is not known about one or more questions that the reviewer has framed.

Note that this definition excludes reviews that just describe texts because the reviewer has not been critical. Such a 'review' simply restates what is in the texts rather than building any argument, targeting any identifiable audience, or focusing on any specific question. Our definition also excludes any review which is destructively critical. A constructively critical account will not indulge in gratuitously negative evaluation for the sake of demonstrating the authors' foolishness and the reviewer's intellectual superiority.

Whether written for assessment or for publication, Critical Literature Reviews are integral to the knowledge-for-understanding, knowledge-for-critical evaluation and knowledge-for-action intellectual projects. They have several features. First, their purpose dictates their focus. Reviews relate to one or more explicit or implicit review questions that may be:

- *Substantive* (about some aspect of the social world).

- *Theoretical* (about concepts, perspectives, theories or models that relate to some aspect of the social world).

- *Methodological* (about the approach to conducting an empirical or theoretical enquiry).

The attempt to address review questions drives the critical reading and self-critical writing process by providing:

- A criterion for selecting some texts for inclusion, rejecting others and homing in on a few of the most relevant selected texts for in-depth Critical Analysis.

- A rationale for reading selectively within any text, saving the time that reading the whole text in detail would take.

- A starting point for a Critical Synopsis (Critical Synopsis Question A) or for a Critical Analysis (Critical Analysis Question 1) of what has been read.

- A focus for synthesizing findings into a logically structured account that puts forward a convincing argument.

Second, in order to answer each substantive, theoretical or methodological review question, Critical Literature Reviews synthesize claims to knowledge from a range of relevant texts. Reviewers attempt to demonstrate to the target audience the basis of their informed judgement about what is known, how strong the evidence is and what is not known from others' work. Third, they enable reviewers to demonstrate the scientific or social significance of their review question and why an answer is worth seeking. The significance of a substantive review question may be as a contribution towards the development of research or practice knowledge in the field of enquiry. The significance of a theoretical review question may be further theory development, and that of a methodological review question may be the justification of the research methods chosen for empirical work. Finally, Critical Literature Reviews enable reviewers to locate their own work within the wider body of knowledge in the area to which the substantive, theoretical or methodological review questions are applied.

Producing a high quality Critical Literature Review is a challenging but rewarding task. As with a Critical Summary or a Critical Review of a text, you can help yourself to focus with precision by clarifying your review question at the outset, even if you find that you need to refine it as you go along. Then sustain that focus as you develop the warrant of your argument through to the conclusion. Another tip is to be consciously constructive when evaluating the literature, ensuring that your judgements are clearly backed by what you have found. Suppose you discover that existing knowledge relevant to your review question is not particularly robust or conceptually coherent. Make this claim, but also indicate the evidence that warrants your claim being accepted. Then be prepared to suggest how, as appropriate, the knowledge base could be enhanced, practice improved, or theory developed.

AIMING HIGH

You will probably have sensed from your critical reading of the literature that there is a big difference between the best and the worst literature reviews that you have encountered. It is worth noticing, and applying, the best features of a high-quality review self-critically to your own writing. In our view, a high-quality Critical Literature Review is likely to be:

- *Focused* on an explicit substantive, theoretical or methodological review question.
- *Structured* so as to address each review question in a logical sequence (see Chapter 12).
- *Discerning*, so that some texts are given a more in-depth consideration than others, according to the reviewer's judgement of their centrality to the review questions.
- *Constructively critical*, evaluating the extent to which knowledge claims and the arguments they support are convincing, or whether a theoretical orientation is coherent.
- *Accurately referenced*, so that each source can be followed up by readers of the review.
- *Clearly expressed and reader-friendly,* with interim conclusions and signposting, to help readers get the reviewer's message easily and follow the development of the argument.

(Continued)

> *(Continued)*
>
> • *Informative*, providing synthesis through a strong conclusion which summarizes the reviewer's judgement about how the cited literature answers the review question, indicating the strengths and weaknesses of the evidence, and arbitrating between any opposing positions reviewed.
> • *Convincingly argued*, expressing the reviewer's 'voice' authoritatively because the conclusion is adequately warranted by evidence from the literature or the reviewer's experience.
> • *Balanced,* indicating that the various viewpoints expressed in the literature have been carefully weighed and that the reviewer's judgements are demonstrably based on a careful assessment of the relevant strengths and limitations of the evidence presented in that literature.

Structuring a Critical Literature Review from completed analyses

Here we suggest a straightforward way of constructing a self-contained Critical Literature Review. It enables you to build an account based directly on completed Critical Synopses and Critical Analyses. Essentially, it combines the structure we offered for a Comparative Critical Summary of several texts from Part One with the structure for a Comparative Critical Review of several texts from Part Two.

In preparation for writing a Critical Literature Review using this structure, you will need to have identified your review question, accessed relevant texts, completed a Critical Synopsis for each one and completed a Critical Analysis for those that turn out to be most central to your focus. If you have attached a copy of each Critical Synopsis or Critical Analysis to the front of your texts, you can divide this material into two sets:

• Critical Synopses, and their texts, that are relevant but not central to answering your review question.

• Critical Analyses, and their texts, that are most central.

You can now compare and contrast your Critical Synopsis and Critical Analysis forms, in order to determine what range of answers you have amassed to each of the Critical Synopsis Questions and, for the most central texts, the corresponding Critical Analysis Questions. Identify what the pattern of answers is: the most common, the range, the most unexpected, and so on. This information will provide you with a basis for your account of what is known and the limits of what is known regarding the answer to your review question. You can easily select from the Critical Summaries and Critical Analyses anything that you wish to highlight, and you can go back to the original texts if you want more detail.

We will indicate, below, what each section in our basic Critical Literature Review structure covers. In writing your own review using this structure you would, of course, need to create your own heading for each section (as we did in the previous chapter with our Critical Review of Wallace's article).

Structure for a Critical Literature Review using Critical Synopses and Critical Analyses

Title – use keywords indicating the focus for the study.

Introduction

- A statement of purpose – your focus, designed to answer one or more named review questions (Critical Analysis Question 1, Critical Synopsis Question A).

- Justification of the significance of your focus (e.g., its importance for improving practice).

- The scope of the review – the range of literature reviewed (e.g., concentrating on research reports, focused on business organizations) and why this range was selected for review.

- Limitations of the review (e.g., mainly concerned with a small number of key texts, restricted to sources from only one part of the world, confined to books and academic journal articles, based on what you could access from the Internet).

- Signposting – indicating how each of the remaining sections of the review will contribute to answering your review question.

Sections building up the warrant of your argument	Based on answers to Critical Analysis Questions for central texts	Based on answers to Critical Synopsis Questions for more peripheral texts
• An introduction to the texts being reviewed.	2, 3	B

(Continued)

(Continued)		
• The authors' main claims relevant to your review question.	4	C
• Evaluation of the authors' claims, including any counter-evidence.	5–9	D
Final section setting out the conclusion of your argument		
• Summary of your evaluation of literature reviewed to assess the texts' combined contribution to answering your review question.	10	E

You may wish to extend the conclusion by:

• offering your self-critical reflection, in retrospect, on the strengths and limitations of your review (e.g., why it may have been difficult fully to answer your review question);

• highlighting possibilities for further work (e.g., research and theory-building) that you judge to be needed and, if appropriate, implications for policy and practice.

References

• A list (in author alphabetical order) of the texts to which you have referred, following the normal conventions for compiling a reference list.

What might such a Critical Literature Review look like?

Your entire critical literature review constitutes one or more arguments: a conclusion for each of your review questions, backed up by evidence that forms the warrant for it. Using the structure we have just described, the warrant of your argument can be built up by writing paragraphs that synthesize your answers to particular Critical Analysis and Critical Synopsis Questions. Here is a fictional example, comprising part or all of each section. (We have indicated in square brackets and italic script how this account embodies elements of the structure outlined above.)

Learning the noun genders in a foreign language: a Critical Literature Review

Introduction This review aims to shed light on why noun genders are so difficult for adult learners of the German language to master, and to consider how noun gender teaching might be improved *[statement of purpose]*. There are three genders in German: masculine, feminine and neuter and, although some nouns have features that indicate their gender, most do not and simply have to be learned *[justifying the significance of the focus]*. In order to understand more about this feature of German, the review explores the published literature in relation to two questions: (a) why are noun genders difficult to learn? and (b) how are they most effectively taught *[review questions]*. Since it is not just German that has noun gender, research on other languages has been included *[scope of the review]*, even though it is possible that not all of the problems and solutions are transferable across languages (Tauber, 1991) *[limitation of the review]*. For clarity, the main texts under scrutiny are first introduced and the basic claims about noun gender learning are compared. Next comes a discussion of the strengths and weaknesses of the main claims, including a brief account of other published works that appear not to align with them. Finally, conclusions are drawn about the extent to which the reviewed texts shed light on the two review questions *[signposting]*.

Research into noun gender learning [introducing the texts] Despite the immediacy of the challenge of noun gender from day one in many languages, there have been surprisingly few studies conducted on why gender is difficult to learn and how it might be better taught. Exceptions are the longitudinal study of Welsh noun gender learning by Jones (2004), the comparative study of classroom and naturalistic learners of German by Nussbaum (1998) and the classic study of French gender carried out by Barthes and his team in the 1970s (e.g., Barthes et al., 1979). Although old, this study is still identified by many as a landmark in language learning research. Several other works also have some bearing on the questions addressed here. Tauber (1991) explains some of the similarities and differences between the noun gender systems of different languages. Jennings (2003) identifies noun gender as one of several hurdles that have to be crossed in first language acquisition. Meanwhile, Vrey and Lambert's (2005) normative approach to their 'revolution in language teaching' sets aside noun gender entirely, as 'an unwelcome and unnecessary distraction from the real fabric of the language' (p. 81).

Jones (2004) collected data from ... .

Like Jones, Nussbaum (1998) was interested in the first year of language learning, though her focus was German, making this comparative study particularly relevant to the present review questions ….

In contrast, Barthes and colleagues (1979) focused on … and they investigated how ….

Why are noun genders difficult to learn? [main claims relevant to the first review question]   All three studies just described propose that the age of learning plays a part, though Jennings' (2003) identification of gender as difficult for young children somewhat contradicts this. According to Nussbaum (1998), it is also *how* learners are first exposed to noun genders that determines how much effort they have to put into learning them (p. 36) … .

How are noun genders most effectively taught? [main claims relevant to the second review question]   We turn now to the effective teaching of noun gender. Jones (2004) claims that teachers should attempt to distract learners from the noun genders until later classes. This proposal, however, does not sit comfortably with Barthes et al.'s (1979) data on what learners naturally pay attention to. For their own part, Barthes and colleagues lay out a detailed set of guidelines for teachers, including four pages on gender. This level of attention contrasts starkly with Vrey and Lambert's (2005) total exclusion of it in their programme … . Meanwhile, Nussbaum's (1998) contribution to answering this question is to note that 'more research is needed on what kind of exposure is most effective for learning' (p. 43).

Strength and limitations of the evidence [evaluation of claims and any counter-evidence]   At first glance, there seems to be consensus that noun gender learning is difficult – whether this implies that it should be carefully taught (Barthes et al., 1979), postponed (Jones, 2004) or ignored (Vrey and Lambert, 2005). However, there are important differences between the accounts, particularly in relation to the sort of intellectual project in which the authors are engaged. Only Nussbaum's study is fully centred in knowledge-for-understanding, while Jones (2004) and Barthes et al. (1979) share with Vrey and Lambert (2005) a strong interest in influencing practice and policy. As a result, all of these studies, it might be argued, demonstrate a vested interest in a particular methodology. It is perhaps not unrelated to this agenda that these are the studies in which the conclusions are made with most confidence, while Nussbaum (1998) remains tentative about what her findings mean … .

… As noted earlier, care must be taken before assuming that the problems that a learner of, say, French has with noun gender are the same as those for a learner of German. As Tauber (1991) points out, 'our nomenclature for the phenomenon of word class tends to falsely impress upon us similarities between languages that all have 'genders' of 'masculine' and 'feminine' (p. 911). Despite the evident dangers of a too simplistic equation of languages, Jones (2004) repeatedly draws backing for his claims about Welsh from research literature into other European languages, somewhat weakening his claims ... .

Conclusion [combined contribution to answering review questions]   Inspired by the problems of learning German, this review has focused on establishing why noun gender is difficult for adults to master and how it is best taught. It has been revealed that, in fact, answers derived from languages other than German may not necessarily be wholly generalizable to it. This proviso notwithstanding, there does seem to be general consensus that something about the learning experience of the adult creates particular problems, even though children also struggle with noun gender (Jennings, 2003). It may relate to how adults pay attention to information, or to the absence of the opportunity in the classroom to focus on using language for communication.

The question of how noun gender is best taught remains unanswered, though there is no shortage of practice-focused and policy-focused commentators willing to propose teaching solutions, sometimes (as shown earlier) without much convincing evidence to support their claims ... .

There is evidently still much scope for research into these questions *[reflections]*. Carefully controlled comparative longitudinal studies, though difficult to conduct, would be of particular benefit. More work is needed, also, into how similar languages are in regard to how their noun genders are learned. An additional variable, apparently little considered in the literature, is the effect on the learning of one set of noun genders (say, German) of already knowing another set in one's first language (say, French). Finally, robust studies of the efficacy of different teaching methodologies are also urgently required. To sum up, there seems to be no magic bullet for the learning of noun gender and, until one is found, the learner may have to take the advice of Barthes et al. (1979), and 'study, study, study' (p. 561).

References [list of all texts mentioned, alphabetically by author, according to standard conventions]

(NB: The texts and ideas in this example are fictional.)

Extending the structure for a review constructed from your completed analyses

This basic structure can be elaborated for a Critical Literature Review where you have multiple review questions, by dedicating a separate section to developing an argument for each review question in turn. These arguments together comprise the warrant for the overall conclusion of the Critical Literature Review as a whole. Each section can itself be divided into an identical sequence of subsections, though obviously the content of each section will be different. The structure might then be:

Title – keywords indicating the focus for the study.

Introduction

- Statement of purpose – say, three review questions that all relate to the overall focus (Critical Analysis Question 1, Critical Synopsis Question A).

- Justification of the focus, scope and limitations.

- Signposting to the remaining sections which indicates how each section will contribute part of the warrant for your conclusion to the Critical Literature Review as a whole.

Section addressing the first review question

Subsections building up the warrant of your argument for this section	Based on answers to Critical Analysis Questions for central texts	Based on answers to Critical Synopsis Questions for more peripheral texts
• An introduction to the texts being reviewed.	2, 3	B
• The authors' main claims relevant to your review question.	4	C
• Evaluation of the authors' claims, including any counter-evidence.	5–9	D
Final subsection setting out the conclusion of your argument answering this review question		
• Summarizing your evaluation of the reviewed texts' combined contribution to answering your **first** review question.	10	E

Section addressing the second review question

Subsections in the same sequence as above, leading to the conclusion of your argument answering the **second** review question	Based on answers to Critical Analysis Questions for central texts	Based on answers to Critical Synopsis Questions for more peripheral texts

Section addressing the third review question

Subsections in the same sequence as above, leading to the conclusion of your argument answering the **third** review question	Based on answers to Critical Analysis Questions for central texts	Based on answers to Critical Synopsis Questions for more peripheral texts

Conclusion for the whole Critical Literature Review

- Your summary account of how the conclusions of your arguments answering the three review questions relate together to provide a warrant for your conclusion to the review as a whole.

- Your self-critical retrospective reflections on the strengths and limitations of your review.

- Possibly, implications arising from your review for future research, theorizing or policy-making.

References

- A list (in author alphabetical order) of the texts to which you have referred, following the normal conventions for compiling a reference list.

If you foresaw the relevance of a text to more than one review question, you will have been able to expand your Critical Analysis or Critical Synopsis of the text to cover all the questions. However, sometimes, a new review question will arise only after you have completed the Critical Analysis or Critical Synopsis. In such instances, you may need to complete a new form (or add to the old one) to ensure you have material relevant to this new review question.

Structuring a Review informed by Critical Analyses and Critical Synopses

The structure we have described above is useful but rather inflexible. In a more flexible approach, you might still draw on material from your Critical Analyses and Critical Synopses, but not all of it and not in any fixed sequence. Here, your Critical Analyses and Critical Synopses *inform* the content of your review but no longer dominate its structure. Parameters bounding your creativity in designing Critical Literature Review structures are set by the essential ingredients needed to develop a convincing argument. We suggest that any structure must include:

1 An introduction setting out and justifying your review questions.

2 A warrant comprising a critical account of whatever evidence you have found in the literature relating to these review questions.

3 A strong conclusion that is backed by your warrant.

4 Your reference list (so that readers can follow-up your sources).

Illustrative structure of a Review informed by Critical Analyses and Critical Synopses

There is scope for a variety of structures within these parameters. Here is one illustration, developed for an 8,000-word assignment for a professional doctorate programme. In this example, the review questions, and therefore the structure required in order to address them, have flowed from a substantive concern to improve the role of school leadership in encouraging teachers' commitment to their job within a developing country. While there is a large literature from organizational contexts in developed countries, it has become clear that very little exists for such contexts in developing countries. As with the previous structure, this one is designed to seek to answers to three related review questions. But it looks quite different.

Title – keywords indicating the focus for the study.

• 'The Impact of Leadership on Teachers' Motivation and Job Satisfaction: Implications for Schools in a Developing Country.'

Introduction

• Statement of purpose – to examine what is known and the limits of what is known about the possible impact of leadership on teachers' motivation and job satisfaction, in order to assess what practical implications there may be for improving leadership practice in schools within a developing country. The review therefore seeks to answer three review questions (Critical Analysis Question 1, Critical Synopsis Question A):

1   What is meant by concepts of leadership, motivation and job satisfaction, and how are they assumed to relate to each other?

2   How strong is the evidence from educational organizations and elsewhere that leadership can positively influence the motivation and job satisfaction of those for whose work leaders are responsible?

3   To what extent does the evidence for leaders having a positive influence on the motivation and job satisfaction of those for whose work they are responsible apply to schools in a developing country?

- Justification of the focus, scope and limitations.

- Signposting to the remaining sections, indicating how each section will contribute part of the warrant for the conclusion of the Critical Literature Review as a whole.

Section on defining leadership, motivation, job satisfaction and their inter-relationship

- Signposting – how this section will be divided into two subsections to address the first review question.

*Material warranting a conclusion that answers the **first** review question, drawing on answers from Critical Analyses and Critical Synopses*	*Drawing on answers to Critical Analysis Question for central texts*	*Drawing on answers to Critical Synopsis Questions for more peripheral texts*
• Subsection A: the main ways in which the concepts of leadership, motivation and job satisfaction are defined, and common assumptions about their interrelationship, especially how directly leadership impacts on either motivation or job satisfaction.	**4, 6**	**C, D**
		(Continued)

(Continued)		
• Subsection B: conclusion about the degree to which leadership is commonly and convincingly conceived as impacting directly on motivation and job satisfaction.	**10**	E

Section on evidence for the impact of leadership on motivation and job satisfaction

- Signposting – how this section will be divided into three subsections to address the second review question.

Subsections presenting material to warrant conclusions that combine to answer the **second** review question, drawing on answers from Critical Analyses and Critical Synopses	Based on answers to Critical Analysis Questions for central texts	Based on answers to Critical Synopsis Questions for more peripheral texts
• Subsection A: author's main claims about the impact of leadership on motivation and job satisfaction.	4	C
• Subsection B: evaluation of these claims, including any counter-evidence.	5–8	D
• Subsection C: conclusion summarizing how strong the evidence is from educational organizations and elsewhere that leadership can positively influence motivation and job satisfaction.	10	E

Applicability of the evidence to schools in a developing country

Material warranting a conclusion that answers the **third** review question, drawing on answers from Critical Analyses and Critical Synopses	Based on answers to Critical Analysis Questions for central texts	Based on answers to Critical Synopsis Questions for more peripheral texts
• Subsection A: evaluation of the extent to which evidence from developed countries for leaders having a positive influence on motivation and job satisfaction applies to schools in a developing country.	9	D
• Subsection B: conclusion about the extent to which school leaders in developing countries may positively influence teachers' motivation and job satisfaction.	10	E

Conclusion for the whole Critical Literature Review

- A summary account of how the conclusions of the arguments answering the three review questions relate together to provide a warrant for the conclusion to the review as a whole:

  1 The way leadership is conceived to impact directly on motivation and job satisfaction.

  2 The strength of the evidence for this impact.

  3 The degree to which contextual differences between developed and developing countries may affect the applicability of claims about this impact to schools in a developing country.

- Reflections, in retrospect, on the strengths and limitations of the review.

- Recommendations for training and other support for school leaders in a developing country.

- An indication of what further research may be needed to explore the relative importance of particular contextual factors potentially affecting the impact of leadership on teachers' motivation and job satisfaction in developed and developing countries.

References

- A list (in author alphabetical order) of the texts to which reference is made, following the normal conventions for compiling a reference list.

Developing independence as a critical reviewer of literature

The sequence of structures we have introduced in this chapter allows for your growing competence in conducting Critical Literature Reviews. All three structures will help you keep the range of literature within manageable bounds by focusing on one or more review questions. The first two structures, because they most closely follow the logic of the Critical Analysis form, offer maximum security for the first-time reviewer. They enable you to:

- Lay out side-by-side your completed Critical Analyses and Critical Synopses of individual texts.

- Scan and synthesize your responses to specific Critical Analysis and Critical Synopsis Questions, using the sequence presented in the relevant forms.

- Translate a synthesis of your responses to each of these Critical Analysis Questions and Critical Synopsis Questions directly into your review.

- Build up logically the warrant of your argument as you write down the synthesis to each Critical Analysis Question and Critical Synopsis Question in sequence, culminating in a conclusion where you indicate what answer the literature gives to your review question.

However, security comes at the price of rigidity. As you gain experience you can afford to work more independently. You can work out how to develop the warrant and conclusion of the argument you wish to make by designing your own structure (within the parameters we outlined earlier) to address your review questions in whatever sequence works best.

Your skills as an increasingly sophisticated critical reader and self-critical writer will stand you in good stead for the most complex of reviewing tasks facing most postgraduate students: incorporating distributed literature reviews as an integral part of a dissertation. We now turn to this task.

12 Integrating Critical Literature Reviews into your Dissertation

This chapter focuses on the contribution of Critical Literature Reviews to a larger-scale investigation. As a critical reader, you may have noticed just how powerfully the published literature can support an author's argument. The literature offers an immensely rich (though not unlimited) source of evidence, ranging over theorizing, empirical research and engagement with practice, and extending way beyond the direct experience that any single individual could have. So as a critical reader you will value it when authors' references to the literature demonstrate that their claims are consistent with what others have found. A skilled use of the literature by authors is part of the reason why you find their argument convincing. Equally, you may be impressed when you see authors drawing on the literature to expose, through counter-evidence, the limitations or flaws in another author's (or indeed their own) claims.

As a self-critical writer (whether of reviews, essays or other written products) you will consciously search the literature for whatever useful evidence you can find there. You will employ this evidence as part of your warrant to make your claims in the conclusion of your own argument as convincing as possible for your target audience. So long as you can successfully keep your critical engagement with the literature within manageable bounds, you will have access to a crucial source of support for whatever argument you wish to develop about the social world.

How can you best harness the literature to back your argument when this literature is playing a support role to your own original investigation rather than being the sole focus? You may already have had some experience, especially if you have completed an assignment where you reflected critically, with reference to the literature, on a piece of data that you had been given or had collected yourself. However, it is only with an extended piece of work such as a dissertation (or, in some countries, a thesis) that the challenge is fully confronted.

For your dissertation you will typically be required to conduct an enquiry centred on your original empirical investigation into an aspect of the social world, locating it within the existing research. (If your dissertation is to be based solely on library research, it obviously amounts to an extended Critical Literature Review. You could take as your starting point the ideas at the end of the previous chapter for structuring a review flexibly to suit your review questions.)

In this chapter we make an important distinction between the unfolding process of hands-on research and the structure of the account that ultimately reports it. We show how you can minimize the difference between your experience of doing the research and what you are finally in a position to report about it, by integrating the different constituent activities as you go along: the critical reading, empirical investigation and the drafting of your account. We offer our view of what makes for a high-quality written account of a dissertation, highlighting the importance of Critical Literature Reviews in one or more locations in the narrative. We then discuss how your account should link together in a logical sequence, developing a convincing *overall* argument. Your Critical Literature Reviews, and the critical reading on which they depend, are vital for making the logic of your account compelling to your examiners.

If you are planning your own dissertation, we invite you to consider the extent to which your study could be structured along the lines we describe. Maybe your investigation could be made to fit exactly or maybe you would wish to adapt the structure. Either way, working through the logic of developing your overall argument will help you realize the full potential contribution that your critical reading and your construction of Critical Literature Reviews can make in building a strong warrant for your eventual conclusion.

The reality of the study process versus the written account

There will inevitably be some difference between your experience while you are working through the research process and what you finally write about it. Early on, it is common to feel quite confused. Clarification comes with time, because you are learning as your enquiry unfolds. Your focus may be diffuse at first, perhaps based on a hunch that some social practice needs improving or that some phenomenon exists which can be observed or measured. As you begin reading round this topic, the amount of literature may seem to be ever-expanding until you establish your review questions. Later on, the research methods you adopt may turn out to produce a mass of data that seems to take forever to analyze, but produces quite a succinct outcome. Even when writing up your findings, you go through stages of being unclear how one section fits with other sections. Your fullest understanding about what you are doing comes only when you complete the final written account, because only then do you bring all of your assembled learning together.

Your final account of what you have done and what you have learned must be focused and logical, progressively developing and providing backing for the overall argument you are putting forward. To save unnecessary work, everything you have written should be linked to your focus. So it is worth making the process of investigating as close to the written account as possible. You cannot know before you start exactly what you will find – what your conclusion will be – but you can frame your questions in such a way that you know what *sort* of conclusion you will have. For instance, by asking 'is learning by heart an effective method for increasing vocabulary knowledge in a foreign language?' you can know from the start that your conclusion will be some version of a 'yes', 'no' or (more likely) 'it depends on X'. With planning focused on clear questions, you can ensure that your critical reading and empirical research are playing their part in generating the material you need for your written account.

The more carefully planned and focused your investigation is from the beginning, the easier it will be to conduct the empirical research while writing draft sections of your account as you proceed. You will always be working towards a defensible final account that will stand up to the critical scrutiny of examiners. Therefore it is important that (once you have done any initial background reading) your focused critical reading is always directed towards writing a draft of some part of your written account. We recommend that you begin drafting this account from the outset of your study, amending and adding to it as your understanding of what you are doing and knowledge of the field increases. Expect to revise the draft of your introductory chapter several times as you gain clarity about your focus.

Maximizing your chances of convincing your examiners

It is widely expected that a dissertation will include critical reviews of literature bearing on three aspects of your enquiry:

1   The *substantive* focus – the particular topic (or issue) that constitutes the substance of the investigation.

2   The *theoretical* issues – how particular concepts, perspectives, theories or models guide and inform the study, and what their strengths and limitations are.

3   *Methodological* approaches to conducting an empirical investigation – in one field a particular methodology might be accepted as standard practice. In another, there may be more methodological debate amongst academics. Either way, you will need to establish which approach is most appropriate for your purpose.

(Recall that we briefly referred to these distinctions in the previous chapter when discussing the need to focus a Critical Literature Review on specified review questions.) For a dissertation, each aspect merits its own Critical Literature Review. You should expect critically to engage with literature in justifying your investigation of the substantive topic, your choice of theoretical orientation to frame your research and the interpretation of your findings, and the methodological approach and detailed methods through which you gather your data. Reference to this literature may be made at various points during your investigation, and within your written account – wherever it helps to develop your warrant for the eventual conclusion of your overall argument. Thus, you are unlikely to have all of your critical evaluation of the literature in one huge chapter called 'Literature Review'. Rather, you will mention relevant literature wherever necessary to contribute to building your argument. In compiling our 'top ten' list of the features of a high quality dissertation, we have indicated in *italic* script how Critical Literature Reviews and reference back to them are distributed across the written account.

A high quality dissertation: 'top ten' features

1   A logical argument, developed from the title to the end of the account, which provides a strong warrant for the claims to knowledge made in the conclusion. It should be possible to capture this argument in a sentence and it will be the core of the abstract if one is required.

2   A clearly-focused substantive topic about an aspect of the social world, justified as a significant focus of investigation by *reference to relevant literature*.

3   Explicitly stated aims for the investigation, the achievement of which will contribute towards answering a well-defined broad central question.

4   *Critical Literature Reviews relating to the substantive area, the theoretical orientation, and the methodology and methods of data collection and analysis. Each Critical Literature Review is driven by review questions* linked to the broad central question, with clear connections drawn between existing knowledge and the present investigation. Answers to the review questions lead to the specification of detailed research questions or hypotheses.

5   A well-structured and explicit design for the empirical study, an appropriate methodological approach, detailed methods and carefully designed research instruments for answering the research questions or testing the hypotheses.

6   A set of data that is analyzed thoroughly to indicate what answers have been found to the research questions or hypotheses. Clearly set out procedures for data preparation, summary and analysis.

7   Discussion of the findings and analysis, explicitly relating back to the research questions or hypotheses, and to the *Critical Literature Review on the substantive area*.

8   A reflective conclusion, making *brief reference to the Critical Literature Reviews on the substantive, theoretical and methodological areas*, that summarizes the study's contribution to answering the broad central question, the study's strengths and weaknesses, any problematic issues that arose, implications for future research and (if appropriate) recommendations for policy or practice.

9   Accurate referencing, both in the text and in the reference list so that, in principle, any *reference to the literature* may be easily traced and followed-up.

10   Clear expression with attention to writing style, punctuation, spelling and grammar, so that the account can be easily understood.

Bear these features in mind when planning the structure and presentation of your dissertation. You will also find it useful to refer repeatedly to the statement of criteria used in assessing your work. This statement is likely to be included in the students' handbook for your programme. Ensure that your written account meets each of the criteria stated there, because your examiners' assessment will be guided by them.

Integrating literature into the logic of your overall argument

You can make the most of your critical reading if each text you read and each area you review has potential for contributing to the development of your overall argument. Clearly, you cannot know in detail what your argument will contain before you have done any reading or data collection, so you cannot initially be sure how relevant a particular text is to this argument. But you can establish early on which areas of literature you need to review and – by formulating focused review questions – how the results of your reviews will enable your overall argument to develop effectively. You need to maintain a sense of the logical sequence of steps required to build the warrant for a convincing conclusion in your final written account. That way, you can plan how to keep the research process and the written account closely aligned.

Some ideas in our 'top ten' list you have met before (such as review questions). Others, that are new, we introduce below. The structure that we advocate as a framework for building up the logic of your argument is widely used in the social sciences and humanities. (Alternative structures are possible, of course. Whatever structure you use, it will still be vital to work out the logic of your argument and how your critical reading will contribute to it.)

Figure 12.1 depicts the progression of the logic in summary form. The chapters that are commonly used to structure the written account are listed down the left-hand side, labelled according to their function in developing the overall argument. (You may, of course, choose chapter names that reflect the content itself, e.g., 'Why are Noun Genders Difficult to Learn?' for a chapter reviewing the literature on that topic.) Down the centre of the diagram, we have listed the sequence of elements contained in each chapter, as they contribute to developing the logic of the overall argument. On the right-hand side we have indicated how everything written in the first five chapters contributes to the warrant, backing up the claims made in the conclusion chapter. Note how the arrowed boxes containing these key elements become progressively narrower, then broaden out again as you scan down towards the conclusion. We use this depiction to signify how you may:

- Begin with a general orientation towards a broad topic.

- Select a small number of specific aims that can contribute to an understanding of that topic.

- Identify a small number of review questions that represent one way of achieving the aims.

- Select one or more research questions from amongst the many arising from the Critical Literature Reviews.

- Focus tightly on a particular data set, collected and interrogated using particular approaches.

- Critically consider how the answers to the research questions relate back to the literature.

- Reconnect with the general orientation by evaluating the achievement of the aims and the contribution made to addressing the topic.

Let us explore the sequence of elements at a general level before we examine them in detail below. The research topic is firmed up as a *central question*, expressed in general terms (we first mentioned this in Chapter 3). The dissertation as a whole will make some modest contribution towards answering it. The central question drives the investigation, which is designed to achieve specific *aims*. They concern the conducting of a small-scale empirical study in a particular context, informed by a specified theoretical orientation, and using a specified methodology and methods of data collection. In order to identify the research design best able to achieve these aims, *review questions* are identified, which drive the Critical Literature Reviews. They are undertaken to find out what is known from other authors' work. This information may offer pointers for the focus of the empirical research, any associated theoretical orientation and the methodological approach. An outcome of the Critical Literature Reviews is to identify detailed *research questions* that the empirical research will seek to answer. The research questions dictate the specification of the *instrument items* (e.g., specific questions in an interview or survey, or experimental stimuli) for the data collection. Responses to the instrument items are analyzed to *answer the research questions*. The findings are also interpreted and

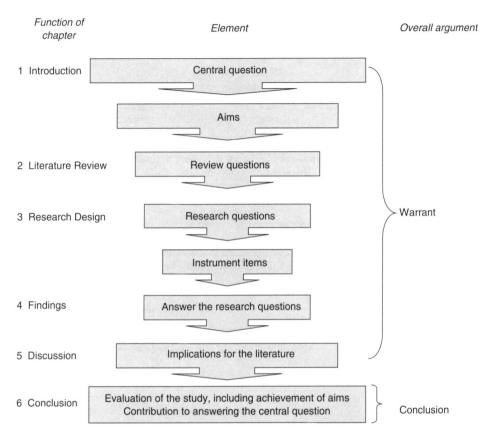

Figure 12.1   The logic of the overall argument in a dissertation

discussed by relating them to relevant literature already reviewed, to show how they are supported by others' work or offer a challenge to it. The conclusion summarizes what has been found out and evaluates how well the research has been conducted, including *how far the aims have been achieved*. The *contribution* of the findings to *answering the central question* is asserted. So we come full circle:

- The investigation begins by posing the central question, signalling the journey towards a conclusion.

- The warrant for the conclusion is built-up through the Critical Literature Reviews, the empirical research and relating of the findings to others' work.

- The conclusion shows how far the findings have contributed to answering the central question.

Figure 12.2 fills out the picture in Figure 12.1 by dividing the development of the argument into six sequential steps. Each step will normally be written up in a particular

Chapter function and step	Element

1 Introduction: identifying the focus of the investigation.

> **Central question**
> Substantive topic, in general terms, with *reference to literature.*

> **Aims**
> Substantive (to study the topic in a specific context).
> Theoretical (conceptual tools to study the topic).
> Methodological (approach and methods to study the topic).

2 Literature review: critically reviewing to inform the content of the empirical work.

> ***Review questions***
> *Substantive aim (issues connected with the substantive topic).*
> *Theoretical aim (the framework and concepts to study the topic).*

> **Research questions**
> Investigating the substantive topic in a specific context.

3 Research design: building towards data collection.

> ***Review questions***
> *Methodological aim (approach and methods to study the topic).*

> **Instrument items**
> To answer the research questions (investigating the substantive topic in a specific context, employing concepts of the theoretical framework).

4 Findings: presenting data.

> The findings for the instrument items answer the research questions and contribute to achieving the substantive aim.

5 Discussion: interpreting data.

> **Implications of answers to the research questions *for the literature reviewed* (substantive topic)**
> The impact of the theoretical framework and data collection methods on the findings with *reference to literature*

6 **Conclusion:** drawing warranted conclusions.	1 A summative claim about what has been found out.
	2 How far the findings answered the research questions and the substantive aim has been acheived.
	How far the theoretical aim has been achieved by using the theoretical framework.
	How far the methodological aim has been achieved through the design and data collection instruments.
	Evalution of the theoretical framework, research design, the overall success of the investigation and what has been learned.
	3 The degree of certainty with which the findings from the specific context can be generalized in contributing to answering the central question.
	4 Suggestions and recommendations for future research, policy or practice supported by the findings.

(References, appendices)

Figure 12.2 Developing the logic of the overall argument in a dissertation

chapter. We have indicated in *italic* script where the Critical Literature Reviews contribute to developing the warrant that backs the sets of claims in the conclusion chapter.

We can now show, step-by-step, how to use the logical progression to bring together the research process and the overall argument in your written account. It demonstrates how planning, drafting and note-taking are of considerable support to the conceptualization of what can be a complex integration of ideas and procedures.

Step 1: identifying the focus of the enquiry

Start writing the first draft of your introductory chapter before you have done anything more than background reading, to help you clarify the focus of your investigation. Include your initial attempt at formulating your *central question*. Posing a central question is a potent way of giving direction to your thoughts. Typically, postgraduate students wish primarily to address a substantive topic in their field of enquiry (rather than developing or testing theory, or trialling a new method of data collection or analysis). You may not know what contribution your study will make yet, but you can anticipate that you will obtain some findings that will contribute towards answering your central question. Articulating the central question constitutes the first stage in building up the warrant for your eventual conclusion.

Initial reference can be made to the literature from the substantive topic area (based on your background reading). This will help focus your search for specific review and research questions, while justifying the scientific or practical significance of the central question. Justify to your target audience why the focus of your investigation is important, by indicating how it can add to knowledge in the field of enquiry. The central question indicates to readers that you are concerned with a topic of wider significance than simply your own small-scale investigation in a particular context. The central question is not specific to the context that you will be investigating and it provides your link from, and back to, the generalization and abstraction necessary to locate your work within the wider domain represented by the literature.

While a central question is a good starting point for focusing an investigation, it does not indicate how you are going to work towards your contribution to answering it. Sharpen your initial focus by identifying the three specific *aims* that your investigation is designed to achieve:

- Your *substantive aim* – precisely what you intend to find out about the substantive topic (e.g., determine factors affecting the effectiveness of some aspect of a practice in a specific context).

- Your *theoretical aim* – what concepts and, perhaps, over-arching theory you intend to use to achieve your substantive aim (e.g., employ a particular set of concepts as a framework for investigating your chosen aspect of practice in this specific context).

- Your *methodological aim* – how you are going to find out what you need to know in order to achieve your substantive aim (e.g., employ a particular methodological approach, research design, and methods of data collection and analysis to investigate your chosen aspect of practice in this specific context).

In attempting to achieve your three aims, you need to think through how you will address any issues (or problems) to which your effort may give rise. The relevant literature may inform your understanding of these issues. Achieving your substantive aim raises the issue of deciding exactly which aspects of your substantive topic to investigate in detail in the specific context for your investigation. Achieving your theoretical aim raises the issue of acknowledging the strengths and limitations of the theory or set of concepts you plan to employ. Achieving your methodological aim raises the issue of assessing the validity of the assumptions underlying your methodological approach, and the strengths, limitations and fitness-for-purpose of the methods you plan to employ.

The nature of the central question simultaneously affects what your aims are and reflects your intellectual project. To communicate your rationale effectively for the central question you have chosen, it is worth indicating what your intellectual project is and what your values are in relation to the topic you are investigating. For instance, if your interest is in improving in-service training for social workers, you may be pursuing knowledge-for-action from a positive value position towards this practice. However, if your interest is in finding out whether women and men interpret second-hand car advertisements differently, you may be pursuing knowledge-for-understanding from a relatively impartial value position.

Attempting to specify your substantive, theoretical and methodological aims in the first draft of the introductory chapter can help you to think through what you are going to do. The central question and aims can always be refined in a later draft in the light of your continuing reading and research design work.

SIGNPOSTING FOR EFFECTIVE COMMUNICATION WITH YOUR EXAMINERS

As a critical reader, you will have appreciated authors who communicate their messages clearly. A dissertation is a long piece of work, so your examiners may easily lose track of what you are doing, why and where your work is leading to.

It is in your interests to assist them, by using regular signposting in your text. Keep in mind the question: what do the examiners need to know next? Provide them with clear indicators that enable them to make connections between one section or chapter and whatever follows. There is an old saying: 'First, tell them what you are going to tell them. Then tell them. Finally, tell them what you've told them'.

This is not an instruction to be unnecessarily repetitive, but continually to gauge your target readers' capacity to follow your account and to help them do so. At the end of the introduction and the end of each subsequent chapter, your conclusion can include a brief summary of what has been discussed or presented and (except for the last chapter) an indication of what will come in the next chapter. At the beginning of each chapter (except the introduction) outline very briefly what the chapter will cover. The small amount of repetition incurred is more than compensated for by the value of keeping your critical readers fully in the picture. Furthermore, if you find yourself struggling to provide a succinct description of what you have said, or are going to say, it may be an indication of insufficient clarity in your thought or structure.

Step 2: critically reviewing literature to inform the content of the empirical work

You will recall that in Chapter 11 we discussed the role of formulating *review questions* as a means of focusing a self-contained Critical Literature Review. In such a review, you build the warrant of your argument towards a conclusion that provides an answer to each of your review questions. In the more extensive investigation that constitutes a dissertation, the review questions are a product of the broader agenda of the study. The initial choice of topic (framed by your central question) and your decisions about how you are going to investigate it (framed by your aims) play a major part in determining the review questions for the Critical Literature Reviews, since these reviews are designed to inform your empirical investigation.

One or more review questions will relate to issues connected with achieving your substantive aim through your empirical investigation. You will direct some of your critical reading and associated Critical Synopses and Critical Analyses towards answering each review question. The Critical Literature Review you conduct may form one or more sections in a literature review chapter. Each section will develop its own argument. The account of what you found in the literature provides the warrant for your section conclusion, answering the review question that drives it.

Similarly you will probably pose one or more review questions about the theoretical orientation, related to your theoretical aim (e.g., what is meant by a particular set of concepts and how they may be employed as a framework for investigating your chosen aspect of the practice in this specific context). The Critical Literature Review generated in this way may also appear in the literature review chapter, since the theoretical orientation is often closely tied to understanding the literature in the substantive area of investigation. However, for clarity it is useful to have a dedicated section for the review questions about the theoretical orientation, and sometimes it makes sense to put them in a chapter of their own.

As you read and follow-up references to further work, you should look out for any major 'landmark' texts that bear directly on your empirical investigation. These are particularly important works that have shaped in a big way what is known about the topic. You can thereby ensure that your written review acknowledges and evaluates the ideas or evidence that they contain. The evaluation can take account of what others say about these texts, but you should aim to draw your own conclusion, based on the strength of the arguments that you identify. Paying attention to landmark texts will help you to convince your examiners that you have conducted a thorough search and are aware of leading authors' work. As you assemble your various Critical Analyses and Critical Synopses, you will be able to identify themes amongst the claims relevant to your review questions. In writing your account of what you have found, you can draw attention to these themes and their contribution to answering your review questions.

Your substantive and theoretical Critical Literature Reviews may valuably inform your empirical work. The answers to the review questions you have obtained give you a sound basis for formulating your more specific *research questions* (sometimes expressed as hypotheses) in the light of what the literature has revealed. Your data collection instruments will be designed to answer your research questions, themselves informed by the relevant literature.

Identifying your research questions in this way builds up the warrant of your overall argument a little further. You will be able to demonstrate to your examiners that you have taken into account what is already known from others' work and, perhaps, you will fill a gap in that knowledge by investigating this particular context. So, by reading critically and constructing the first draft of your literature review chapter (or chapters) before you finalize your research design, you are in a good position to ensure that your investigation builds on others' work and that you demonstrate this to your examiners.

Step 3: building towards data collection

The literature has an equally important part to play in informing the design of your empirical investigation. This time the review question or questions you pose will concern:

- Methodology – the philosophical assumptions about the nature of the social world that are framing your approach to empirical work.

- Your choice of methods, including their strengths, limitations and fitness-for-purpose as means of seeking answers to your research questions.

The critical review of the relevant methodological literature is likely to form a section in your research design chapter rather than an earlier dedicated literature review chapter. You may also refer to methodological literature in later sections to justify particular design and procedural decisions. The literature you draw on will include, but need not be restricted to, research methods textbooks. Others' research may offer you a methodology to adopt or methods to emulate. Nor need you look only within your own substantive area for such inspiration, since many approaches are relatively generic and transferable.

As always, your written account must develop an argument that justifies your conclusion to the section. To draw warranted conclusions about your choice of methodology and methods you will be critically evaluating others' accounts about conducting empirical research: methodological paradigms, data collection and analysis methods, sampling and piloting, and ethical issues. Your literature-backed conclusion will help to convince your examiners of your reasons why you have adopted your methodological approach, and why your chosen methods for data collection and analysis stand a strong chance of answering your research questions fully.

In the light of your earlier Critical Literature Review of relevant theory, you may now construct a theoretical framework of linked concepts appropriate for your methodological approach. This framework relates to the formulation of your research questions. These research questions, in turn, determine the detailed design of your data collection instruments, such as interview schedules, observation guides, or questionnaires. Each item included in the instrument is designed to make some contribution to answering a research question. For example, an interview schedule might include questions on each factor that has been identified in the literature as playing a role in organizational effectiveness, in order to answer the research question 'What do members of this organization believe influences the effectiveness of their practice?' The answer to each research question is intended to tell you something about the substantive topic in the particular context of your empirical work, which in turn relates, via your theoretical orientation, to your central question. Thus, decisions made about the design of the research instrument directly affect your ability to arrive at a convincing conclusion to your work as a whole.

Providing a step-by-step account of the empirical research procedures is essential for convincing your examiners that you knew what you were doing and why you were doing it. In principle, you should give enough information for someone else to be able to replicate your work accurately.

It is equally crucial that you make explicit your procedures for checking, summarizing and analyzing data, to pave the way for the presentation of your findings. Your examiners need convincing that the claims you are making on the basis of your analysis are well-grounded in the procedures you have adopted. (If the data include quantifiable variables, it is necessary to explain which statistical procedures and tests you are conducting and why. Procedures for coding and analyzing qualitative data are less standardized than for quantitative data, adding to the importance of setting them out.)

Making your research design, rationale and procedures clear will together add substance to the warrant for your overall argument. You will be indicating to your examiners that you chose your approach with care, took what is known about different approaches into account in making this choice, and thought through in detail how you were going to conduct and analyze your empirical research.

Step 4: presenting data

The data you gather and, consequently, your account of what you found, are essential to developing a convincing overall argument. They constitute the empirical evidence on which the overall argument ultimately rests. The supporting evidence that the literature can offer is also very important. But the core of the warrant in an account of an empirical investigation obviously lies in the empirical findings. The presentation of your findings must be structured so as to summarize the results that provide answers to your research questions. Together, the answers to your research questions contribute to the achievement of your substantive aim (identified in Step 1).

Note that reviews of the published literature have no place here. It is only you that can say anything about what you have found. Relating your findings to the literature – an integral part of discussing them – is certainly important. But it is the next logical step in developing your overall argument (Step 5 below), so save it until after the findings have been presented.

PRESENT THEN DISCUSS OR PRESENT-AND-DISCUSS?

One adaptation of our advice on presenting data before discussing it is to combine the account of your presentation of findings with your discussion of them in one or more 'findings and discussion' chapters. In this approach, the findings that answer a particular research question are *presented* and followed immediately by the relevant *discussion*. The sequence is then repeated for the next research question and so on. The logic is still 'present first, then discuss', but the present-discuss sequence is used in turn for each research question, rather than listing all the findings first and then engaging in all the discussion. Which structure to adopt will depend in part on the extent to which your raw results are as discrete in nature as the questions they are used to answer. Some data sets cannot be divided up at the reporting stage, and the global picture of what you found needs to precede any attempt to pick out patterns that address the research questions.

NOT DISCUSS-AND-FORGET-TO-PRESENT!

With a present-and-discuss structure, beware of failing to present all of your data because you are too preoccupied with the discussion. In the logic of developing your overall argument, the findings are the sole source of evidence from your own empirical investigation. So the warrant for your eventual conclusion about the outcomes of your study and their contribution to answering your central question depends on this evidence. Your examiners are unlikely to be convinced if your account makes claims about how your findings are supported by or challenge what others have reported in the literature, but omits to supply the evidence of what you found.

Step 5: interpreting data

The warrant your findings offer for the conclusion to your overall argument can be considerably enhanced if you relate what you found to what others have found or, perhaps, did not think of looking for. Since all your research questions are directed towards your central question, it is necessary also to discuss the combined significance of your answers, taken together. In short, you need to use reference back to literature in your earlier substantive Critical Literature Review, and maybe other literature as well, to demonstrate the extent to which your findings are consistent with or challenge what is known and not known about the topic.

Your empirical work may be small-scale but in contributing to answering your central question your findings do add something to knowledge about the substantive topic. They may also add to the accumulation of knowledge about other related social phenomena and practices. You need to convince your examiners of the extent to which your findings have wider significance for contexts other than the one you investigated empirically. The literature can help you demonstrate this significance. You may be able to show that other researchers have found similar things, that your findings fill a gap in knowledge about the topic, or even that your findings contradict what others have found and so raise questions about the convincingness of their research.

Equally, you will want to convince your examiners that you have been rigorous in your data collection and analysis, and that you are also aware of the limitations of what you have done. So it is important to reflect self-critically on the impact of your theoretical framework on the findings. (For instance, this framework may have directed attention towards some aspects of the empirical phenomenon while downplaying other aspects which a different theoretical orientation might have picked up.) Similarly, it is important to reflect self-critically on how your findings may have been affected by the data collection and analysis methods. (Suppose that your data collection methods relied solely on informants' perceptions about their practice. A limitation would be that there was no check on whether their perceptions matched what they actually did.) You may wish to make brief reference to relevant theoretical and methodological literature that you critically reviewed earlier.

Acknowledging the likely effect of your theoretical orientation and methods on your findings may seem to undermine the warrant of your overall argument because you are admitting to limitations in your empirical work. But you actually *strengthen* your warrant because you demonstrate that you are realistic about what you have achieved, aware of the compromises you made and are appropriately cautious about the certainty and generalizability of what you have found.

Step 6: warranting your final conclusions

The literature review, empirical research design, execution and analysis are all geared to developing the warrant of your overall argument. Now you are in a position to take the final step: pulling the different aspects of the study together in articulating a strong conclusion about how your investigation has contributed to answering your central question.

In our view, there are four components to a strong conclusion in a dissertation, each of which depends either directly or indirectly on your critical reading of the literature and your self-critical engagement with your own work. The components are:

1 A summative claim about the answers to your research questions and how they relate to the existing literature.

2 A set of self-critical reflections on what you have achieved, including what limitations you have identified and what you have learned from your experience of conducting research.

3 An evaluation of the extent to which the answers to your research questions contribute to answering your central question, in terms of both their reliability and their generalizability.

4 A look towards the future, to consider what subsequent research might usefully focus on and (if appropriate) how your own investigation might inform practice or policy.

Component 1   The summative claim reflects the conclusions to your findings and discussion chapter(s) and should briefly pick out the key claims and observations from the literature that informed the formulation of your research questions. In this way, you show your examiners that you have located your own findings appropriately within the wider context of research.

Component 2   The reflective component is not always particularly visible in published research but it is essential in work for assessment, since examiners must gain a clear idea of the learning process that you have gone through. You need to consider:

- To what extent have you achieved your three aims (substantive, theoretical and methodological)? You can gauge this by looking at the wording of your aims to see if there is anything that you were unable to achieve. Where you have fallen short in one or more of your aims, you need to explain why and make a frank assessment of the extent to which this situation has compromised your study.

- What is your evaluation, now, of the theoretical framework and design of your empirical investigation? Did they enable you to find out and interpret what you hoped? Did the approach you took inhibit you from seeing the full impact of any important variable or factor? How might the research design be improved if you were to repeat the investigation?

- How do you assess your overall success in conducting the research? Although things may not have gone perfectly, there is no need to frame your account over-negatively. Your examiners are interested only in how much you have *learned* from anything that went wrong.

Component 3   There are two key evaluations to make, based on the two dimensions of variation amongst knowledge claims that we introduced in Chapter 7. They are: your degree of certainty that your study has answered your research questions reliably and adequately; and the extent to which you believe that your findings can be generalized beyond the context in which you operated, to the broader contextual domain covered by your central question.

The certainty that you express in your findings having provided reliable and adequate answers to your research questions is a product of the reflections you have just made on your approach and practice. To gain another perspective on the same issues, imagine that someone else is about to do a piece of research that will address the same research questions, using the same framework and approach as you did, and a data source (informants, text or whatever) that meets the same criteria as those that you specified. How certain are you that this new researcher would come up with the same results as you? Asking this question may help you to separate out features in your findings that you feel are robust and likely to be found by anyone, from others that you suspect are a product of some unintentional circumstance.

As regards generalizability, the issue is the extent to which your findings reflect more general patterns, so that they can be judged representative of the wider domain encompassed by your central question, either directly, or at a more abstract level. No two contexts or situations are identical and it is a matter of assessing whether details of your own research context affect the extent of generalization that it is reasonable to make. Examine the wording of your central question and research questions: identify how the narrow context of the latter potentially maps onto the wider context of the former and where aspects of the wider context are most likely to fall outside of anything that your study has explored.

It normally pays neither to be overconfident about your conclusions, nor to over-generalize. The more modest claims are often the most plausible. Authors who admit to limitations in what they did and state that their results *might* indicate something more general, or that there *may* be applications of their findings to new contexts, are often more convincing than those who propose that they have definitely *proved* something of major general significance.

Component 4   The section where you focus on future research, policy and practice is of considerable importance. Placing it at the end has strategic value, particularly if your investigation has been only partly successful. Since it looks forward, it enables you to end on a positive note, with new ideas. Note that suggestions for future research and recommendations for changes in practice or policy amount to claims about what should be done. To convince your readers that they should accept these claims, very briefly warrant each claim by referring back to your data and to the literature.

The end of your conclusion chapter is the end of your narrative, but not the end of your piece of work nor, indeed, the end of the warrant for your overall argument. The reference list is the final point where your critical reading of the literature contributes to convincing your examiners. It enables them to follow up your literature sources, and its accuracy and completeness is indicative of the thoroughness of your investigation. Similarly, any appendices (such as examples of your research instruments) add to the warrant supporting your conclusion and must also be presented with care.

Applying your critical frame of mind

We have now shown in detail how specific areas of the literature are integral to developing a strong and coherent overall argument throughout a dissertation. Making effective use of Critical Literature Reviews to support a larger enquiry requires thoughtful initial planning, continual monitoring and regular adjustment as the research process proceeds towards producing the written dissertation to be assessed. The earlier you establish your focus, start planning the structure of your written account and begin drafting sections of it, the more you take charge and harness the literature for your purposes, so making efficient use of your time. Habitually applying the critical frame of mind that you have been developing throughout your postgraduate studies, both to the literature you critically read and to the account that you self-critically write, will enable you to make what is a complex undertaking as straightforward as possible.

All our advice on structuring can do no more than act as a guide for you to learn-by-doing as you work on your own dissertation, but we can offer a few props to help you along the way. That is the focus of the next chapter.

13 Tools for Structuring a Dissertation

We offer here three tools to help with developing an argument through the research process and with producing a written dissertation. They relate directly to the discussion in the previous chapter. First, we offer a means for you (and your supervisor) to keep track of the development of your overall argument as you plan your investigation and write your dissertation. Second, we describe an outline structure for a dissertation that reflects our six steps for integrating Critical Literature Reviews into the development of an argument. Finally, we suggest a way of applying a simple test to your written account, to check for flaws in the logic of your argument and for any material that may be irrelevant to it.

Checking the logic of your developing argument

The 'Logic Checksheet' is a means of ensuring that you gain focus early on, so that you build up the logic of your research effort – and hence the written account – as you go along. You and your supervisor can also use it to check that you have not left out any steps in the logic or links between the steps. A blank form of the full Logic Checksheet is given in Appendix 4, and we provide here the first part of a completed one. (You may also wish to download the Logic Checksheet template from the Sage website www.sagepub.co.uk/wallace.) It will give you a feel for the way the focus narrows, as the Critical Literature Reviews contribute to answering the review questions and prepare the ground for the empirical investigation, especially by helping identify suitable research questions that frame the data collection instruments. (As we saw in Figure 12.1, the narrow scope of the investigation itself then broadens out again as its implications and applications are considered.)

Our illustration is based on a study that pursues knowledge-for-action. The substantive topic is how women who work as administrators in British universities might face and overcome barriers to their career progression. The normative purpose is to inform practice in order to improve the extent to which women administrators can achieve their full potential.

Building towards the focus of the data collection instruments

Chapter	Element of logic	Content in this dissertation
	Title (keywords in the central question).	Title: *Factors Affecting the Aspirations to Senior Administrative Responsibility, and the Career Progression, of Women Administrators in British Universities.*
1 Introduction	Central question (substantive topic, stated in general terms).	Central question: *What barriers may inhibit women administrators in British universities from aspiring to, and progressing in, their career towards achieving a senior administrative position, and how may these barriers be overcome?*
	Substantive aim (substantive topic, specific context).	Substantive aim: *To investigate the facilitatory factors that have enabled women who have achieved senior administrative positions in British universities to overcome any barriers to achieving these positions.*
	Theoretical aim (concepts guiding investigation of the substantive topic).	Theoretical aim: *To adopt a framework based on the key inhibitory and facilitatory factors that are identified in the literature as affecting women's careers in educational management in general, and use it to see how far they apply to the situation of career administrators in British universities in particular.*
	Methodological aim (design and methods to address the substantive topic).	Methodological aim: *To design a small-scale qualitative investigation which will gather, through interviews, the perceptions of fifteen women who succeeded in becoming senior administrators in British universities, about how barriers to their achievement of these positions were overcome.*
2 Review of Literature	Review questions: substantive aim (issues related to the substantive topic).	Review question(s), substantive aim: 1. *What does the literature reviewed suggest are the barriers that inhibit women from aspiring to become senior administrators or managers, and what are the barriers that those who aspire to these positions then face?* 2. *What does the literature reviewed suggest are the facilitatory factors that support women's aspirations to become senior administrators or managers, and help them to overcome the barriers they then face?*

(Continued)

Chapter	Element of logic	Content in this dissertation
		3. Within the education sector, what does the literature reviewed suggest are the strategies of women senior administrators or managers who succeed in overcoming the barriers to their aspirations and subsequent career advancement?
		4. To what extent are these factors and strategies applicable to the aspirations and career progression of women administrators in British universities?
3 Research Design	Review questions: theoretical aim (selecting the theoretical framework and defining concepts).	Review question(s), theoretical aim: 1. What conceptualizations have been employed to characterize factors facilitating or inhibiting women's aspiration towards senior administrative or management positions and their career progression into these posts?
	Review questions: methodological aim (issues relating to the methodology and methods).	Review question(s), methodological aim: 1. What are the strengths and limitations of interviews as a method for gathering data on informants' perceptions?
	Research questions: substantive aim (reflecting answers to the review questions).	Research questions: 1. What do women in senior administrative positions in British universities perceive to be the barriers that they had to overcome in order to aspire to and achieve their present position? 2. What do these women perceive to be the key facilitatory factors helping them to aspire to, and then overcome the barriers to, achieving their present position? 3. What strategies did these women use to overcome barriers to their aspiration and subsequent career advancement? 4. Were any of these strategies different from the strategies identified in the literature as being used by women who succeed in becoming senior administrators or managers in settings other than British universities and, if so, what were the unique features of the British university context that led to these strategies being used?

The second part of the Logic Checksheet is not exemplified here because it comprises a series of tickbox questions. They prompt you to justify to yourself what you should include in the findings, discussion and conclusion chapters of your written account.

As with other forms in this book, the Logic Checksheet is just a way of helping you structure your thinking. You may wish to adapt it to suit the development of your argument. However, working through the checklist before deciding to adapt or discard it will ensure that you do justify the reasoning for your decisions.

Possible outline structure for a dissertation

There are various possibilities for structuring a dissertation, depending on the methodological approach and the way the logic of the argument is developed. Our 'top ten' features of a high quality dissertation, description of the logic of developing your overall argument and Logic Checksheet, all reflect a widely employed structure for an empirical investigation.

We offer here the outline for our recommended structure, indicating the likely location of the main text components and highlighting in *italic* script the various places where Critical Literature Reviews may be located or referred back to. (You should, of course, also check the regulations of your institution for indications of what must be included and where.)

Title

- Containing keywords that reflect the central question you are seeking to answer, expressed in general terms.

Abstract

- A brief summary (around 200 words) of the purpose of the study, empirical work and your conclusions.

Acknowledgements

- Any acknowledgement you wish to make of the support of individuals (e.g., your supervisor, your family) and of the cooperation of informants.

Chapter 1: Introduction

- A statement of purpose – to contribute to answering a central question expressed in general terms, typically about a substantive topic in your field of enquiry.

- A statement of the more specific aims of your research – substantive, theoretical and methodological.

- A justification of the significance of the central question, *with brief reference to relevant literature*.

- A statement of your value position in relation to this topic, as it shapes the focus of your enquiry.

- A summary of the broad issues (or problems) that will need to be addressed in order to achieve your three aims (above), *giving brief reference to relevant literature*:

  - substantive (indicating why it may not be straightforward to decide which aspects of the substantive topic identified in the central question should be investigated in detail);

  - theoretical (indicating why the choice of theoretical framework may not be straightforward);

  - methodological (indicating why the choice of methodology and methods may not be straightforward).

- A brief description of the context of your enquiry. If you are investigating practice in a country other than the one in which you are studying, you may wish to outline the national context as it relates to your central question, possibly with *reference to relevant literature*. Doing this will familiarize your examiners with the context and enable them to appreciate any significant differences between this context and those which they know well.

- A brief final section in which you outline the rest of the study – providing signposts to the content of the remaining chapters, and how these chapters develop your argument about the contribution your investigation will make to answering your central question.

Chapter 2: Literature Review

- A chapter-introduction offering signposts to what will be covered in each section.

- *A Critical Literature Review addressing review questions relating to your substantive aim and associated issues,* leading to a summary conclusion of your position, as determined by the answers you obtained.

- *A Critical Literature Review addressing a review question (or questions) relating to your theoretical aim and associated issues,* leading to a summary conclusion about the nature of the framework that you will need to guide your empirical investigation (and whether you will be adopting or adapting an existing framework, or developing your own).

- A brief chapter-conclusion in which you identify one or more detailed research questions (alternatively expressed as hypotheses to be tested) in the light of the answers obtained to your review questions.

- A signpost stating how the Research Design chapter will take the next step towards seeking answers to your research questions.

Chapter 3: Research Design

- A chapter-introduction setting out what you are going to cover in each section, indicating how you will employ your theoretical framework to address the research questions through your research design.

- The theoretical framework that you are using to help you understand and analyze the substantive topic relating to your central question.

- A *Critical Literature Review of the literature addressing a review question (or questions) relating to your methodological aim and associated issues*, considering how other researchers have approached these issues and have investigated similar substantive topics, leading to a summary conclusion of your position, as determined by the answers you obtained.

- An account of your methodology and methods, including as appropriate:

  - a justification for the methodological paradigm within which you are working;

  - detailed methods of data collection you are using and your justification for using them;

  - specification of the sample of informants and your rationale for selecting them from the wider population;

  - a summary description of your data collection instruments indicating how research questions (or hypotheses) about the substantive topic are addressed, and your rationale for using the instruments chosen;

- a summary of the data collection effort (e.g., piloting, the number of interviews or the number of individuals surveyed);

- a summary of how the data are to be analyzed (e.g., statistical methods, use of matrices for qualitative data);

- ethical factors taken into account, and how (e.g., confidentiality of interviews);

- the timetable for the research process (e.g., timing of first and second rounds of interviews).

- A chapter-conclusion reflecting on the strengths and limitations of your design (e.g., reliability, internal and external validity, sample size relative to population size), and indicating that you will evaluate the design in the concluding chapter in the light of your experience with implementing it.

- A signpost stating how the findings chapter will present the result of implementing this design as the means of answering your research questions.

Chapter 4: Findings

- A chapter-introduction where you set out the ground to be covered in each section.

- A summary of all the findings, as relevant to answering each research question (or hypothesis) in turn, possibly supported by tables and matrices, diagrams and quotations from informants.

- A concluding summary of key findings and emerging issues or themes that you have identified.

- A signpost stating how these issues or themes will be taken up in the discussion chapter.

Chapter 5: Discussion

- A chapter-introduction, setting out the ground to be covered in each section.

- A discussion of your findings and the answers they give to your research questions, including the implications *for the literature on the substantive topic that you critically reviewed earlier.*

- A brief reflection on how your theoretical framework may have impacted on the findings, *referring to theoretical literature you critically reviewed earlier.*

- A brief reflection on how your choice of data collection methods may have impacted on the findings, *referring to methodological literature you critically reviewed earlier.*

- A chapter-conclusion summarizing how the findings support or challenge what other authors have reported in the literature on the substantive topic and your evaluation of the possible impact of your theoretical framework and data collection methods on what you found (and possibly did not find because you did not look for it).

- A signpost stating how you will draw conclusions about the contribution of your findings to answering your central question in the Conclusion chapter.

Chapter 6: Conclusion

- A chapter-introduction where you set out the ground to be covered in each section.

- A summative claim about the answers obtained to your research questions and how they relate to the literature, *referring back briefly to your Critical Literature Reviews.*

- Self-critical reflections on the extent to which you have achieved your substantive, theoretical and methodological aims, limitations of your work that you have identified, what you have learned from the experience of researching and how the research design could have been improved.

- An evaluation of the extent to which the answers to your research questions contribute to answering your central question, in terms of both the degree of certainty and generalizability.

- A look towards the future, to consider what subsequent research might usefully focus on, and (if appropriate) how your own investigation might inform practice or policy. Any recommendations should be backed by very brief reference to your evidence and *literature on the substantive topic*.

- A final statement asserting, in summary, the contribution of your study to answering the central question posed in the introductory chapter and reflected in the title of the dissertation.

Reference List

- Contains all works to which reference is made in the text, but not background material to which you have not made direct reference.

- Presented in author alphabetical order and in the required format.

Appendices

- For example, research instruments, letters to informants, examples of raw data.

- Labelled in a way that helps the reader identify the material and relate it to one or more particular locations in the main text (where there should be reference directly to it).

ADAPTING THE STRUCTURE

Although our outline has six chapters, labelled according to their function, your dissertation could have more where appropriate for the story you wish to tell. If so, ensure that each chapter makes its distinctive contribution to the developing logic of your overall argument, with its own chapter-introduction, chapter-conclusion and signposts. Where research is composed of several independent data sets (or substantially different analyses of the same dataset), each one may need to be justified and reported separately. This can be achieved by repeating the structure for Chapters 3 to 5 for successive (sets of) research questions. Such repetition will work best if it can be shown how one set of research questions derives from the answers to the previous set, or if each new account picks up on one of an original set of research questions identified at the end of Chapter 2. If necessary, Chapter 2 itself can also be part of the repeated process, so that more than one Critical Literature Review is presented, as appropriate to the changing focus of the progressing investigation.

Tracking the logical flow of your overall argument

The structure we have just outlined provides a framework that encourages you to develop a logical overall argument through your dissertation. Every part of a defensible account of empirical research should link logically together, from the title, with its keywords indicating the focus of the study, through the central question being addressed, the Critical Literature Reviews, the research design, the data collection instruments, the presentation and discussion of the findings, the conclusion and any recommendations, to the reference list and any appendices. The 'Linkage Tracker Test' (below) prompts you to look for these links in your written text and to detect any gaps. It is worth applying the Test to everything you draft as you go through the research process, and also to the complete draft of the dissertation, as you prepare it for submission.

The 'Linkage Tracker Test' to check the developing logic of your overall argument

The Linkage Tracker Test assesses the relevance of any piece of your text to the story you are telling. How well do all the parts of the written account of your investigation link together? As critical readers of your work, supervisors and examiners are likely to notice any digressions and any claims that have not been adequately backed up. To apply the Linkage Tracker Test to your draft written work, select any piece of the text (this includes tables, figures, references and appendices). Then ask yourself two questions:

1 **Why is this material here?**

2 **How does this material contribute to the development of my overall argument?**

The answers should be clear to you and to your reader. If not, how can you make them so? Is the material in the right place? Would removing it help you to sustain a tight focus?

The beginning of the end, or the end of the beginning?

Applying your critical frame of mind in using or adapting these tools will enable you to build up a convincing argument. For many postgraduate degrees, the assessment of the written account you have submitted is accompanied by a *viva voce* oral examination or public defence. Having read the text you submitted, your examiners will ask you probing questions about your work. Their role is to assess the extent to which you have met the examination criteria. As sceptical but fair critical readers and interviewers, they want be in a position to pass your dissertation. Our advice on structuring is designed to help you to help them do so. The more you can show in your text that you have met the examination criteria – by developing a soundly argued account, presenting and interpreting reliable data, and recognizing the limitations of what you have achieved – the easier you will find it to convince your examiners during the viva or defence. You will have pre-empted many of the critical questions they are likely to ask. So you will be in a position during the viva to confirm and elaborate on what you have already stated in the text. This will help to consolidate the examiners' impression that you understand what you did and why, and have learned through self-critical reflection on your experience.

For some postgraduate students, getting the dissertation submitted and passed is the end of their academic apprenticeship and the end of their interest in academic study. For others, however, it comes near the beginning of an academic career. If you are among the latter group, you will find that critical reading and self-critical writing are transferable skills that will stand you in good stead as an academic. If you would like to know more, turn to the final chapter.

14 Building your Academic Career on Critical Reading and Self-Critical Writing

Critical reading and self-critical writing skills are central to evaluating and developing arguments. After working through this book, you should be well-prepared for a diversity of professional academic tasks. The nature of your primary role as an academic scholar will determine the tasks you are expected to undertake. Several of them will require you to engage critically with written material. You will also find yourself creating various written accounts in which you attempt to convince your target audience of an argument that you develop: unpublished reports, articles submitted for publication in academic journals, applications for research grants and so on. As your academic expertise becomes known within your field, further activities will be added, as you are invited to act (often anonymously) as a peer reviewer, assessing the quality of other academics' written efforts – including conference paper proposals, journal articles and research grant applications.

If your professional role includes teaching, you will expect to help your postgraduates to sharpen their own critical reading and self-critical writing skills, and you will be assessing their written assignments, and supervising and examining their dissertations. You may, perhaps, also act as a mentor for your less-experienced academic colleagues, providing advice and support as they develop their skills in writing publications and grant applications.

Professional writing is subtly different from postgraduate writing, as each audience demands its own emphases and coverage. However, there are many parallels. You can apply the techniques presented in this book in writing texts for any purpose where a convincing argument composed of well-warranted conclusions is required.

Table 14.1 illustrates how centrally important critical reading and self-critical writing skills are in academic work. It confirms the value of transferring and further refining these skills for your own use and of helping others to learn them too.

Transferring and further enhancing your critical reading and self-critical writing skills in developing your own scholarship will be of immediate advantage if you are just starting out as an academic. Here are three brief illustrations.

Table 14.1 Critical reading and self-critical writing skills in academic work

Academic role	Indicative Task	Contribution of critical reading skills	Contribution of self-critical writing skills	Target audience
Scholar	Writing a paper for an academic publication.	Critical Analyses and Critical Synopses of texts.	Creating a Critical Review of a text or a Critical Literature Review, integrating Critical Literature Reviews into the argument of a research or theoretical paper.	Academic peer reviewers, other academics.
	Applying for a research grant.	Critical Analyses and Critical Synopses of texts.	Integrating short Critical Literature Reviews to support an argument about how projected out-comes and impacts will be achieved.	Academic peer reviewers, grant allocation committee members.
	Peer-reviewing a paper submitted to an academic journal.	Critical Analysis of a text.	Critical Review of a text.	The author of the paper, editorial board members.
Teacher	Teaching study skills.	Support for learning to read critically.	Support for learning to review literature critically and to develop a convincing argument.	Postgraduate students.
	Examining a dissertation.	Critical reading to assess the quality of the argument.	Verbal feedback to the author, a written report giving reasons for your judgement.	The author of the dissertation and other academics involved.
	Mentoring colleagues who are writing for publication.	Support for learning to read critically, critical reading to assess the quality of the argument.	Support for learning to develop a convincing argument through a written account, feedback to the author.	Academic colleagues

Writing academic journal articles

If you have been studying for a doctoral degree, you may be keen to get summary accounts of your work published in academic journals. You will be aware, from critical reading, how academic authors most effectively develop and communicate a convincing argument. In the same way, your argument must now convince the critical readers who peer review your submitted article. Their job is to recommend whether it should be accepted, revised or rejected. They typically write a short anonymous review that the editors may feed back to you when they inform you of their decision. You are entitled to expect peer reviewers to act with integrity, as sceptical but fair evaluators. Good practice demands that their judgements about your work should be explicitly warranted with evidence, so that you know how to amend it when required to do so. (Note that most submissions require further work on the basis of the peer reviews, so you need not feel discouraged if your paper is not accepted first time.)

The journal editors will probably ask the peer reviewers to refer to specified criteria, which might include judgements about whether the work:

- Focuses on a significant issue in the field of enquiry covered by the journal.

- Is supported by literature and is scholarly.

- Develops and appropriately supports a central set of claims.

- Demonstrates theoretical and methodological rigour, as appropriate.

- Makes an original and interesting contribution to knowledge in the field.

- Has relevance to an international audience.

- Is written in an appropriate style.

The criteria vary between journals, so it is well worth checking them – look on the inside cover of a hard copy or on the relevant website. You may also want to look at articles published in past issues of the journal to see how the criteria are embodied in practice.

Writing research grant proposals

Parallels with your postgraduate work may seem less obvious initially. Whereas most academic writing consists of an account of what has already been done, a research grant proposal focuses on what you promise to do in the future in return for receiving funding. However, it is still academic discourse and many of the same ideas about structuring your written account and ensuring that it meets assessment criteria apply equally here. Your task is to develop a strong argument and communicate it sufficiently well to convince your assessors to recommend the funding of your project. They need easily to see, through the formulation of your argument and the way you structure your account, that you have a strong case for funding and that your proposal meets the criteria stipulated by the funder. You need to indicate the projected outcomes of your empirical investigation and any potential impacts on, and benefits for, important stakeholders. You must also demonstrate that you are competent to deliver the important outcomes you promise, that they will potentially impact on important users of the research, and that you will make efficient use of resources.

Your claims to competence and potential efficiency in conducting the research are warranted not only by the content of your proposal and your curriculum vitae, but also the presentation. An orderly proposal that contains clearly explained and fully warranted arguments will be interpreted as evidence of your ability to work through a problem and organize your thoughts coherently.

In short, a convincing argument in a research proposal will contain a conclusion about the projected outcomes and potential impacts, warranted as strongly as possible by the account of the focus, aims, approach, costing and so on. Evidence that helps to build a strong warrant may include a brief Critical Literature Review to demonstrate that there is a gap in existing knowledge, or to justify a chosen theoretical or methodological framework.

If you are successful in winning the funding, you will soon be embarking on a new empirical investigation informed by the literature. In due course your own published accounts will become part of that literature, for others critically to read and evaluate in their own reviews.

Assessing others' work

Once you are established in your academic career, you will be asked to evaluate other authors' work. You may be acting as a peer reviewer or referee (in your role as an academic scholar) or as a tutor, supervisor or examiner (in your role as a teacher). We have already noted that when you write, you are entitled to expect the critical readers who assess your work to be fair and respectful, sceptical, open-minded and empathetic. Furthermore, you will know from experience how important it is for a writer's self-esteem and ability to learn, that assessments are not biased, unnecessarily heavy-handed or devoid of indications about how to improve. Now, in your role as a critical reader, you will surely wish to adopt a constructively critical attitude.

The assessment process often involves critical reading of others' writing and a written report of some kind. The report may be as informal as feedback notes for a student on how to improve a draft, or as formal as an assessment decision (or recommendations for such a decision) that go to an independent body and are fed back to the author anonymously, if at all. Your responsibility in all cases is to evaluate the arguments you read, with reference to assessment criteria where provided. It also entails developing your own argument, giving reasons – the warrant – for your judgements. The constructive purpose of academic assessment means it needs to be formative in spirit, especially where what you write is fed back to the authors. An awareness of, and sensitivity to, the fact that the authors comprise part of your target audience is therefore of considerable importance. You have an opportunity to support authors' professional learning by offering a brief warrant for your judgement of their efforts.

As with other academic writing, assessing work and giving supportive feedback is a highly skilled task that takes some time to learn, so you are likely to benefit from taking a self-critical approach towards the writing that you do (and also towards the verbal feedback that you give) as an assessor. You might wish to invite a trusted and experienced colleague to act as your mentor by critically reading, and giving you feedback on, your draft reports.

Academic success and academic learning

Anyone who takes up an academic career soon realizes that even though the apprenticeship of their postgraduate study is over, learning how to operate with integrity as an effective and successful academic has scarcely begun. Transferring critical reading and self-critical writing skills offers a sound starting point for continuing to develop your critical frame of mind through good academic practice. As an academic, you are very largely in charge of the opportunities for learning that you create both for yourself and for those whom you teach. The challenge is to maximize your potential to learn from these opportunities. Over to you.

Appendices

Appendix 1

'One Word or Two? Psycholinguistic and Sociolinguistic Interpretations of Meaning in a Civil Court Case,' by Alison Wray and John J. Staczek [abridged version of the article in *The International Journal of Speech, Language and the Law* (2005), 12 (1): 1–18, published by the University of Birmingham Press.]

Abstract

What relative weighting should be given, in a court case, to psycholinguistic and sociolinguistic explanations of an alleged offence? We review the case of an African-American Plaintiff, who claimed that her receipt at work of a framed document with the title 'Temporary Coon Ass Certificate', from a white male supervisory-level employee in the same company, constituted racial discrimination in the workplace. Dialect research conducted by JJS, as expert witness for the prosecution, demonstrated that the dialectal use of 'coonass' (as it is more commonly spelled) to refer to Cajuns (white settlers of French descent) was restricted to the states of Louisiana and south-eastern Texas. It was argued by the prosecution to be unreasonable to expect someone from another part of the United States to know the meaning of the word. The jury found in favour of the Plaintiff. The prosecution case rested upon the premise that when a word is unknown, it will be interpreted by breaking it down into smaller units, in this case 'coon' and 'ass', both derogatory terms, the former strongly racist. We explore the psycholinguistic rationale for this assumption, and its converse, that when a word is well-known to an individual, (s)he may fail to see how it is constructed.

Introduction

This paper discusses a 1996–7 case of alleged racial harassment in the workplace, based upon a perceived use of language in an offensive manner. The African-American Plaintiff filed the action, alleging that her employer, the US Department of Energy, created a hostile work environment. The case was heard in the United States District Court for the District of Columbia.

The Plaintiff claimed that, on returning from vacation, she found in her desk drawer a framed certificate with the title 'Temporary CoonAss Certificate' and her name printed on it. The document was signed by a white Department of Energy employee based at a workshop in east Texas, the site of a recent team visit that the Plaintiff had been unable to attend. The Plaintiff, upon receiving the certificate, 'immediately experienced emotions of shock, outrage and fury, and felt the certificate and the statements contained therein constituted a serious racial slur' (communication from the clerk of the Plaintiff's attorney to JJS, as expert witness for the Plaintiff, 7 August 1996). The Plaintiff sought internal remedies in the form of sanctions against the sender and alleged that: 'the Defendant condoned the hostile environment by failing to discipline the sender or take other remedial action' (ibid). In September 1997 the jury found in favour of the Plaintiff and awarded some $120,000 in compensatory damages against the US Department of Energy.

The Plaintiff was not the only Department of Energy employee to receive such a certificate, and was one of two African-Americans in this round of certificate distributions. In court testimony, the sender stated that he had picked up a bulk load of certificates in 1985 at the World's Fair in New Orleans.

Q   You've given out 'Coonass Certificate' [sic] just like the one you gave to [the Plaintiff] for 10 or 11 year [sic], it that right?
A   That's correct, sir.
Q   And what you did, I gather, is you got a package of 'Coonass Certificates' from a restaurant, is that right?
A   Yes, sir … I picked them up, brought them to the site. I made changes to them, basically about where they came from, took 'Plantation House' off, and at that point in time I put 'Tex-Oma-Complex' on the bottom of them.
(Trial Transcript: cross-examination of Defense witness by Plaintiff's attorney, 21 August 1997, p. 37.)

Since acquiring the certificates, he had issued them regularly, with the implicit approval of his supervisors:

Q   And the supervisors you've had over that 11-year period that you've been giving out the 'Coonass Certificate,' has any of your supervisors said to you, 'Don't give out these Coonass Certificates'?
A   No, sir.
Q   Have any of them said the 'Coonass Certificate' is racially offensive?
A   No, sir.
(Trial Transcript: cross-examination of Defense witness by Plaintiff's attorney, 21 August 1997, pp. 39–40.)

Certificates were issued after site visits made by teams from other company offices. The meaning of the term 'coonass' as 'white Cajun' (see below) was allegedly explained during the visits. The Plaintiff was sent a certificate in error, since her name appeared on the list of attendees even though she did not participate in the visit.

Interpreting 'Coonass'

We shall examine, below, sociolinguistic and psycholinguistic factors that play a role in the interpretation of a word's meaning. First, however, we examine the printed evidence, since dictionaries are in general, and certainly were in this case, viewed as a key source of authoritative information.

The term 'coonass' (non-hyphenated) appears in two dictionary sources: *The Historical Dictionary of American Slang (HDSA)* and *Dictionary of American Regional English (DARE)*. Its primary meaning is given as a term for Louisiana Cajuns. Although the term 'Cajun' is historically complex with regard to racial group and social status, Cajuns are classically defined as the white descendants of settlers in Acadia, a former French colony of eastern Canada, who were deported by the British, or relocated voluntarily, to the south-western territories, including Louisiana, in the mid-eighteenth century (*American Heritage Dictionary of the English Language (AHDEL)* 1992: 9). DARE attests that the usage of 'coonass' is confined to Louisiana and south-eastern Texas, though it is also known to regional speakers in Mississippi, Arkansas and Alabama. Research to determine this regional distribution was based on formal interviews with informants in the South.

In addition to the core definition, however, the following specific entries are notable:

- 'Coonass is still a pejorative for any low-life individual, especially Negroes' (DARE informant, File eKY).

- 'The term 'coonass' ... may have been a racial allusion suggesting a Cajun-black genetic mixture' (HDAS informant, Dormon, 1983: 87).

The combined evidence above suggests that 'coonass' has two meanings, the second alluding to, if not actually referring to, African ancestry. However, the status of the latter entries is questionable, as we shall see presently. Unequivocal, though, is the offensive meaning of the separate terms 'coon' and 'ass'. A wide range of standard and specialist dictionaries give as one meaning of 'coon', 'a Negro', and indicate that it is a slang and derogatory term. Its origin is consistently reported as a shortened form of 'raccoon', itself a word of Algonkian Indian origin. 'Ass' is identified in HDAS as a US version of British 'arse', the buttocks or rump. As such it is considered a 'vulgarism' (HDAS). AHDEL gives the definition 'a vain, self-important, silly, or aggressively stupid person', based on a primary meaning of 'donkey'.

What sort of quality of evidence is obtained from dictionaries, though? In the course of questioning, the expert witness for the defendant made a number of observations regarding the validity of dictionary definitions:

' … these dictionaries are only as good as the people they're talking to.…These are not definitions. These are recorded testimonies of what people think these things mean'.

(Trial Transcript: direct examination of expert witness for the Defense, 22 August 1997, p. 44.)

Referring to the DARE and HDAS:

> 'Those two dictionaries are based on interviews with people, asking them what regional or slang terms mean to them. The reason for that is because these terms are not – have no standard accepted meaning.'
>
> (Trial Transcript: cross-examination of expert witness for the Defense, 22 Aug 1997, p. 60.)

As the observations of this expert witness indicate, care needs to be taken with dictionary entries where there is no evidence of general consensus within a speech community, or where there are grounds for doubting the validity of the statement that the dictionary cites. Specifically with regard to the two attestations, above, that 'coonass' can imply African ancestry, it is possible that the claimed extension of the term to black people is a *post hoc* rationalization based on folk etymology. In actual fact, the consensus across dictionaries, including both HDAS and DARE, is that 'coonass' has an etymology in which 'coon' does not figure at all, being, rather, the corruption of the French 'connasse', a vulgarism used as an insult.

Dictionaries, then, can offer valuable insights into the historical origin and at least some current perceptions of a word's meaning. However, there is more to meaning than this. The instructions to the expert witness for the prosecution were to ascertain 'not the specific meaning of 'Coonass' within Cajun circles, but … what the words 'Coon' and 'Ass' generally mean, how they are generally intended and received, and the hurtful potential of these words' (Memorandum from the clerk of the Plaintiff's attorney to expert witness for the Plaintiff). Dictionaries can give only limited insight into these matters, since they are unable to comment on meanings of words *in use*, that is, in relation to (a) the text in which they occur, (b) their role in a particular communicative act, or (c) the social context that might determine why a speaker/writer chooses one term over another, and how a hearer/reader interprets it.

Sociolinguistic considerations

Language, whether oral or written, exists within a context of use. Both speakers and hearers bring to their understanding of a word or phrase a knowledge founded on a socialization, education and experience that may be totally or partially shared, or not shared at all. The term 'coonass' is clearly dialectal and, as such, certain questions follow:

- How is the word likely to be interpreted by an individual who does not come from, and has not lived in, the region in which the word is customarily used?

- What contextual and other considerations might come into play when such a person is interpreting the term?

Regarding the first question, the Plaintiff, an African-American woman living and working in Washington D.C., was neither from the dialect area in which the term 'coonass' was in use (Louisiana and south-eastern Texas), nor from one of the 'dialect contact areas' (Mississippi, Arkansas and Alabama). Dialect contact areas are locations where, usually because of geographical proximity and/or cultural or commercial links, dialect forms might often be heard, even if not used by the local population. Should the Plaintiff, then, reasonably be expected to have known what 'coonass' meant? During cross-examination, the expert witness for the defendant stated:

> ' … it's not unreasonable to think that people – not only people in South Louisiana and East Texas would be familiar with the term…People all over the place know this.'
>
> (Trial Transcript, cross-examination of expert witness for the defense by Plaintiff's attorney, 22 August 1997, pp. 49–50.)

That is, this expert witness considered unfamiliarity to be the exception rather than the rule. In contrast, the view of the expert witness for the Plaintiff was that the term as a reference to a Cajun could not be expected to have widespread recognition across the United States.

How can this difference of opinion be interpreted? The expert witness for the Plaintiff had carried out some informal and random sampling of African Americans and White Americans in the Washington D.C. area, to determine their understanding of the term 'coonass'. He found that almost all of those questioned perceived a racial overtone in the term and viewed it as offensive and disrespectful.

In contrast, the expert witness for the Defense was himself a South Louisianan of French Acadian descent – that is, of Cajun ancestry. He then, originated from, and resided well within, the dialect area in which the term was in use and he was, as a result, highly familiar with it. This fact is apposite because the issue was whether a member of a speech community is able to assess the extent to which people who are not members of that speech community share its lexical inventory. In other words, how aware are dialect speakers about (a) which words in their vocabulary are dialectal, and (b) how widely known they are beyond the immediate area? If we do not perceive the need for remedial action, we are unlikely to undertake it. It is, consequently, significant that the expert witness for the Defense stated:

> 'Frankly, I didn't look for definitions of 'coonass' because I know what it means.'
>
> (Trial Transcript: cross-examination of expert witness for the Defense, 22 August 1997, p. 43.)

Turning now to the second question, words do not operate in isolation. They are interpreted in relation to other words with which they occur and also the situational and social context in which they are used. We may reasonably conjecture that had the Plaintiff not been African-American, she would probably have reacted to receiving the certificate with bafflement rather than distress. Even taking into account the generalized understanding of 'ass' as a derogatory term, the fact that the Plaintiff's case was one of racial harassment indicates that she reacted predominantly to seeing the word 'coon'. Indeed, in court she stated:

> 'When I pulled [the certificate] out, the first thing I saw was 'coon'. I didn't see 'temporary'. I didn't see 'ass'. All I could see was 'coon' … I was shocked. I was outraged.' (Trial Transcript: direct examination of the Plaintiff by Plaintiff's attorney, 20 August 1997, p. 36.)

Thus, her own ethnic identity formed part of the context within which her reading of the words 'coonass' caused offence. The contention of the prosecution was that the sender should have been aware of, and sensitive to, the possibility that these context parameters could lead to an interpretation of the phrase as offensive. In other words, even though he had no reason to anticipate that *anyone* would receive a certificate without having had the term explained to them during their visit, nor that if anyone did do so, they would be African-American, the potential for the phrase to cause offence should have been taken into account when he decided to send the certificates.

An examination of the certificate itself, however, reveals some counterbalancing factors. Firstly, it is to be signed by 'a certified coonass', implying that if an insult is intended, even in jest, that insult falls first, and more heavily, on the sender than the recipient. More than that, it indicates that the certificate represents a gesture of inclusion, not exclusion, that is, it is welcoming the recipient into membership of a group, not labelling him or her as a member of an outsider group. Secondly, the smaller print on the certificate indicates that the sentiments in the definition of a 'certified coonass' are predominantly positive – that is, the description is complimentary. Thirdly, several words co-occurring with 'coonass' in the text ('boudin', 'crackins', 'crawfish etouffee' and 'gumbo') are clearly dialectal and their presence arguably heightens the impression that 'coonass' itself might be.

Psycholinguistic considerations

Wray (2002) begins her book *Formulaic Language and the Lexicon* with the following anecdote:

> In a series of advertisements on British TV early in 1993 by the breakfast cereal manufacturer Kellogg, people were asked what they thought Rice Krispies were made of, and expressed surprise at discovering the answer was rice. Somehow they had internalized this household brand name without ever analyzing it into its component parts (p. 3).

Why should this happen? She proposes that: '… overlooking the internal composition of names is a far more common phenomenon than we might at first think … [and] it is actually very useful that we can choose the level at which we stop breaking down a chunk of language into its constituent parts' (p. 3–4). In the course of her book, Wray draws on an extensive critical examination of the research literature to demonstrate that the internal composition of phrases and polymorphemic words is, indeed, often over-looked, and also develops a psychological model of how we learn and store lexical material, that accounts for why it comes about (see later).

In the trial, the expert witness for the Defense was asked whether he viewed 'coonass' as a single word or two words. In reply, he compared it to the word 'firefly': "'firefly' is not 'fire' or 'fly'; it's a 'firefly'. It's an expression used together." (Trial Transcript: direct examination of the expert witness for the defense, 22 August 1997, p. 14). In the case of 'firefly' there is, of course, a clear hint as to why it gained its name, that relates to its component parts. However, internally complex words and multiword phrases often have an apparent etymology that is misleading, with subcomponents that do not represent what they seem to. Thus, the 'ladybird' or 'ladybug' is so-called not because it is female or resembles a lady, but because it was traditionally a creature of 'Our Lady', the Virgin Mary (compare German 'Marienkäfer', 'Mary's beetle'). A 'penknife' is not a knife that is the size or shape of a writing implement, but a knife orig-inally designed for sharpening quills ('pen' = 'feather').

What of 'coonass', then? If we set aside the single proposal, discussed earlier, that the term takes the form it does because it first referred to black Cajuns, and if we follow instead the more reliable etymology from French, then 'coonass' is no more made up, historically, of 'coon' and 'ass' than 'carpet' is made up of 'car' and 'pet' or 'browsing' is made up of 'brow' and 'sing'. We must recognize a direct link, within the dialect area of its use, between a French word for a part of the body and a consistently applied deroga-tory term for an immigrant group of French settlers from Canada and their descendants. Any association with African-Americans is after the event and imposed by outsiders.

But does that make the externally imposed, albeit historically false, interpretation any less real to those who make it? More appositely here, does the 'innocent' etymology of a word or phrase excuse insensitivity on the part of its contemporary users? In order to assess this issue, we need to return to Wray's proposal that words and phrases are not always broken down into their smallest components. She identifies several interrelating reasons why that might occur. One is well-exemplified above: in many cases an appar-ently polymorphemic word does not, in fact, break down in components that help one work out the meaning. The same applies to phrases, from the clearly irregular 'by and large' through to many multiword expressions whose internal oddity we could easily overlook (e.g., 'perfect stranger'; 'broad daylight'; 'in order to'). In these instances, there will be no benefit in examining the word or phrase too closely. However, that cannot be the root of the issue, for how would the user *know* that the word or phrase was partly or entirely non-compositional, unless by attempting to do that analysis?

Wray's explanation is that when we encounter new words and phrases, we only break them down to the point where we can attribute a reliable and useful meaning, and then we stop. She terms this strategy *needs only analysis* (Wray, 2002: 130–2). Needs only analysis suggests that people who have been raised in Louisiana or southeast Texas will, having encountered the term 'coonass' and having accepted without question that it refers to a Cajun, have had no reason to engage in further analysis of it. This could go some way to explaining how the sender of the 'coonass' certificate apparently failed to anticipate the possibility of a misunderstanding. Furthermore, it could account for why the expert witness for the Defense felt that he did not need to look the phrase up: 'because I know what it means', and why he described the racial interpretations as 'not standard meanings' (Trial Transcript, cross-examination of the expert witness for the Defense, 22 August 1997, p. 44).

In contrast, someone who does not know the word, has an additional 'need', and will therefore engage with more analysis, by breaking down the incomprehensible whole into comprehensible parts, naturally using the 'word' break as the morphological boundary. The result is two words with independent meanings, 'coon' and 'ass'. The decoding that is required by a person encountering 'coonass' for the first time is minimal: no more than the recognition that there are two components, both derogatory, implying that their combination must also be so.

What of the sender? Although he may never have needed to break down 'coonass' into its components to derive meaning, nevertheless, he would presumably only need to have once caught sight of the word 'coon' on its own on the certificate to have noticed, and quite differently computed, its meaning as a separate item. Yet he appeared never to have made the connection between 'coon' and 'coonass':

Q   You're familiar with the term 'coon', aren't you?
A   Yes, sir, I am.
Q   You understand that that has a racially-derogatory meaning?
A   Yes, sir, I do.
Q   And you knew that the term 'coon' has a racially-derogative meaning to African Americans at the time that you prepared the certificate that's been marked as Plaintiff's Exhibit Number 1, isn't that true?
A   That's correct.
    (Trial Transcript: cross-examination of Defense witness by Plaintiff's attorney, 21 August 1997, p. 40.)

His claim is particularly striking in view of the fact that he had actually handed a certificate to another African-American employee, yet still did not see a connection between 'coonass' and 'coon' (Trial Transcript: cross-examination of Defense witness by Plaintiff's attorney, 21 August 1997, p. 42). This makes most sense from the perspective of *needs only analysis*, and would be a case of 'constituent blindness' brought about by the strong and consistent association of a specific meaning with the composite word 'coonass'. More accurately, it would be 'pseudo-constituent blindness' since 'coon' and 'ass' are not, historically or actually for the dialect speakers, constituents of the whole. For such individuals to see 'coon' and 'ass' in 'coonass' is – a word break notwithstanding – comparable to a standard English speaker noticing 'sea' and 'son' in 'season'.

Conclusion

So, what does a word mean? We operate within, and across, speech communities. Whatever we may intend by a word, we must be constantly aware of how it is, or could be, received by others. Nevertheless, we may, for good psycholinguistic reasons, be blind to the internal construction of a word or phrase in our own variety. Meanwhile, that same internal construction may be all too plain to those unfamiliar with the item. The user of the construction may discover the other possible interpretations only by chance. Is it then reasonable for a court to expect that a word with strong local cultural associations will always be recognized as potentially ambiguous, even though, within its own realm of application, it is not?

The judge and jury are put into a difficult situation in such cases, assuming that they take both parties to have made an innocent interpretation of the disputed term. The Judge, in his summing up, stated:

> [T]o determine … whether the Temporary Coon Ass Certificate was racially offensive, you should consider [the sender's] intent to discriminate or not to discriminate against blacks, the subjective effect of the forwarding of the certificate on [the Plaintiff], and the impact it would have had on any reasonable person in [the Plaintiff's] position. (Trial transcript: Summary of the Judge, 25 August 1997, p. 19.)

The Judge allows for the possibility that while the sender's intent was non-discriminatory, the impact on the Plaintiff was nevertheless one of deliberate discrimination. Achieving a ruling therefore entailed deciding which of the two was more justified in their blindness to the other's perception. For linguistic awareness cuts both ways: the sender might have been expected to have an awareness of non-dialect users' interpretations of 'coonass', but, similarly, the recipient might have been expected to spot, from the various indicators, that she was reading an unfamiliar dialect term.

This linguistic awareness, we have argued, may rest on more than the words themselves. The Plaintiff's initial sight of the certificate, when the word 'coon' was all she saw, may have blinded her to the possibility that 'coonass' meant something other than 'coon' + 'ass'. Meanwhile, the sender did not deny familiarity with the word 'coon' and its racist meaning, only any awareness that 'coonass' might be construed by a person who did not know the term, as containing the word 'coon'. We propose that her constituent awareness, and his constituent blindness, are entirely natural consequences of linguistic processing.

Just how a court should handle such psycholinguistic considerations is another matter. They could clearly have some bearing on the issue of intent but it could still be argued that, however explicable the oversight might be in psycholinguistic terms, it is part of the educational level required of a manager or supervisor that he or she will be language-aware in relation to differences between linguistic varieties used, and encountered, in the work place. At the very least, the outcome of this case suggests that individuals in a socially responsible position are expected to appreciate the singularity of their own dialect or slang forms to a sufficient extent that they will refrain from using them with people likely to be unfamiliar with – or to misconstrue – their meaning.

References

American Heritage Dictionary of the English Language (1992) (3rd edn). Boston: Houghton Mifflin Co.

Dictionary of American Regional English (1985) Volume 1. Cambridge, MA: The Belknap Press of Harvard University Press.

Dormon, J. H. (1983) *The People Called Cajuns: An Introduction to an Ethnohistory*. Lafayette, LA: The Center for Louisiana Studies.

Historical Dictionary of American Slang. Volume 1: A-G (1994) New York: Random House.

United States District Court for the District of Columbia (1997) Transcript of Trial (Civil Action No. 96–401) Before the Honorable Harold H. Greene, United States Judge and a Jury, August 1997.

Wray, A. (2002) *Formulaic Language and the Lexicon*. Cambridge: Cambridge University Press.

Appendix 2

'Sharing Leadership of Schools through Teamwork: a Justifiable Risk?' By Mike Wallace [abridged version of the article in *Educational Management and Administration* 2001, 29 (2): 153–167, published by Sage.]

Abstract

This paper develops the empirically-backed normative argument that ideally school leadership should be shared among staff, but the extent of sharing that is justifiable in practice depends on diverse contexts of schools, and consequent risks – especially for headteachers – that may inhere in the endeavour to share leadership. Findings are discussed of research into senior management teams (SMTs) in British primary schools showing how the headteachers variably shared leadership by setting parameters for teamwork according to a differing mix of belief in a management hierarchy and in equal contribution of team members. A model is put forward which links interaction between headteachers and other SMT members according to their belief in a management hierarchy and in equal contribution with different levels of team synergy. A contingent approach to sharing school leadership is justified on the basis of this model and implications for training are identified.

Sharing leadership – in principle

The purpose of this paper is to develop the normative argument that school leadership should ideally be extensively shared but, because school leaders do not live in an ideal world, the extent of sharing which is justifiable in practice depends on empirical factors. In other words, championing of shared leadership draws on principles which are contingent on the situation, not absolute. Specifically, I wish to explore empirical factors connected with the contexts of schools and consequent risks – especially for headteachers – that may inhere in their endeavour to share leadership. Findings will be discussed from research into senior management teams (SMTs) in British primary schools, whose role is to support the headteacher in leading and managing the institution. Typically, they consist of the headteacher, deputy head and other teachers with the most substantial management responsibility. Team members are variably involved in making policy and routine management decisions on behalf of other staff, whose views are represented in some measure. The term 'management' in the label 'management team' therefore refers both to leadership (setting the direction for the organization) and to management activity (orchestrating its day-to-day running). A combined cultural and political perspective was employed to investigate how the 'culture of teamwork' expressed in SMTs embodied contradictory beliefs and values. These beliefs and values reflected the wider social and political context, which impacted reciprocally on team members' use of power, and affected the extent to which leadership was shared between team members.

Several principles have been advanced to support the claim that school leadership should be shared relatively equally amongst staff. Most centre on staff entitlement. First, staff are entitled to contribute to decisions which affect their work and to be empowered to collaborate in creating an excellent institution. Shared leadership is morally just (Starratt, 1995; Sergiovanni, 1996) in a democratic country where individual rights are accorded high priority. Second, since staff give their professional lives to their school, they are entitled to enjoy the comradeship that working with colleagues can engender. Participating in shared leadership has intrinsic value, potentially, as a fulfilling experience for all involved (Nias et al., 1989; Wallace and Hall, 1994). Third, staff are entitled to gain this experience to further their professional development and career aspirations. It offers individual team members a potent opportunity for workplace learning, whereby they may improve their performance in their present role and prepare for promotion. A fourth principle looks to staff obligations as student educators. Adult working relationships in schools play a symbolic part in fostering children's social development. As role models, staff have responsibility to express in their working relationships the kind of cooperative behaviour they wish their students to emulate.

A fifth principle focuses on valued leadership outcomes rather than the process. Shared leadership is potentially more effective than headteachers acting alone. Staff are interdependent: every member has a contribution to make as leadership tasks can be fulfilled only with and through other people. Achieving extensive ownership of policy decisions is therefore necessary if staff are to work together to implement them. Empowerment through mutual commitment and support enables staff to achieve more together than they could as individuals (Starratt, 1995; Wallace and Hall, 1994). In these circumstances they can achieve an optimum degree of *synergy*, which may be defined as group members combining their individual energies to the best of their ability in order to achieve shared goals. Advocates assume that staff will adhere to these principles if given the chance: those offered their entitlement will take it up; they will act as good role models for students; and they will collaborate and generate synergy.

Prescription versus practice

Such ideas are embedded in normative theories of educational leadership from which prescriptions for practice are derived (Starratt, 1995; Sergiovanni, 1996), informing the school restructuring movement in North America (Pounder, 1998) and advocated for the UK by a few commentators (Southworth, 1998). They commonly refer to notions of transformational leadership and organization-wide learning originating with the world of business (e.g., Senge, 1990; Conger and Kanungo, 1998). Principals (head-teachers) are urged to promote transformation of the staff culture through articulating a vision of a desirable future state for the institution; garnering colleagues' support for it; and empowering them to realize this shared vision through developing management structures and procedures emphasizing professional dialogue, teamworking and mutual support. How principals should behave, according to these theories, reflects assump-tions about the real world of schools which include:

1 Principals possess freedom to determine their vision, their strategy for inspiring colleagues to share it, and the means for implementing it through their practice.

2 It is possible to engineer change in a teacher culture with predictable results.

3 Elements of the teacher culture are mutually compatible and individual interests are reconcilable, facilitating transformation that results in unity of purpose.

4 Empowerment of teachers leads to their actions to realize the vision proffered by principals.

Should these assumptions prove unrealistic, it follows that the principles on which the normative theory rests must be compromised if it is to have prescriptive value. That transformational leadership is deemed exceptional enough in North American schools and industries to merit books and training programmes promoting it suggests that the assumptions behind transformational leadership do not obtain in North America. Their applicability to the UK is even more questionable.

First, British headteachers have lost their freedom to be visionaries because of central government reforms. 'National standards for headship' (Teacher Training Agency, 1998: 4) require that 'the headteacher provides vision, leadership and direction for the school and ensures that it is managed and organized to meet its aims and targets.' The content of these aims and targets is largely determined by a central government engaged in a nationwide school target-setting exercise and imposing what, when and how literacy and numeracy must be taught in primary schools. Headteachers are expected both to articulate and gain colleagues' support for government ministers' edu-cational vision and to ensure its implementation.

Second, research on schools implies that the teacher culture is not directly manipu-lable through leadership, though it is open to change (e.g., Nias et al., 1989). Attempts to stimulate cultural development may precipitate cultural change in unforeseen and undesired directions (Wallace, 1999). Hargreaves (1994) found that attempts in North America to foster a collaborative teacher culture merely engendered 'contrived collegiality' – a poor substitute for the genuinely collaborative culture which he argues may arise spontaneously.

Third, teacher cultures frequently contain incompatible elements: contradictory beliefs and values coexisting in tension. An earlier study of secondary school SMTs (Wallace and Hall, 1994) showed how their culture of teamwork encompassed two contradictory sets of beliefs and values. SMT members believed in a *management hierarchy* topped by headteachers, since they are in charge of running the school under supervision from the governing body, and have a unique ability to affect colleagues' careers through their contribution to staff selection and development. The sense of hierarchy was reinforced by the system of graded posts for staff, representing differential status, salary and responsibility levels. Senior staff are entitled to oversee the work of junior colleagues for whose work they are responsible. At the same time, team members believed in the ability of all their number to make an *equal contribution* to teamwork, being entitled to have an equal say in working towards consensual decisions whatever their status in the management hierarchy. Headteachers were hierarchically superior as creators, developers and leaders of their SMTs, but also were team members whose opinion carried equal weight with that of colleagues.

Fourth, empowerment of other staff does not guarantee that they will take up this entitlement in a manner acceptable to headteachers. Research shows that a significant minority of SMT members remain uncommitted to teamwork (e.g., Weindling and Earley, 1987; Wallace and Hall, 1994). Even where commitment is uniform, SMT members other than the headteacher may use power accompanying their team membership to act in ways that lie outside the limits of practices that accord with the headteacher's 'comfort zone' (the range of others' acceptable behaviours).

Under the structure of authority in British schools, the decision over how far to share leadership has long lain with headteachers. Research over recent decades suggests that perhaps the majority actually behaved more in accordance with the 'headmaster tradition' born of nineteenth century public schools (Grace, 1995). Many primary heads identified closely with 'their' school, confining shared leadership to empowering colleagues to deliver their agenda (Hall and Southworth, 1997). In a hands-off political climate, headteachers enjoyed considerable agency, empowered to adopt their idiosyncratic construction of headship, often entailing restricted sharing of leadership which cast their colleagues exclusively in the role of followers. However, research also suggests there was limited followership, teachers publicly toeing headteachers' official line in the 'zone of policy' (Lortie, 1969) while, behind the classroom door in the 'zone of practice', they also possessed sufficient agency discreetly to do their own thing.

Central government education reforms have changed all that. Local administration has been largely replaced by additional central government authority to direct educational essentials like curriculum and to determine standards through legislation and financial incentives, complemented by devolution of authority to headteachers (within centrally determined limits) over inessentials like the operating budget. The most compelling reason for sharing leadership is now less a matter of principle than of pragmatism in a hostile environment. Headteachers must share leadership and their colleagues must deliver. The former are ever more dependent on the latter to contribute their specialist expertise in implementing mandated reforms, to feed this expertise into the leadership process as they gain experience with new practices, and to assist with monitoring implementation.

Headteachers now have less room to manoeuvre. Their notion of headship is increasingly constructed for them by external forces, and they can no longer afford *not* to accept the risk of sharing leadership in some degree. Yet an ironic consequence of central government strategy is to render sharing leadership as risky for headteachers as it is necessary. While they still enjoy exclusive authority to decide how far to share leadership, they are also held uniquely accountable for the outcomes of their decision. Reforms designed to strengthen external accountability, like national assessment of pupil learning and regular inspection of schools (both involving publication of results), have increased the vulnerability of the very headteachers on whom central government ministers depend to implement reforms. Headteachers alone are charged with legal responsibility for running the school within the oversight of the governing body. The accountability measures have increased the likelihood that headteachers will be publicly vilified if evidence is revealed of failure to implement central government reforms or to reach stipulated targets for educational standards.

Headteachers are confronted by a heightened dilemma: their greater dependence on colleagues disposes them towards sharing leadership. In a context of unprecedented accountability, however, they may be inhibited from sharing because it could backfire should empowered colleagues act in ways that generate poor standards of pupil achievement, alienate parents and governors, or incur inspectors' criticism. If this is the reality of schooling, how far should headteachers be expected to risk sharing leadership, since it could negatively affect their reputation, colleagues' work and ultimately children's education? If the risk of ineffective leadership can be reduced by limiting the amount of sharing, is it justifiable for headteachers to adopt a contingency approach, varying the degree of sharing as the situation evolves?

The case of primary school SMTs

The remainder of the paper seeks a tentative answer to these questions by considering evidence on the operation of primary school SMTs. First, relevant aspects of the research design and the combined cultural and political perspective framing the investigation are outlined. Second, findings are reported showing how the headteachers variably shared leadership by setting parameters for teamwork according to a differing mix of belief in a management hierarchy and in equal contribution of team members. Third, a model is put forward which links different levels of team synergy with interaction between headteachers and other SMT members, according to their belief in a management hierarchy and in equal contribution. Finally, a contingent approach to sharing school leadership is justified on the basis of this model and implications for training are identified.

The research, funded by the Economic and Social Research Council, investigated SMTs in large primary schools. (For a full account, see Wallace and Huckman, 1999.) Institutions with over 300 students were selected because SMTs in them would proba-bly constitute a subset of the teaching staff. A key criterion for selecting SMTs was members' unified professed commitment to a team approach. Headteachers at potential sites were contacted and individual SMT members' stated commitment confirmed during a preliminary visit. Focused, interpretive case studies of four SMTs (labelled as Winton, Pinehill, Kingsrise and Waverley) were undertaken over the 1995/96 academic year. Data sources comprised 58 semi-structured interviews (eight with headteachers, 20 with other members of the SMTs, 26 with a sample of other staff, and four with chairs of school governing bodies); non-participant observation of twelve SMT meet-ings and ten other meetings where SMT members were present; and a small document archive. Research questions for the case studies were derived from a literature review, the previous study of secondary school SMTs and an initial postal questionnaire survey of headteachers, to which interview questions related. Fieldnotes were taken during case-study observations and tape-recorded interviews. Summary tapes were prepared and transcribed with reference to fieldnotes, schedules and documents. Data analysis entailed compiling interview summaries that fed into site summaries, forming the basis for cross-site analysis. Tables were constructed to display findings, the data set was scanned to explore the contextual complexity of specific interactions and explanatory models were developed.

The cultural and political perspective guiding the research integrates concepts about teacher professional cultures and micropolitics. It focuses on the reciprocal relationship between culture and power: cultural determinants of differential uses of power and uses of power to shape culture (Wallace, 1999). Culture informs deployment of power which, recursively, contributes to the maintenance or evolution of this culture. A simple definition of *culture* is 'the way we do things around here' (Bower, 1966): beliefs and values about education, leadership and relationships common to some or all staff in a school. A *culture of teamwork* may develop among SMT members which comprises shared beliefs, values and norms of behaviour about how they work together. As indi-cated above, a pivotal feature of the culture in the case studies was the interplay between uses of power according to belief in the management hierarchy and in the enti-tlement of all team members to make an equal contribution to the SMT. The uneasy coexistence of these beliefs is a consequence of the flow of wider social and political forces for cultural change and continuity going back to the headmaster tradition (based on belief in a strict hierarchy); the subsequent upsurge of demands from teachers to share in leadership (reflecting belief in equal rights as colleagues to participate in schools located within a democracy); and the new 'managerialist' belief in public sector managers' right to manage (Whitty et al., 1998), to achieve goals set by their political bosses (reasserting belief in hierarchy but with headteachers now in the middle of the chain of command).

Following Giddens (1984), a definition of *power* as 'transformative capacity' – use of resources to achieve interests – is employed. This conception was selected to encompass interactions which vary between synergistic, where staff pull together to achieve the same goal, and conflictual, where they pursue incompatible goals. Power may be divided (Bacharach and Lawler, 1980) into *authority* – use of resources legitimated by beliefs and values about status, including the right to apply sanctions; and *influence* – informal use of resources without recourse to sanctions linked to authority (although other sanctions may be available). Headteachers' conditions of service give them exclusive authority over other staff, but teachers may wield influence in seeking to support or undermine headteachers. The latter have recourse to authority and influence to promote a particular culture of teamwork within the SMT but cannot guarantee it will happen. Controlling other staff is, for headteachers, more a matter of *delimitation* – allowing for different behaviour within the boundaries of their comfort zone – than of establishing directive control. Changing beliefs about the redistribution of authority and influence between headteachers, their colleagues and other stakeholders reflect the impact of externally imposed reforms which delimit the agency of headteachers and other staff along quite narrowly defined boundaries. Headteachers may have created their SMTs, but not under conditions entirely of their own choosing.

A balancing act

The four headteachers had authority to decide, according to their professional beliefs and values, whether to adopt a team approach to leadership and how far to share leadership within it. SMT operation at Winton was relatively egalitarian, with a strong emphasis on equal contribution by all members to a wide variety of team tasks. In the other three schools it was more hierarchical, with deputies being more involved than other members in a narrower range of tasks. The headteachers enjoyed very different degrees of freedom to choose their team mates. The headteacher at Pinehill was newly appointed from elsewhere and inherited other members of the SMT. The headteachers of Kingsrise, Waverley and Winton had been in post for some years. They had both created their SMT and played a major part in selecting all team colleagues when vacancies had arisen, so had been able to appoint colleagues who subscribed to their conception of teamwork.

Elements of a management hierarchy were intrinsic to headteachers' design of the team structures. The spread of individual management responsibilities among team members gave them joint oversight of other staff (Table 1). Senior teachers were either responsible for a group of classes (e.g., the junior department) or for a specialism (e.g.,

Table 1 Case-study SMT membership

Status level of SMT members	Winton (4 members)	Pinehill (6 members)	Kingsrise (7 members)	Waverley (5 members)
Headteacher	1	1	1	1
Deputy Head	2	1	1	1
Senior Teacher	1	4	5	3

students with special needs). The extent to which headteachers shared leadership depended on the balance they sought between expressing belief in the management hierarchy and in equal contribution of team members in the SMT's operation. The headteacher at Winton had created a small team to facilitate extensive sharing consistent with her belief in promoting an equal contribution by all members, who could take initiatives and engage fully in debate. The hierarchical approach that she had rejected as tokenism, where a headteacher would merely seek support for his or her agenda, was close to that embraced by the other headteachers – who opted for larger teams.

How limited headteachers' power can be to set parameters for SMT operation when inheriting a team was demonstrated at Pinehill. The new headteacher attempted to impose his authority to introduce a more hierarchical mode of operation on other members of the existing team. The previous headteacher and deputy had been absent for long periods and other members of the SMT had enjoyed the opportunity to make a relatively equal contribution to teamwork. Several would not, initially, accept the more restricted contribution the new headteacher allowed them. Department leaders used influence by offering minimal compliance to the headteacher while complaining to other teachers behind his back, generating a widespread perception of a disunited team.

Varying the balance between equal and hierarchical sharing

Different degrees of sharing were expressed through several aspects of the teams' practice. First, the extent and boundaries of team tasks diverged. At Winton, the headteacher encouraged all other SMT members to participate fully in most leadership tasks, extending to developing policy proposals. At Pinehill, team tasks excluded curriculum matters (which were addressed by a parallel group consisting of the headteacher, deputy head and a teacher designated as curriculum leader). Monitoring implementation of decisions extending to classroom observation was being developed through training for the headteacher and deputies at Winton. The headteachers of the other schools had accepted that this potentially threatening level of internal monitoring was a task for them alone. They were not sole determinants of the limits of SMT practice. Reticence among SMT colleagues to monitor the performance of other staff reflected their allegiance to the wider staff professional culture, which accorded individuals considerable classroom autonomy. These SMT members had used influence to voice their unease and realize their interest in avoiding an unwelcome task. The notion of a management hierarchy suited them here: they could argue it was not their job, as junior members, to monitor colleagues.

Second, the headteachers variably empowered team colleagues to contribute to tasks they did share. While the headteacher at Winton encouraged SMT colleagues to take initiatives within broad boundaries (such as piloting a system for improving student discipline), the other headteachers confined sharing to consulting team colleagues on their prespecified agenda. Where all members participated in making team decisions, the norm was universal that a working consensus must be achieved. Debate leading to a decision at Winton, however, commonly comprised 'open consultation' where all members were encouraged equally to offer ideas. The other headteachers tended to opt for a more hierarchical approach of 'bounded consultation', where they put forward their proposed decision and sought colleagues' comments before taking it to a meeting with other staff. Pooling information to build an overview was a feature of the four teams, but the flow of information and opinion was multidirectional at Winton and channelled more unidirectionally in the other SMTs towards what the headteacher wished to know.

Third, there was varied appreciation of individual members' complementary knowledge and skills. SMT members at Winton were aware of the complementarity of their expertise connected with their individual management responsibility, and of contrasting skills linked to personalities which were required to balance creative thinking with getting tasks completed. Awareness of complementarity in the other teams was restricted largely to knowledge connected with the hierarchical distribution of individual management responsibilities, suggesting that their contribution to the team did not run as deep.

While the team approach at Winton expressed belief in equal contribution of SMT members most fully, expression of belief in a management hierarchy was not only enshrined in the structure but was also reflected at times in the team's practice. Observation of Winton SMT meetings indicated that members other than the headteacher expressed their belief in the management hierarchy by ensuring that their contribution stayed inside the implicit boundaries set by her. They would check voluntarily that she was comfortable with the course of action they were advocating. The culture of teamwork shared throughout this team included the norm that the headteacher had authority as formal leader within the management hierarchy to pull rank, but only for contingent situations where equal contribution did not result in consensus. The flexibility with which all team members were able to switch between the two contradictory beliefs as circumstances changed was one foundation of synergy for this SMT. Unified commitment to combining individual energies in pursuit of a shared goal was not jeopardized when the prevalent norm of equal contribution was temporarily replaced by reversion to hierarchical operation. Team colleagues' willingness to switch in this way reduced the risk for the headteacher of losing control that relatively equal sharing can bring. The culture of teamwork here was sophisticated enough for contradictory beliefs and values to coexist without conflict, mutually empowering all members.

Sharing leadership though teamwork

The headteacher at Winton shared most leadership tasks, shared them with all her SMT colleagues, and did so relatively equally. While the other headteachers empowered their team colleagues to make a more restricted contribution as equals (especially to debate and some decisions), they shared fewer leadership tasks, shared less with more junior colleagues, and shared tasks unequally with all other members. The agency of all four headteachers was similarly delimited by national contextual factors connected with central government reforms, but differently by school level factors – notably the opportunity to create their team and choose its membership. The headteachers retained sufficient agency to employ their authority in orchestrating alternative approaches to sharing leadership within the SMT, dependent on their contrasting balance of belief in a management hierarchy and in equal contribution. Their team colleagues likewise had agency to use influence in making a supportive or resistant response to headteachers according to the balance of their own adherence to these contradictory beliefs and values. The agency of headteachers and their colleagues may have been more tightly delimited by reforms but it was still significant. The new central government promotion of a management hierarchy had yet to eliminate adherence to more egalitarian norms whose origin predates the reform era.

Figure 1 is a model explaining what occurred within the agency of the headteachers and other SMT members. It compares norms relating to belief in a management hierarchy and in equal contribution to which the headteacher subscribes (the left and right hand columns) with the equivalent norms to which other SMT members subscribe (the upper and lower rows). Each cell depicts the combination of norms held by the headteacher and other SMT members. (For simplicity, it is assumed that all other SMT members share allegiance to the same norm at any time.) The *upper left cell* represents the situation at Kingsrise and Waverley, whose headteachers adopted a strongly hierarchical team approach which their SMT colleagues accepted. Interaction was harmonious since there was congruence between norms followed by all members. The headteachers took a low risk of loss of control by restricting other members' contribution. The potential for SMT-wide synergy was also only moderate because the range of shared tasks over which their energies could be combined was limited. Other members were not encouraged to take initiatives or to contribute their ideas, beyond responding to the headteachers' proposals.

Norms	Headteacher	
	Management hierarchy	*Equal contribution*
Management hierarchy	**Moderate SMT synergy** • Headteacher operates hierarchically, • other members accept head-teacher's seniority, • other members contribute few ideas, • working consensus achieved, • outcomes acceptable to headteacher.	**Low SMT synergy (disengagement)** • Headteacher encourages other members to make an equal contribution, • other members prefer headteacher to operate hierarchically, • other members contribute few ideas, • willingness to compromise in favour of headteacher, • outcomes acceptable to headteacher.
Equal contribution	**No SMT synergy (open conflict)** • Headteacher operates hierarchically, • other members do not accept headteacher's seniority, • other members contribute few ideas, • no consensus achievable, • outcomes not acceptable to headteacher.	**High SMT synergy** • Headteacher encourages other members to make an equal contribution, • other members wish to make an equal contribution, • all members contribute many ideas, • outcomes acceptable to headteacher.

(Left margin label: Other SMT members)

Figure 1   Modelling interaction between the headteacher and other SMT members

The *lower right cell* represents the situation at Winton, where the headteacher encouraged other members to make an equal contribution and they were willing to do so. Here the potential for SMT synergy was high because all members were involved in a wide range of tasks and were encouraged to contribute all of which they were capable, including taking their own initiatives. The risk of the headteacher losing control remained low only as long as other members sought outcomes within the headteacher's comfort zone and were willing to compromise if necessary to achieve this situation.

Interaction is harmonious in both cells where there is congruence between the norms followed by all members, but the level of synergy is potentially greater where all involved can make an equal contribution. The solid arrow linking the *upper left and lower right cells* indicates how a team may sustain harmonious interaction and reap as much synergy as is possible at any time through all members working towards making an equal contribution. If the contingency arises where one or more other members advocate action lying outside the headteacher's comfort zone, harmony may be sustained if they can accept the headteacher withdrawing a decision from the team and making it unilaterally, as the team leader who is externally accountable for the work of the SMT. The key to smooth operation and maximizing synergy is for both headteacher and other SMT members to be flexible enough to switch together temporarily, for such contingencies, from adherence to the norm of equal contribution to the norm of a management hierarchy.

The remaining two cells depict how synergy may be compromised through disjunction between norms followed by the headteacher and other SMT members. The *lower left cell* covers situations where the headteacher operates hierarchically by pulling rank according to his or her position in the management hierarchy. But other members do not accept this move, because it transgresses their belief in their entitlement to make an equal contribution. Conflict may ensue, as at Pinehill after the arrival of the new headteacher when other members found his strongly hierarchical approach to leadership unacceptable. The *upper right cell* covers situations where the headteacher encourages colleague members to make an equal contribution, but they act according to their subordinate position in the management hierarchy. The result is disengagement of other members, as they withhold from making the contribution fostered by the headteacher. Such a situation arose in the more hierarchical SMTs where headteachers encouraged other team members to participate in monitoring other staff but they declined the invitation, implying it was the headteachers' task as top manager.

From practice to prescription: a contingent approach to sharing leadership

This model indicates how different approaches to sharing leadership in the case study SMTs proved significant for the degree of synergy attainable. While the arguments put forward earlier for the principle of sharing school leadership widely and equally are persuasive as far as they go, they fail to take into account two features of the real world, at least in Britain: the risk that sharing will result in ineffective leadership which is unacceptable because of its negative impact on students' education; and the strict hierarchy of accountability where the headteacher may have to answer for empowering colleagues to make an equal contribution if things are deemed to have gone wrong. The research implies that prescriptions for school leadership should be informed by evidence, and so rest on principles that are context-sensitive: the approach advocated will therefore be contingent on circumstances. For the UK, evidence-based principles might be:

1 School leadership should be shared widely and equally to maximize the potential benefit for children's education and for teachers' job satisfaction and professional growth.

2 Headteachers have responsibility for promoting shared leadership but the right, because of their unique accountability for doing so, to delimit the boundaries of sharing and to have the final say where there is disagreement over leadership decisions.

3   Other teachers have the right to participate in school leadership but the responsibility, because of the headteacher's unique accountability for their work, to ensure that they operate within the boundaries set, including letting the headteacher have the final say where there is disagreement over leadership decisions.

These principles would justify British headteachers working towards the most extensive, equal sharing of leadership possible to maximize potential for synergy, while allowing for contingent reversal to hierarchical operation to minimize the risk of disaster. Such a context-dependent prescription runs counter to the more generic prescriptions portrayed in North American normative theories like transformational leadership and organizational learning, whose applicability to the UK environment was questioned earlier. Arguably, such theories beg for elaboration and refinement to reduce their cultural relativity, so that they embrace more of the complexities of leadership in different real world situations and have wider applicability between contexts.

Finally, school leadership training and informal learning support should include raising participants' awareness of their contradictory beliefs and values. Assistance could be offered with learning to live with this contradiction and to switch between alternative beliefs and values as contingencies arise. Rather than offering simplistic advice (until recently, in Britain, pushing towards context-free equal sharing of leadership), headteachers could be advised to adopt a contingent approach, depending on an ongoing situational analysis.

The approach to training and shared leadership practice suggested here flies in the face of most training in the UK and elsewhere, which tends to reduce the complexity of leadership to a single formula for action. This research shows that real life is not so straightforward and the sooner training catches up with this complexity, the better. It is ironic that another UK reform – preparatory training for aspiring headteachers, introduced in 1997 – is cast so much in terms of hierarchy, reversing trainers' equally simplistic earlier orientation. The central government project of 'modernizing' the teaching profession, reflecting a hierarchical approach to leadership in the service of New Labour educational goals, may be challenged: it inhibits headteachers and their colleagues from sharing leadership in ways that maximize everyone's potential contribution. An approach to sharing leadership which works towards equal contribution, with an occasional regression to hierarchy, may be where the synergy lies that could really make a difference to the quality of school leadership, and so help raise educational standards. Yet the training syllabus focuses closely on the headteacher as directive top manager (Teacher Training Agency, 1998). Sharing leadership through an SMT scarcely makes it onto the new training agenda. Where is the justice in that?

References

Bacharach, S. and Lawler, E. (1980) *Power and Politics in Organizations.* San Francisco: Jossey-Bass.

Bower, M. (1966) *The Will to Manage.* New York: McGraw-Hill.

Conger, J. and Kanungo, R. (1998) *Charismatic Leadership in Organizations.* Thousand Oaks, CA: Sage.

Giddens, A. (1984) *The Constitution of Society.* Cambridge: Polity Press.

Grace, G. (1995) *School Leadership: beyond Educational Management.* London: Falmer.

Hall, V. and Southworth, G. (1997) 'Headship: state of the art review', *School Leadership and Management, 12* (2): 151–70.

Hargreaves, A. (1994) *Changing Teachers, Changing Times: Teachers' Work and Culture in the Post-Modern Age.* London: Cassell.

Lortie, D. (1969) 'The balance of control and autonomy in elementary school teaching', in Etzioni, A. (ed.), *The Semi-Professions and their Organization.* New York: Free Press.

Nias, J., Southworth, G. and Yeomans, R. (1989) *Staff Relationships in the Primary School: a Study of Organizational Cultures.* London: Cassell.

Pounder, D. (ed.) (1998) *Restructuring Schools for Collaboration.* Albany, NY: State University of New York Press.

Senge, P. (1990) *The Fifth Discipline: the Art and Practice of the Learning Organization.* London: Century Business.

Sergiovanni, T. (1996) *Moral Leadership: Getting to the Heart of School Improvement.* San Francisco: Jossey-Bass.

Southworth, G. (1998) *Leading Improving Primary Schools: the Work of Headteachers and Deputy Heads.* London: Falmer Press.

Starratt, R. (1995) *Leaders with Vision: the Quest for School Renewal.* Thousand Oaks, CA: Corwin Press.

Teacher Training Agency (1998) *National Standards for Headteachers.* London: TTA.

Wallace, M. (1999) 'Combining cultural and political perspectives: the best of both conceptual worlds?' in Bush, T., Bell, L., Bolam, R., Glatter., R. and Ribbins, P. (eds), *Redefining Educational Management: Policy, Practice and Research.* London: Paul Chapman.

Wallace, M. and Hall, V. (1994) *Inside the SMT: Teamwork in Secondary School Management.* London: Paul Chapman.

Wallace, M. and Huckman, L. (1999) *Senior Management Teams in Primary Schools: the Quest for Synergy.* London: Routledge.

Weindling, D. and Earley, P. (1987) *Secondary Headship: the First Years.* Windsor: NFER-Nelson.

Whitty, G., Power, S. and Halpin, D. (1998) *Devolution and Choice in Education.* Buckingham: Open University Press.

Appendix 3

CRITICAL ANALYSIS OF A TEXT

1 **What review question am I asking of this text?**
   (e.g., What is my central question? Why select this text? Does the Critical
   Analysis of this text fit into my investigation with a wider focus? What is my
   constructive purpose in undertaking a Critical Analysis of this text?)

2 **What type of literature is this?**
   (e.g., Theoretical, research, practice, policy? Are there links with other types of
   literature?)

3 **What sort of intellectual project for study is being undertaken?**

   (a) How clear is it which intellectual project the authors are undertaking? (e.g., Knowledge-for-understanding, knowledge-for-critical evaluation, knowledge-for-action, instrumentalism, reflexive action?)

   (b) How is the intellectual project reflected in the authors' mode of working? (e.g., A social science or a practical orientation? Choice of methodology and methods? An interest in understanding or in improving practice?)

   (c) What value stance is adopted towards the practice or policy investigated? (e.g., Relatively impartial, critical, positive, unclear? What assumptions are made about the possibility of improvement? Whose practice or policy is the focus of interest?)

(d)   How does the sort of intellectual project being undertaken affect the research questions addressed? (e.g., Investigation of what happens? What is wrong? How well a particular policy or intervention works in practice?)

(e)   How does the sort of intellectual project being undertaken affect the place of theory? (e.g., Is the investigation informed by theory? Generating theory? Atheoretical? Developing social science theory or a practical theory?)

(f)   How does the authors' target audience affect the reporting of research? (e.g., Do the authors assume academic knowledge of methods? Criticize policy? Offer recommendations for action?)

4   **What is being claimed that is relevant to answering my review question?**

(a)   What are the main kinds of knowledge claim that the authors are making? (e.g., Theoretical knowledge, research knowledge, practice knowledge?)

(b)   What is the content of each of the main claims to knowledge and of the overall argument? (e.g., What, in a sentence, is being argued? What are the three to five most significant claims that encompass much of the detail? Are there key prescriptions for improving policy or practice?)

(c)   How clear are the authors' claims and overall argument? (e.g., Stated in an abstract, introduction or conclusion? Unclear?)

(d)   With what degree of certainty do the authors make their claims? (e.g., Do
they indicate tentativeness? Qualify their claims by acknowledging
limitations of their evidence? Acknowledge others' counter-evidence?
Acknowledge that the situation may have changed since data collection?)

(e)   How generalized are the authors' claims – to what range of phenomena
are they claimed to apply? (e.g., The specific context from which the
claims were derived? Other similar contexts? A national system? A
culture? Universal? Is the degree of generalization implicit? Unspecified?)

(f)   How consistent are the authors' claims with each other? (e.g., Do all
claims fit together in supporting an argument? Do any claims contradict
each other?)

5   **To what extent is there backing for claims?**

(a)   How transparent are any sources used to back the claims? (e.g., Is there any statement of the basis for assertions? Are sources unspecified?)

(b)   What, if any, range of sources is used to back the claims? (e.g., First-hand experience? The authors' own practice knowledge or research? Literature about others' practice knowledge or research? Literature about reviews of practice knowledge or research? Literature about others' polemic? Is the range of sources adequate?)

(c)   If claims are at least partly based on the authors' own research, how robust is the evidence? (e.g., Are there methodological limitations or flaws in the methods employed? Do the methods include cross-checking or 'triangulation' of accounts? What is the sample size and is it large enough to support the claims being made? Is there an adequately detailed account of data collection and analysis? Is there a summary of all data that is reported?)

(d)   Are sources of backing for claims consistent with the degree of certainty and the degree of generalization? (e.g., Is there sufficient evidence to support claims made with a high degree of certainty? Is there sufficient evidence from other contexts to support claims entailing extensive generalization?)

6   **How adequately does any theoretical orientation support claims?**

(a)   How explicit are the authors about any theoretical orientation or conceptual framework? (e.g., Is there a conceptual framework guiding the data collection? Is a conceptual framework selected after the data collection to guide analysis? Is there a largely implicit theoretical orientation?)

(b)   What assumptions does any explicit or implicit theoretical orientation make that may affect the authors' claims? (e.g., Does a particular perspective focus attention on some aspects and under-emphasize others? If more than one perspective is used, how coherently do the different perspectives relate to each other?)

(c)   What are the key concepts underpinning any explicit or implicit theoretical orientation? (e.g., Are they listed? Are they stipulatively defined? Are concepts mutually compatible? Is the use of concepts consistent? Is the use of concepts congruent with others' use of the same concepts?)

7   **To what extent does any value stance adopted affect claims?**
   (a)   How explicit are the authors about any value stance connected with the phenomena? (e.g., A relatively impartial, critical, or positive stance? Is this stance informed by a particular ideology? Is it adopted before or after data collection?)

   (b)   How might any explicit or implicit value stance adopted by the authors be affecting their claims? (e.g., Have they pre-judged the phenomena discussed? Are they biased? Is it legitimate for the authors to adopt their particular value stance? Have they over-emphasized some aspects of the phenomenon while under-emphasizing others?)

8   **To what extent are claims supported or challenged by others' work?**

(a)   Do the authors relate their claims to others' work? (e.g., Do the authors refer to others' published evidence, theoretical orientations or value stances to support their claims? Do they acknowledge others' counter-evidence?)

(b)   If the authors use evidence from others' work to support their claims, how robust is it? (e.g., As for 5(c).)

(c)   Is there any evidence from others' work that challenges the authors' claims, and if so, how robust is it? (e.g., Is there relevant research or practice literature? Check any as for 5(c).)

9   **To what extent are claims consistent with my experience?**

10 **What is my summary evaluation of the text in relation to my review question?**

(a)   How convincing are the authors' claims and why?

(b)   How, if at all, could the authors have provided stronger backing for their claims?

Appendix 4

CHECKLIST: DEVELOPING A LOGICAL OVERALL ARGUMENT IN A DISSERTATION

Building towards the focus of the data collection instruments

Chapter	Element of logic	Content in this dissertation
	Title (keywords in the central question)	Title:
1 Introduction	Central question (substantive topic, stated in general terms)	Central question:
	Substantive aim (substantive topic, specific context)	Substantive aim:
	Theoretical aim (concepts guiding investigation of the substantive topic)	Theoretical aim:
	Methodological aim (design and methods to address the substantive topic)	Methodological aim:
2 Literature review	Review questions: substantive aim (issues related to the substantive topic)	Review question(s), substantive aim:
	Review questions: theoretical aim (selecting the theoretical framework and defining concepts)	Review question(s), theoretical aim:

Chapter	Element of logic	Content in this dissertation
3 Research design	Review questions: methodological aim (issues relating to the methodology and methods)	Review question(s), methodological aim:
	Research questions: substantive aim (reflecting answers to the review questions)	Research questions:

Focusing the data collection instruments

Chapter 3: Research design	Tick

Do the data collection instrument items contribute to answering the research questions related to the substantive aim?

Do the data collection instrument items employ the concepts of the theoretical framework?

Is there any reference to the inclusion of the data collection instruments, and possibly to raw data, in the appendices?

Focusing the presentation of the findings

Chapter 4: Findings	Tick

Do the findings for each data collection instrument item contribute to answering a research question related to the substantive aim?

Are the findings given for the items relating to each research question in turn?

Are all the findings reported, whether in full or in summary?

Focusing the discussion of the findings

Chapter 5: Discussion	Tick

Does the discussion show how the answers the findings give to the research questions contribute to achieving the substantive aim?

Are the implications explored of these answers to the research questions for the literature on the substantive topic that has been reviewed?

Does the discussion consider how the theoretical framework may have affected the findings?

Does the discussion examine how the data collection methods may have affected the findings?

Drawing conclusions

Chapter 6: Conclusion	Tick

Is a summative claim made about the answers obtained to the research questions and how they relate to the existing literature?

Is a conclusion drawn about the extent to which the substantive, theoretical and methodological aims were achieved, any limitations of the study, what has been learned from the experience of conducting the research, and how the research design might be open to improvement?

Is a conclusion drawn about the extent to which the answers to the research questions contribute to answering the central question, in terms of the degree of certainty about the findings and the degree to which they can be generalized beyond the empirical context?

Are any suggestions or recommendations for different audiences supported by brief reference to the evidence of findings and, if appropriate, literature reviewed?

Signposting throughout the text to highlight the logic of the overall argument developed

All chapters, reference list, appendices	Tick

Is it stated at the end of the introductory chapter how the overall argument to answer the central question will be developed in the remaining chapters?

Is there an introduction to each of the other chapters indicating what will be covered in each section?

Is there a statement at the end of each of the other chapters, except the conclusion, indicating how the logic of the overall argument will be taken forward in the next chapter?

Are all references to literature in the text accurately listed in author alphabetical order in the reference list so that readers may, in principle, find these references?

Are all appendices clearly labelled so that their contribution to the development of the overall argument is clear?

Index

abstraction
  level of, 73–4
academic traditions and styles, 7–8
applications of critical reading
  academic journal articles, 179
  peer evaluation, 180–1
  research grant proposals, 179–80
argument
  definition, 27–8
  development of, 39–40
  incomplete or flawed, 30–31
  logic of, 151–5, 166–9
assessors
  characteristics of, 41–2
  how to convince, 149–50
assumptions, 68–9
audience
  characteristics, 41–2
  sense of, 40–1

Butters (2004)
  use in examples, 50–1, 53–7

certainty, 72–5
concepts, 63–5
conclusion (component of argument)
  definition of, 27, 153
  identification of, 30
conclusion (of dissertation)
  structure of, 162–5
critical analysis questions
  blank form, 209–18
  effective use of, 93–9
  example, 101–13
  exercise, 99
  purpose of, 92–3
  relationship to critical synopsis questions, 92
  sub-questions, 94–8
  use in critical literature Review, 134–5
critical literature review
  definition of, 130–3
  example of, 136–8
  flexible approaches to, 141–6
  integration into dissertation, 147–65
  role in informing empirical work, 157–9
  role in informing methodology
    and methods, 159–60
  structure of (multiple review
    questions), 138–40
  structure of (single review question), 133–5

critical reading
  applications, 177–81
  definition of, 7
  what to read, 15–17
critical review (single text)
  example of, 119–22
  structure of, 116–8
  the 'perfect' review, 122
critical review (comparative)
  structure of, 123–5
critical summary (single text)
  examples of, 45–7, 50–2
  structure of, 43–4
critical summary (comparative)
  examples of, 53–7
  structure of, 48–50
critical synopsis questions, 31–4
  blank form, 34–5
  example answers, 36–7
  relationship to critical analysis questions, 91–2
  use in critical literature review, 134–5
critical synopsis of a text, 34–7

data
  interpretation of, 161–2
  presentation and discussion of, 160–1
dissertation
  logical structure of, 151–5
  outline structure of, 169–74
  tools for structuring, 166–76
  top ten features of, 150–1

evidence
  relationship to theory, 20

focus of enquiry, 155–7

generalization, 72–5

ideologies, 68–70
instrumentalism, 84–8
intellectual project
  characteristics, 86–7
  five sorts of, 72, 84–9, 90–1
  identification of, 85–9
internet as a resource, 21–4

knowledge
  practice, 78–9
  research, 78

knowledge *cont.*
  theoretical, 76–7
  three kinds of, 71, 76–9, 90
knowledge-for-action, 84–9
knowledge-for-critical evaluation, 84–9
knowledge-for-understanding, 84–9

langford (2000)
  use in examples, 52, 53–7
linkage tracker test, 175
literature
  four types of, 72, 79–84, 90
  policy, 80, 82–3
  practice, 80–3
  research, 80–3
  theoretical, 80–3
logic checksheet, 166, 168–9, 219–21

mental map for exploring the literature
  components of, 71–90
  definition of, 62
  key, 62
metaphors, 66–7
methodological aim, 156
models, 67–8

noun gender example, 136-8

opinion
  definition of, 28

perspectives, 65–6
phonics example, 5, 6, 28–9, 40
postgraduate study
  expectations for, 8–9

questions
  central question, 27

review question, 27
reflexive action, 84–9

self-critical writing, 6–7
  applications of, 177–81
  definition of, 7
  getting started, 39–47
  link with critical reading, 11–13
self-evaluation tasks
  academic style, 7–8
  how critical are you?, 12–13
signposting, 157
study process
  relationship to written account, 148–9
substantive aim, 156

task-driven reading, 10–11
theoretical aim, 156
theories, 67–8
tools for thinking, 62–70, 76, 90
types of literature
  data-driven, 20–1
  policy, 21
  practice, 21
  readers, handbooks, encyclopedias, 18–19
  research, 20–1
  textbooks, 17–18
  theoretical, 19–20

variation
  two dimensions of , 71, 72–5, 90

Wallace (2001)
  text, 195–208
  use in examples, 64, 66, 68, 69, 74–5,
    79, 83, 88–9, 101–13, 119–22
warrant
  definition of, 27–8, 153
  identification of, 30
  linking to conclusion, 30
Wray & Staczek (2005)
  text, 185–194
  use in examples, 36–7, 45–7, 53–7